IN A DOOR, INTO A FIGHT,
OUT A DOOR, INTO A CHASE

In a Door, into a Fight, Out a Door, into a Chase

Moviemaking Remembered by the Guy at the Door

by William Witney

with a foreword by Francis M. Nevins, Jr.

McFarland & Company, Inc., Publishers
Jefferson, North Carolina, and London

LIBRARY OF CONGRESS CATALOGUING-IN-PUBLICATION DATA

Witney, William, 1915–
    In a door, into a fight, out a door, into a chase : moviemaking
remembered by the guy at the door / by William Witney
      p.   cm.
    Includes index.

    ISBN 0-7864-2258-0 (softcover : 50# alk. paper) ∞

    1. Motion picture serials—United States—History. I. Title.
PN1995.9.S3W48   2005
791.43'6—dc20   95-18171

British Library cataloguing data are available

On the cover: William Witney (drawing by Dave Holland, director of
the Lone Pine [California] Film Festival)

Manufactured in the United States of America

McFarland & Company, Inc., Publishers
  Box 611, Jefferson, North Carolina 28640
   www.mcfarlandpub.com

To Jack and Dene Mathis—without their help,
pictures, cajoling, threats, etc.,
this book would never have seen the light of day;
and to my wife, Beverly, for her patience, with love;
and to Kathleen Harrell, my right arm

Acknowledgments

*T*hanks to William C. Cline for pushing me up the long hill that led to Jefferson, North Carolina; Francis M. Nevins, Jr., for his flowery foreword; Dave Holland for forgetting to draw in the wrinkles when he sketched the drawing on the cover; Jim Stringham for opening up his still collection to me; Herb Kirkpatrick and Republic Pictures, Inc.; and last but not least to all the nice serial and western film buffs I've met at the film festivals.

Contents

Foreword

*T*he media have a rule that what can't be said in a ten-second sound bite can't be said at all. My sound bite for Bill Witney takes a lot less than ten seconds if you talk fast: He's the Hitchcock of the pure action film.

William Nuelsen Witney was born in Lawton, Oklahoma, on May 5, 1915. His family moved to California when he was an infant and his Polish-American father died when Bill was five. In 1933 Witney got a job as office boy at Mascot, the Poverty Row studio that specialized in cliffhanger serials. Two years later, when Mascot was merged into the newly formed Republic Pictures, Bill was promoted to script clerk and then to film editor. In 1937, during a crisis on the Utah location of Republic's serial *The Painted Stallion*, Witney was asked to take over as director for one day—a day that launched the career of Hollywood's number one actionmaster.

In his early and middle twenties, he directed or co-directed twenty-three Republic serials, scenes from which are echoed in the Star Wars and Indiana Jones movies and in many other contemporary cliffhangers with megamillion dollar budgets. After serving in a marine combat photography unit in World War II, Witney came back to Republic and, in 1946, took over the studio's Roy Rogers pictures, directing twenty-seven consecutive features with Roy in five years. In the fifties Witney's output was more varied: nine Westerns with Rex Allen, dozens of episodes of Republic television series such as *Stories of the Century* and *Frontier Doctor*, and a pair of color features with relatively generous budgets (*The Outcast*, 1954, and *Santa Fe Passage*, 1955). His favorite among all the pictures he's made is Republic's 1956 *Stranger at My Door*, an unsung classic if ever there was one. After Republic folded in 1956, he concentrated on directing episodes of television series: *Zorro, Sky King, Mike Hammer, State Trooper, Coronado 9, Bonanza, Tales of Wells Fargo, The Virginian, Laramie, Branded, Laredo, The Wild Wild West* and *The High Chaparral*, just to name a few. He has been semiretired since the late sixties.

1

One hallmark of a Witney picture is its eye-popping action, providing an endless parade of thrills, chills, spills and stuns shot from every conceivable camera angle. Another Witney trademark is the menagerie. He has loved animals all of his life and has found ways to work dozens of other species besides horses into his Westerns. But the storylines and most breathtaking sequences of his finest films center on horses, and it is no secret to anyone who has known him or seen his work that he adores them.

A third Witney element, found abundantly in the serials he recalls so vividly in this (I hope) first volume of his life story, is a taste for bizarre script material that contributes hugely to making his cliffhangers the finest films of their kind ever made: The near-mystical figure of the woman who rides *The Painted Stallion*; the five indistinguishable Texans who form the collective personality of Witney's version of *The Lone Ranger*; the black-shrouded high-tech adversary The Lightning in *The Fighting Devil Dogs*; the fusion of one man with brains, another with brute strength and a third with almost inhuman agility into the *Daredevils of the Red Circle*; and the unforgettable Don Del Oro in *Zorro's Fighting Legion*, at once a collective personality (whose component parts are also the government of the province of San Mendolito) and an empty god. When popular culture academics rediscover the brawling young rebel who directed these and other cliffhanger classics long before his thirtieth birthday, you will see more than one ponderous tome dealing with the material I have compressed into a paragraph here.

Make that two paragraphs, because I can't resist the urge to share one moment of the near quarter century in which Bill and I have been friends. On a lovely day in 1984 when he was visiting suburban St. Louis and we were strolling around my neighborhood, I asked him how—with neither desire nor training—he had been able to learn the director's art literally in no time at all. I have never forgotten his answer: "It was so easy!" Almost fifty years after his career had begun he still seemed amazed at it. In that season when the hit movie was *Amadeus*, I couldn't help thinking of a precocious infant by the name of Mozart.

Enough of me. Settle back and enjoy yourself as a genial and unpretentious titan by the name of Witney, who seems to have known everyone and seen and remembered everything in the picture business since the dawn of talkies, shares some of his memories and adventures.

FRANCIS M. NEVINS
St. Louis, Missouri
October 1995

Preface

I directed my last picture in 1981. Everyone told me I'd be bored with retirement after the hectic, exciting life I'd led making pictures. Don't you believe it.

After my wife of thirty-five years passed away in 1973, I remarried in 1977 and decided to live happily ever after. And I don't think I've ever been as contented or happier in my life. We moved from the Los Angeles area to the Northern California mother lode country, about forty miles below Lake Tahoe. It is a land of big trees, deer, birds, and nearby lakes.

My wife, Bev, and I have been invited to several western film festivals, and everywhere the nice people I've met have asked the same question: "Why don't you write a book about making the old serials?" There have been numerous books written about the serials, but very few from the people who have made them. As a matter of fact, I guess I'm the last of the breed still kicking around.

Two years ago we were snowed in for a couple of weeks, and to keep busy I decided to start writing—about myself. I wrote about thirty pages and stopped. The I's and me's on the pages stared back at me. Did I do all the things that I'd written about? I knew in my heart that I'd done them. I had been one of the busiest directors in Hollywood for over forty years. There isn't an action sequence ever dreamed up that I hadn't put on film at least once, but writing about "me" doing them was something else.

I called my best friend, Thomas Thompson. Tommy had written dozens of Western novels and screenplays. He started years ago writing for the Western pulp magazines and has every award that a writer could collect. He is even in the Cowboy Hall of Fame. I had met Tommy when he was a story editor on *Bonanza*, and we'd had a thirty-year close friendship since then. I was sure he could answer my questions.

When he answered the phone, I said, "Tommy, how in the hell do you write about yourself?" He said he'd tried it once and had the same problem that I was having. After a lot of thought he finally "saw the light." "You don't write about yourself," he said. "You write about a fictitious character named Joe Blow, Dick Jerk, or Phil Phony. Then when you're finished, just go back and substitute your name for the name you've picked." I've tried it and it worked.

So if you wish to see how the original manuscript read, wherever you see I or me just substitute Joe Blow.

WILLIAM WITNEY
Fall 1995

The Serials Remembered

*T*he company of cavalry sat on tired horses. Both man and beast were too dehydrated to sweat. The tell-tale dried white salt streaks were all that was left from the sweat that had been dripping hours before. Now the sun was dead overhead and showed no mercy as it beat down on their heads on this midsummer day.

The cavalry was lined up in three scraggly rows in front of the headquarters building in the middle of a small compound surrounded by logs that were tied together. The pointed tips of the logs shimmered in the heat as they reached to the sky for some cool air. Every time a horse stomped its foot to dislodge the swarm of flies, a cloud of dust rose in the air that mingled with the flies, then settled quickly on the soldiers' faces and eyes. I sat on a horse in the far back row, too far away to hear what the officers and scout holding a pow-wow on the headquarters building porch were saying, although the few words that drifted back to me seemed to tell us that the fort was expecting an Indian attack. Every now and then a voice would holler, "All right, everybody at attention," and a second later, "Quiet please."

I was pretty sure that we were not in Indian country because the motion picture set was only about a mile from the Mack Sennett Studios. The studio had been built by Sennett in the late twenties on a piece of property donated by a developer in an effort to sell lots in a new subdivision in the San Fernando Valley, just over the hill from Hollywood. They had named the small area surrounding the studio Studio City.

The motion picture facility was now used only by a few "quickie" independent producers. This was 1933, and the once-thriving institution that made the Keystone Kop comedies, the Sennett bathing beauty shorts, the Charlie Chaplin shorts, the Fatty Arbuckle shows and the biggest hit of all, the Mable Norman comedies, was in bankruptcy, a casualty of the Great Depression.

The location was at the end of Laurel Canyon Boulevard. The street was

5

a two-lane asphalt road and one of the only three passes that led out of the San Fernando Valley into the Hollywood area. Today the road is wider, but it has not changed much. You turn south on Laurel Canyon Boulevard from Ventura Boulevard, and about a mile up there is a sharp left turn that takes you through Laurel Canyon. The road that went straight ahead wasn't paved and led into a small valley where someone had built a small stockade fort set before the Depression. Today there are wall-to-wall homes and swimming pools in the area. In those days there was just dust and flies. I'm still not so sure that the old days weren't the best.

We sat on our horses, a bunch of cowboys and one green kid about seventeen—me. I was dressed like a cavalry man and was making five bucks for a day which started before sunup and ended after sundown, with one time out of a half-hour to eat a box lunch that had been sitting in the sun since it was delivered from the caterers about ten o'clock.

The picture was a serial. If you're not too young, you'll remember them: twelve or fifteen chapters, with each chapter played on Saturday afternoon before the main picture. Each chapter ended in the apparent demise of the leading man or lady by the hand of the black-hatted villain. Then the next week you came back to see how they got out of the mess without a scratch, only to get themselves, again, apparently eliminated at the end of the episode.

Reading back on what I just put down on paper, it seems to me that the soap operas of today's television are directly copied from the serials. Instead of action they use sex for the end of each of their episodes to encourage you to return for the next one.

This serial starred Johnny Mack Brown and the title was *Fighting with Kit Carson*. The production company was called Mascot Pictures and was owned by Nat Levine. The company was very small, and for the last four years they had made serials on a very short shoestring budget. The directors were Armand (Mandy) Schaefer and my brother-in-law, Colbert (Bert) Clark. Even then there were two directors on the serials. It was too much to expect one man to shoot a hundred setups day after day, so they alternated days, their day off being spent preparing for the next day's shooting.

As I was sitting there I thought of the old cavalry song, "Cavalry, Cavalry, Trot Trot Trot Trot 'Til Your Ass Is Burning Hot—Cavalry." I also wondered, "If this is the picture business, God deliver me." The day before had been even worse.

I had come up from my home in Coronado, California, to visit my sister Pickie and her husband Bert for a few days. I had been going to a small school in San Diego after graduation from Coronado High School to help me cram for my entrance exams for the U.S. Naval Academy in Annapolis. I had an appointment for the next year, 1934. The school worked like the picture business, starting at sunup and stopping at sundown, with not even a break for a hot box lunch!

Bert was in production on a serial and asked me if I would like to work for a couple of days making chase scenes with the cowboys. I jumped at the chance. I considered myself a pretty good horseman. I had learned from an uncle who was a captain in the army and had been stationed at Fort Sam Houston, Texas. I had lived with him for four years and we rode nearly every day, and we also both showed jumping horses. I had never been on a picture set before and having my nose buried in English, calculus and history books for nearly a year, it would at least be something different. Boy, was it ever!

Bert took me with him the next morning. It was about 4:30 A.M. when we left the house for the location. Bert drove his own car. The road went out Ventura Boulevard through the San Fernando Valley past Sennett Studios to Reseda Boulevard, and then right on Reseda to Devonshire, followed by a left. When it dead-ended at Topanga Canyon, we took a right turn that would take us up through the Santa-Susanna Pass, which drops down on the other side into Simi Valley. About halfway up the hill there was a small sign that read "Iverson Ranch." We turned off the highway onto a narrow dusty road.

Iverson Ranch was a desolate piece of land with some high boulders jutting out of the ground in a disorderly fashion. The rocks were of no particular color, just a dirty brown. It sure didn't look like ranch country to me. The Iverson brothers owned the ranch and rented it out to the studios for a small fee. It was big enough for horse or car chases and there were dirt roads that the studios had cut through and around the rocks over the years. The brothers made a lot more money from renting their ranch to the studios than if they had been trying to farm it. I believe the only thing that would have grown there was rattlesnakes. I am sure of this because there were plenty of them around.

The entire landscape was burned-out brown. The rocks matched the dead grass and even the few oak trees were so dusty their leaves looked dead. Two big trucks and a few cars were parked under one of the trees. Bert pulled the car in beside them and parked. After an experienced glance up at the sky to see how long it would be before the sun came up, he walked to the trucks and I followed. Two men were hooking some steps onto the back of one of the trucks. Bert introduced me to Bill Strohback who was one of the assistant directors. Bert then told me that Bill would tell me what to do. "After the day's work is over, stick around and wait for me," he told me. That was the last I saw of him up close until we got into the car to go home.

Strohback introduced me to the wardrobe man, Ted Towey. When I took a close look at Towey, it was like looking at a map of Ireland. Strohback asked him to outfit me in a settler's outfit, and with that he turned and walked away. Ted sized me up, literally, "About a size medium, I'd say." I nodded. He asked if I were new here and again I nodded. Then Ted said, "Strohback said you were Bert Clark's brother-in-law," and again I nodded. He turned away, muttering with an Irish brogue. It sounded like "oh, shit," but I couldn't be sure. Ted came out of the truck with a settler's outfit, tossed it down to me from the truck and said, "Hang your clothes on a hanger, keep your wallet and anything of value with you."

I looked around and asked if I was the only one here besides the camera crew. Ted grinned a big Irish grin that was as honest as the day was long and answered, "Naw, bus will be along anytime." He gestured with his head and a bus came up the road and pulled in next to the trucks. When the door opened, about thirty sleepy cowboys with big belt buckles and bigger hats got off. I watched silently as they made their way to the truck and Ted handed them all settler's outfits. The changing room turned out to be the great outdoors. As I was changing I asked one of the cowboys where the bathroom was. He looked at me in disbelief, then he turned his head toward the back end of the truck. He spit a five-foot stream of tobacco juice toward it and said, "See that roll of toilet paper hanging on the water can? Grab a wad and you sure as hell won't have no trouble findin' a rock in this miserable place." The changing room and the bathroom were in the same place. There were a lot of westerns being made "in this miserable place," and by the end of a long hot summer it was hard to find a rock that didn't have its own fancy "TP" decorations adorning its base.

Everyone knows that winter follows summer. At "this miserable place" the boiling sun was followed by cold hard winds. If you were unlucky enough to be working out there the first few windy days, I guess the best way to describe it would be like a New York ticker tape parade with the ticker tape being replaced by toilet paper. Someone said to me once, "You work in a very glamorous business." I guess they were right if you think working in horse hockey and toilet paper is glamorous.

Now two big horse trucks pulled up the dusty road and parked under some trees. Each one held about fifteen horses. The wranglers unloaded them and tied them to the side of the truck, and I finally changed my clothes. I noticed that as soon as the cowboys changed into settler's outfits and handed their clothes back to Ted, they went to the horse trucks, untied a horse and led it over to the truck that had a big water can full of coffee and a box of donuts.

I was the last to turn in my clothes. I walked over to the horse truck. There was only one horse left tied to the truck. All the wranglers had joined the cowboys at the truck with the coffee and I stood and looked at the horse and immediately knew why he was last. He was the littlest, scrawniest, poorest specimen I'd ever seen. I looked at the ones the cowboys had in hand over by the coffee truck; some were good, some bad. The worst of the bad was better than the one I had. I untied him from the truck and stood there waiting to see what I was to do next.

The assistant director yelled, "Mount up and follow me." He started to walk up the hill. The sun hadn't shown itself yet, but it would only be a matter of minutes until it peeked over the top. I could see the camera setup pointing to the spot where the sun would crest the hill to greet a new day. I pulled the cinch tight and stepped on the little horse. He bucked and jumped a few times. Later I figured that those two bucks used up all the energy he had for the rest of the day. I joined the cowboys in the walk up the hill.

The director (Bert, my brother-in-law) was waiting for us. He pointed to some rocks and said, "Come from behind those rocks." He pointed at a big bunch of boulders and said, "Come by fast on this side of the camera," and he indicated which side. I followed the rest of the cowboys on up the hill and behind the rocks. We sat on the horses, waiting. When Bert yelled "come on" they all took off. I was last; my horse couldn't keep up despite all my efforts to make him run. I followed the pack; they were so far ahead of me and it was so dusty I couldn't even see the camera. The dust thinned a little and I finally galloped past the camera. Bert took a couple of steps in my direction and yelled, "Damn it to hell! Next time keep bunched up!" I turned the little horse toward him, he took a long look and said, "Oh, it's you."

We stayed in the settler's outfits until around 11:00 A.M., doing chase after chase. I was always last, and so full of sweat and dust that I felt like a big settler's mud pie. Then the assistant director told us to get into the Indian outfits. We changed and once again made chase after chase. This time, instead of fighting to keep the floppy settler's hat that was at least one size too big on my head, I had to fight a fake eagle feather that kept flowing across my eyes. The dust was bad enough; now this damn flying feather was attached to a band that was too small. I wasn't doing any better as an Indian. I was still last and still a mud pie, but this time I was an Indian mud pie!

Around 2:00 P.M. the assistant said, "Get into the cavalry outfits." Again we filmed chase after chase after chase. The hat fit this time, and had no feather, but something else had been added: a saber in a scabbard. That darn scabbard kept wanting to turn upside down, and the saber wanted to fall out. Also, the saddles on the horses had been changed from the conventional western to the cavalry McClellen type. These saddles were designed by General McClellen to go easy on the horse; to hell with the rider! There was a saying in the cavalry: "Ride one of these all day and you're ready to fight anybody." By now I was as tired as the horse. Again I was last, only this time I was a soldier mud pie with a sore butt.

I asked one of the cowboys what the story was about. He said, "As far as I can figure out, the Indians are chasing the settlers and the cavalry is chasing them both." I decided right then and there that I didn't want to see this picture because whoever I was supposed to be, being last all the time, the Indians had sure as hell caught and scalped me. If my horse could have run I might have been able to save myself. I was so pooped by this time that even having my hair lifted by an Indian didn't seem so bad. I had one consolation: my hair was so muddy from dust and sweat that I doubt if an Indian could have found my scalp.

The sun finally went down behind a bunch of big rocks. One cowboy told me they called the area "The Garden of the Gods." I'm sure it was named correctly because I sure thanked the good Lord that this day was over. It seemed to me that I'd been on that poor little horse's back for at least a week. I felt so sorry for him that if I hadn't been so tired I would have let him ride me for the last chase scene. There was still some sun shining up on the hillside and my brother-in-law pointed up to the top of the hill and took off in that direction.

The crew picked up the cameras and reflectors and started after him. I turned to see what the other cowboys were doing. They were getting in their own clothes around the wardrobe truck. I turned to follow them and another assistant director stopped and asked me if I had come to work with Bert. When I said I had, he told me to come with him. He turned and started up to the top of the hill where the last spot of sun was shining brightly.

I stood around on top of the hill and watched them shoot a close shot of an actor. Two cavalry men then rode up the hill leading an extra horse. The assistant told me to get aboard the extra horse, so I walked over, got up on the horse and sat with the other two. Bert walked up to us and pointed out an opening between two big rocks and said, "Come out from between the rocks and gallop down the hill." He pointed in the direction he wanted us to ride.

By now I was an old hand and I knew he'd yell "come on," and I was sure where he would want us to ride. I turned the horse toward the opening between the rocks and the two cavalry men followed me. We lined up out of sight and waited for the director to bring us on. I patted the horse on the neck. This was no old broken down nag this time; he had that "ready to go" feeling. He could see the other horses being loaded into the trucks and wanted to go home with them. I looked over at the other two soldiers. They sat quietly on their horses, each one with a big wad of tobacco in his cheeks. They each spit like they'd done it a million times before.

I looked at the two rocks we had to ride between. There was only room for two horses to get through, and there were three of us. The other two didn't seem concerned. I patted my horse's neck again. I'd been last all day and I was tired of eating all that dust. When I heard the director's yell "come on," I took the end of my reins and hit the horse. He jumped forward, the three of us heading for the opening in the rocks. I reached around and hit him again, and I beat the other two to the opening by a nose. There was a slight jam up and they checked back. I rode on down the hill in the lead on a dead run. I felt like hollering "whoopee!" I was not breathing dust, just clean air.

At the bottom of the hill I pulled up and started to walk my horse back to where the crew was moving on up the hill to follow the sun. The other two soldiers had pulled up with me and as we trotted up the hill they pulled alongside. One of them said, "You could get yourself hurt doing something like that, kid!" I looked at him, grinned, and added, "So could you." By the time we got back up to where the camera and the crew were, the sun had gone down behind the hill. The assistant told the two cowboys to take my horse. That was "a wrap." I thankfully handed the rider my horse's reins and started to walk down the hill to the trucks.

I thanked God it was downhill; I was so tired even then I wasn't sure I could make it. I was wrong; it wasn't a wrap for me. The assistant called me back to where the camera was set up, and stood me about three feet in front of it. The prop man pinned a marshal's badge on my chest, the wardrobe man threw a black cape over my shoulders and pulled the bottom of the cape back and forth a few times. The scene was what they called an insert. The wind was supposed to blow the cape back just long enough to reveal the marshal's badge, then the cape was to settle back into place and hide it. I knew what was going on, but by now it was so dark I couldn't see the trucks down at the bottom of the hill. I figured they must have had some new kind of film. I knew that I could never take a picture with my little Brownie camera in the dark. The cameraman said, "Roll 'em." I heard the camera turning, and then suddenly the whole landscape lit up as bright as day. The prop man had fired a flare. I said, "Well, I'll be damned," and the assistant yelled for me to hold still.

I had to drive the car home that night. I thought I was pooped until I saw Bert. He had been on his feet all day, following the sun to the top of the hill to get the last rays of light that were bright enough to expose a frame of film. It was now 8:30 in the evening. He turned to me and asked if I were tired. That made me laugh, and I told him what I had just been thinking. He had a big smile on his face. He told me that he had seen that big jam up in the rocks and then he asked me if I had any idea who those two cowboys were that I had beat to the opening. I shook my head no, and Bert explained that the short stocky one was Ken Cooper, and the tall thin one was Yakima Canutt. Bert told me that they had both been world champion cowboys two or three times apiece, and they were the best stuntmen in the picture business.

I headed home a couple of days later, back to the second floor of an old building in downtown San Diego, still attending school twelve hours a day, and cramming myself with history, English and algebra. I knew the entrance tests for

Annapolis were going to be rough. The country was still in a hard depression and everyone wanted the free education that the Naval Academy offered. Early in 1934 I received a letter that confirmed my appointment and directed me to take the tests at the post office building in downtown Los Angeles. The test would take seven days some time in the early spring.

When the time came, I again went to Los Angeles to stay with my sister and brother-in-law. Bert was like a father to me. My own father had passed away when I was four and I'd been raised by my mother and two sisters. Pickie (her real name was Frances Louise) had been born in Mississippi and our dad called her his little pickaninny. Both of my sisters were older than me, Pickie by six years, and Julie, the red-headed one, by seven years.

Pickie married Bert when she was quite young. Bert was a few years older. I think there were about seventeen years difference in age between Bert and me. Over the years we had become good friends. When he passed away in 1960 I was still "sonny boy" to him.

Bert was a graduate of Harvard and was a veteran of World War I. He was about five foot ten and soaking wet he didn't top one-forty. He had come to Hollywood to become a writer. Again the Depression held him back. He took any job the studios offered. He did extra work and ran errands, anything to stay in the picture business he dearly loved. He worked as a spear holder on the De-Mille picture, *The King of Kings*. The big sets had long hallways that were lined with Roman soldiers holding spears. I can imagine Bert was always in the distant background because he had to be the skinniest Roman of them all.

He told me a story about the time he was running errands at the Hal Roach Studios. The studios had a comedy gag in an *Our Gang* comedy, and they sent him across town to pick up a prop. Nobody told him what it was; they just handed him a slip of paper with an address on it. When he found the address, the big sign outside read "Los Angeles Alligator Farm." He was sure he had the wrong place, but decided to check it out. Inside there were two men behind the desk. He asked one of them if he had a pickup for the Roach Studios. The man nodded and said, "Is that your car outside?" He pointed to Bert's car and when Bert answered yes the other man in the office went out a side door. The first man shoved a piece of paper over the desk at Bert and said, "Sign here."

As Bert signed the paper, two men walked through the office carrying the biggest alligator he had ever seen. Bert froze as he watched them carry the squirming and kicking animal out the door and toss it into the back seat of the car. It was a touring car with no top. Bert slowly walked to the car where the two men were tying the animal by running some rope through the door handles. One of them said, "The door handles should be strong enough to hold this one." Then turning to Bert he said, "Be sure when you bring him back that his mouth is tied shut with a good strong rope."

Bert looked at the rope that tied the alligator's mouth shut, and at the two beady red eyes that stared at him as he slowly got into the front seat to head back to the studio. On the way back the alligator flipped and flopped in the back. People stared at the car as the creature reared up and shook its head. Bert nearly wrecked the car as he kept trying to keep an eye on the alligator that was keeping an eye on him. Bert watched the door handles very carefully to make certain that they were still attached to the car.

After the prop men got the animal out of the back seat, Bert told them what the man at the alligator farm had said about keeping the creature's mouth tied shut with a good knot. The prop man said, "Right, and you can check it out before we put him in the car!" Bert shook his head and said, "It won't be me that takes him back!" He walked up to the front office and quit the errand-running phase of his movie business career.

School was out. I think it was the summer of 1930. Bert got a job keeping script on a picture called *The Painted Desert*. It was Clark Gable's first picture, and Bert would be away on location in Arizona for a month. Pickie asked me to spend a week with her. A few days after I came to Los Angeles, someone called and said that the cast and crew would be coming home a week early. It seemed there had been an explosion and a lot of people were hurt, but Bert was okay.

The train came in about eleven in the morning. Pickie and I were at the station at ten. The train pulled in, and when it started to unload it looked like a scene in *Gone with the Wind* at the station in Atlanta. People were being carried off on stretchers, with broken arms and legs. The director was on crutches. Heads were bandaged, arms in slings. Bert got off the train under his own power. On the way home he told the story.

In the end of the picture there was to be an explosion on a cliff above the town that the studio had built, and an avalanche destroys the town. The dynamite experts had spent days drilling holes in the top of the cliff. That was supposed to make the explosion blow straight up in the air. What they didn't know was that they had drilled into a soft strata of shale and when the charge was detonated, it blew straight out of the cliff, the explosion taking the line of least resistance. It was like a giant cannon aimed over the crew's heads. Rocks were blown for half a mile. Bert said his World War I experience probably saved his life. He dove behind a big rock and a second later something hit him in the back and knocked the air out of him. It was an Indian taking the same cover he had. He had also taken the falling rocks that were meant for Bert.

During the next year or two, Bert still kept script and finally went to work for a small company called Mascot Pictures. When the president, Nat Levine, found out he could write, he kept him on full time. Bert would work on scripts as a writer, then keep script when the serial went into production. It wasn't long before he was directing.

For seven days I took a bus into downtown Los Angeles to the post office building for the entrance exams, and for seven days the tests got tougher and tougher. I felt I was well prepared for everything but English. The rest of the kids all worried about the math section, but I breezed through that with several hours to spare. It was the English part I worried about. In those days it took three months to get back the test results.

I came back to Bert and Pickie's late on the last day of testing and they had dinner waiting for me. I told them about the three months' wait for the results and Bert said, "Sonny Boy, how would you like to go to work?" I thought about the two days of chase and wait in the sun, but he laughed. "Not as a cowboy this time, but running errands as an office boy." I jumped at the chance. I was so sick of studying twelve hours a day that anything seemed better, and besides, the pay had to be better than the life guard job I'd had at the Coronado beaches the last few summers. I went to work with Bert the next day. The address, I still remember, was 6001 Santa Monica Boulevard. It was the top floor of a building material business whose main entrance was around the corner. The entrance to 6001 was on the corner. There was a glass door between two plate glass windows. Painted on the glass door was a sign, "Mascot Pictures Corp." The door led into a small entryway with a pair of steep rubber carpeted steps that led up to the second floor.

At the top of the stairs was a glass window with a hole in it so you could talk to the person on the other side. A very pretty young girl sat at the telephone switchboard with a headset over one ear and a microphone hanging around her neck. She said good morning to me. She was the telephone operator and receptionist. Her name was Brownie, and she was half Indian, with pretty black hair hanging down below her shoulders testifying to that fact.

The building was long and narrow. Straight ahead was a very large room filled with desks and typewriters. Several smaller office doors opened into it. The windows faced Santa Monica Boulevard and the Hollywood Cemetery was across the street. A long narrow hall with offices on both sides ran from the reception window at right angles to the stenographic room. It was early and the place seemed deserted. I followed Bert through the stenographic room to one of the small offices. Bert opened the door and entered the office. Behind the desk was a short heavy-set man, reading a script. He looked up and said good morning like he meant it. Bert introduced me to Al Levoy. Al was a clean-cut, nice looking man. He sized me up and looked me straight in the eye. He held out his hand; the shake was firm as he said, "Glad to meet you." He then turned to Bert and said, "Thanks for bringing him in. I'll take it from here." Bert closed the door behind him, leaving us alone.

Al sat down behind the desk and pointed to a chair for me. He looked at me in silence for a moment, then said, "I'm going to start you at twenty-five dollars a week." I am sure my eyes showed my surprise—I just couldn't believe it! Twenty-five dollars per week was a tremendous amount of money. I would have been happy with fifteen dollars. He asked me if I had ever run a mimeograph machine. I said I hadn't but I was sure I could learn.

We went through the stenographic room and Al opened the door to the collating room where the scripts were assembled. This room had a mimeograph machine and a wall filled with pigeon holes. There was a young man, maybe a year or so older than me, punching holes in the mimeograph papers and Al introduced us. His name was Connie, and he said, "Hi, welcome to the rat race!" Al smiled and told him to brief me on the office routine, teach me about the mimeograph machine and take me to the garage that was on the next corner. There he was to show me which cars belonged to Mascot Pictures, and how to work the gasoline pumps.

Al took off for his office, and Connie looked at the wall clock. It was about 7:30 A.M. He said to follow him and with that we went back through the stenographic room. There were a few girls standing over a coffee pot that was set in the corner. Connie said hi to them as we went by. On the last door there was frosted glass with printing on it that said "Nat Levine" with the title president under his name.

Connie knocked and when there was no answer he opened the door. He told me to always knock because sometimes Mr. Levine worked all night or got in very early before anyone else. We opened a closet door and took a dust rag from the shelf and dusted off the big desk, the four or five overstuffed chairs that sat along the office walls, and picked up the tray that had a water pitcher and several glasses on it. I followed him outside to a water cooler with a bottle on top. He wiped out the glasses with some paper towels, then refilled the water pitcher, turned and went back into the office. After the tray was placed back on the desk, Connie told me that this would be one of the chores I would be responsible for every morning and that Mr. Levine was very fussy about a clean desk. The rest of the day was spent with Connie briefing me on all the things I was expected to do to help around the office. Connie said he wouldn't be in the next morning because the studio was starting a new serial and he would be keeping script notes.

The next morning I came to work around 6:00 A.M. The front door was open but the place seemed deserted. The telephone operator-receptionist hadn't checked in yet. I went into the mimeograph room and picked up a few papers that were on the floor and threw them in the waste basket. I knocked on Mr. Levine's door. There was no answer so I went in, got the dust rag and carefully wiped off the desk and dusted the chairs. I shook the water pitcher. It was nearly empty, so I picked up the tray, taking it out to the water bottle, carefully cleaned the glasses and put the pitcher under the water bottle spout. It wouldn't fit.

There wasn't enough room between the spout and the drain. Holding the pitcher at an angle I could get a little water in it, but that didn't solve the problem. I knew Connie filled it from the spout, and wished I'd watched him a little closer. Then down below I noticed a small spigot. The pitcher just fit under it if I set it on the floor. That had to be the answer. I turned on the spigot, filled the pitcher, put the lid back on and replaced it on Mr. Levine's desk—so far, so good.

As people started coming in to work, Brownie took her place at the switchboard and one of the girls in stenography made a big urn of coffee. Al Levoy came in and said good morning and gave me some money to run down to the corner drugstore for the trade papers. I had to ask him for the names, and he said the *Hollywood Reporter* and *Variety*. I passed the garage where the company cars were kept. The day before there had been about six cars there; now only one Chevrolet touring car was there. The rest were out on location with the serial.

When I came back with the papers Mr. Levoy had a stack of mimeograph stencils in his hand and asked me to run twenty copies of each. He asked if I'd like him to check me out on the first one and I told him that I sure would. Al had been in the printing business in New York and had edited a small newspaper before going to work for Nat Levine. I soon learned he was Levine's right-hand man. He ran the company, literally, and was the most fair, hard-working, honest man I have ever known.

Al taught me how to riffle the papers before putting them in the machine so they wouldn't stick together. The mimeograph machine was run by a hand crank that turned a big drum with the stencil on it and a new piece of paper automatically went under the drum with every turn. It was a messy job. The ink oozed through the print to make the impression on the paper. It also oozed all over everything else if you weren't careful. Each new stencil had to be properly placed before you could run the number of pages you wanted.

I was busy at the machine when the phone rang in my little office. It was Brownie, and she told me to go into Levine's office right away. She said he was very upset about something. I headed for his office and knocked on the door. A voice hollered "come in" and I opened the door and entered. Mr. Levine was sitting behind his desk. I had seen Mr. Levine before that morning, but only for a glimpse or two as he walked through the office, but now I was surprised at how young he looked. He was a small man with glasses and a pleasant face. I had to guess it was a pleasant face because there was a dark scowl staring at me and a finger pointing to a glass full of water. "Did you fill the pitcher this morning?" he asked. I nodded yes, and then he asked me if I were new here, and this time I replied, "Yes, sir." With his dark scowl and deep voice he asked, "What are you trying to do, poison us all?" With his finger still pointed at the glass, I now took a closer look. The water was filthy, with big green chunks of yuck floating in it.

I said, "I don't understand, sir. I drew it out of the water bottle."I grabbed the tray and beat an exit to the door.

Once in the stenographic room I walked over to the water cooler and studied it. I drew some water out of the lower spigot, and it was the same color as the water in the glass: green. Then I noticed that the receptacle that held the glass as you filled it also acted as a pipeline to the waste water holder below. I pushed on the glass holder and it swung away so there was plenty of room to put the pitcher under the spigot. I took the pitcher and glasses into the restroom and washed the hell out of them, then went back and filled the pitcher with the bottled water.

Again I knocked on Mr. Levine's door and again the voice said to come in. I walked to the desk, set the tray down and poured a glassful of clean water. All three men sat and watched in silence. When I was through I said "sorry" and walked out. As I was headed back to my little office Brownie stuck her head out of her room and asked what was going on. I told her what I had done and I also added that I hoped the next job I got lasted more than one day. As it turned out, this one lasted for twenty years.

There were no set hours to any job in the picture business in those early days. Unions were a thing to come in the near future. The Depression had broken any attempt that had been made to unionize.

I had never worked before, so the long hours meant nothing to me. I got to the office about six and was home by eleven or twelve at night. The last thing I had to do was drive the mail to the Burbank Airport so that it would arrive in New York the next day or so. The first week went by fast. I was so busy trying to keep up with what I was supposed to do and learning about the whys and wherefores of the picture business that Sunday rolled around and I was still a little behind in the mimeograph department.

I went to work as usual at 6:00 A.M. I was busy turning out script changes for Monday in a very empty office when Mr. Levine came bustling through and said good morning as he passed the mimeograph room. Just a few minutes later I smelled smoke. I went out into the hall and smoke was coming out of one of the writers' offices. I ran down the corridor and tried to open the door but it was locked. I ran back to Mr. Levine's office, opened the door and yelled, "The place is on fire!" I grabbed a fire extinguisher and with Mr. Levine following ran back to the door. I asked if I should break it down, got an okay, and took a run at the door. I fell into the room which was full of smoke. The smoke was coming from the couch, and on the couch was a body. I rolled the body onto the floor and hit the couch with the fire extinguisher. It didn't take long before the fire was out.

When I turned to the body on the floor it got unsteadily to its feet and yelled at Mr. Levine and me, and in a slurred voice asked, "What the hell's going on?" That body was drunk as a skunk, and it took a menacing step toward us. I stepped in front of Mr. Levine and he said, "Throw him out!" Then I recognized the body. It was one of the serial writers. He was a feisty five foot six, and I'd never even met him. I asked Mr. Levine if he meant literally, and he said yes.

I grabbed the writer by the seat of his pants and the back of his coat and rushed him down the hall kicking and screaming. When we came to the steps I stopped and informed him, "If you keep kicking and screaming, we're both going to take a hell of a spill." He looked at the stairs. I still had a firm grip on him as he walked down the stairs like a gentleman. I opened the big glass door for him and pushed him out onto the sidewalk. I quickly closed the door and locked it. He stood in the middle of the sidewalk for a moment, and then with a fist raised over his head, charged the doors. I stepped back, expecting him to shatter the glass, but he stopped inches from the door, put both hands on the glass and said very quietly, "This is a hell of a way to treat a friend." He turned and staggered up the vacant street. He was Norman Hall, and he later became a good friend of mine. We worked together many times, and I still say he was a better writer drunk than a lot of them were sober.

Time passed quickly and I met a lot of new people. Nat Levine was only in his mid-thirties, and he surrounded himself with young people. He was easy to talk to and I got to know his wife Francis and his son Arthur. One of my jobs was to drive Mrs. Levine to the market a couple of times a week.

Mascot was shooting their interiors at the Mack Sennett Studios. One of my jobs was to take script changes to the set and sometimes pick up actors and take them to the studio. The set activity, the lights and reflectors, fascinated me. Connie, the boy who broke me in at the office, was still keeping script notes. They had two script clerks on the set. The main clerk was watching to see that the dialogue was correct, that the wardrobe all matched from scene to scene, and that the entrance and exit from one scene to the next was correct, as well as the direction in which the actors were looking.

Connie kept a small printed pad in front of him with a place to put the time, the camera roll number, the scene and take number, and a brief description of the scene and where the dialogue started and stopped. These were turned in to the cutting room every night after shooting to help the cutter assemble the film, which was developed and printed every night. It was then sent to the studio to be reviewed the next day. If the film didn't match the script report, they knew something was missing and had a way to trace and find it. There were thousands of feet of film exposed in a twelve-chapter serial. The cutter ended up with probably a hundred or so small rolls of film on his bench before he started to splice them together. If one roll was missing, it left a hole in the picture, like one piece missing from a jigsaw puzzle.

Each time I'd get on the set I'd talk to Connie and hang over his shoulder.

When the company was on location it was even more fascinating. When the camera setup was moved, sometimes I'd pick up an apple box, a reflector, or help pull a cable from the sound truck to the camera. I got to know most of the crew and admired the way they worked as a team to get things done in the shortest length of time. Time spent on a set was money to this company, which was working on a shoestring, so it meant jobs as well as food on the table. This was a depressed time economically, and the bread lines still hadn't disappeared.

Three months passed and I hadn't even thought about the Naval Academy exam. When a letter came from the Naval Department, I knew it had to be my grades. I stared at the envelope for a long time before I opened it and scanned the grades. I had gotten pretty good numbers in most of the subjects that had worried me; then I turned the page. I couldn't believe what I saw: I had failed math, my easiest subject. I thought back to the day of the test—a five-hour test, which I'd finished in a couple of hours. I was so sure I hadn't made any mistakes that I never went back through to check it.

I was living with my sister and Bert at the time, and they both sat watching me as I thumbed through the report. I handed them the letter and sat down. My sister shook her head and said, "Don't feel too bad. You only failed math and you can try it again next year." Bert said, "Well, sonny boy, it looks like back to school for you." I shook my head and told them I'd had enough schooling the last two years and I was happy with my job. I was going to stay at Mascot Pictures at least a few months more.

Today as I look back into my life, it seems that fate has more to do with steering your path into the future than you do. There were seven friends of mine who graduated with me from high school, passed their tests and graduated from Annapolis. They were among the junior officers who fought the Japanese navy in World War II. There was only one survivor.

Mr. Levine felt that he needed room to expand; instead of paying rent on the Sennett Studio sound stages, he made a deal to lease the studio. The big sign on one of the sound stages which read "Sennett Studios" was painted over with white paint, and the new black lettering stood out like a sore thumb, proclaiming that Mascot Pictures had moved in.

Also a victim of the depression was the large billboard that stood on a vacant lot outside of the studio facing Ventura Boulevard. The weather-beaten picture on it had some men in funny little hats wearing striped blazers. Some of the paper was peeling off, and flapped in the breeze. If you studied it carefully, it was advertising Bing Crosby and the *Rhythm Boys*. The billboard was torn down, and it seemed a sad symbol of the demise of Sennett Studios, which had brought so much laughter to the world, and ended up like this. The studio was still full of the old Sennett props, including two almost look-alike cars, one that headed down the street to squeeze between two streetcars passing each other and the other a tall narrow one that came out of the other end. The prop room was full of stuffed animals, prop snakes and big spiders. The wardrobe was full of Keystone Kop uniforms and the funny high dome hats they wore, and great big pants that Fatty Arbuckle had worn, and the tremendous shoes and canes for which Charlie Chaplin had been famous.

Billy Gilbert, who was the head property master for Mascot, had worked for Sennett in the same capacity. He told me that one day Mack Sennett had brought in a little Englishman named Charles Chaplin. He had signed him to a contract based on his reputation as a comic in England. When he met him he couldn't see anything funny about him and asked Billy to see if he could dress him to make him funny. Billy gave him Fatty Arbuckle's pants, some big shoes that belonged to Mack Swain, the big giant who was a Keystone Kop, and an umbrella stripped of the cloth top. History tells the rest of that story.

Mack Sennett still had an office in the studio and once in a while I would see him wandering around the empty halls, a defeated old man. My heart went out to him. I went out of my way to say hello and over the course of time got to know him. He showed me the swimming pool built in one of the stages where he had made all his bathing beauty shorts. The sign over the stage door read "Neptune Club." He also showed me the room where all the gag writers worked around a big table, with a bar in the corner to help them relax, and his office with the workout and steam rooms. He introduced me to George, the gateman, who had a French accent. George had been one of Sennett's best cameramen before the depression. He remained on the gate for the next fifteen or twenty years.

Mascot's move to the new quarters didn't happen overnight. It was over a period of several months. Every time I went in or out of the studio I couldn't help but notice how the newly painted Mascot Pictures sign stood out against the old paint that was on the outside of the big sound stage.

The serial that was in production during the move was called *Burn 'Em Up Barnes*. It was a race track story starring Jack Mulhall, Frankie Darro and Lola Lane. Bert Clark and Mandy Schaefer were directing. It was my introduction to the process stage, again something totally new for me to learn. Nat Levine had turned over the old swimming pool stage that had been the Neptune Club to a cameraman named Bud Thackery. Bud had engineered a heavy wooden floor over the empty pool, and he built a long narrow tunnel in back of the stage, extending probably one hundred feet. At the back of the tunnel was a projection machine.

Where the tunnel met the stage wall, Bud had installed a semitransparent screen. The camera on the other side of the screen photographed the actors in front of the screen, along with whatever was showing through the screen in back of them. An actor sitting in a car could turn and talk to another actor without the motor noise or traffic noise interfering. All that was required was a process plate to be shot of a moving background along a city street. It could also be used for storms at sea or close shots of someone riding a horse. You didn't see the horse they were riding (unless he was put on a treadmill), but you saw the other horses on the screen running in back of him.

The cameras photographing the actor in front of the transparent screen had to be in electrical interlock with the projector throwing the picture on the screen. When film moves through a camera, each frame stops for an instant and is exposed, forming a picture before it moves on. The movement of the film has to be blacked out. This is done by a revolving shutter that is built into the camera and the projection machine. The electrical interlock assures that the two shutters, the one on the projection machine and the one on the camera, are synchronized to open and close at the same time. Your eye doesn't see the movements of the film because the screen goes black when the light is blocked out by the shutter. You have in your eye something called retention of vision. Just close your eyes for a second and note that what you just looked at remains for an instant before it fades away.

All of the race car close-up shots of Jack Mulhall driving were made on the process stage. I remember that they had a motorcycle hanging on wires in an almost vertical position. Jack Mulhall was supposed to be going down a steep hill. The process plate had been made by panning (moving) the camera down a steep cliff at a very fast pace. Jack climbed up on the motorcycle and everything was ready for the shot. The prop man was just out of camera range, spinning the front wheel, with a fan blowing white dust over the whole motorcycle while Jack leaned forward.

They rolled the camera. Jack leaned further forward as the director yelled at him over the fan noises. Something happened to the wires: one broke, then another, and the motorcycle came crashing down, hit the stage floor and broke through with Jack still in the saddle. As it disappeared into the old swimming pool, all hell broke loose. Ladders and ropes appeared out of nowhere as they brought Jack up out of the hole, shaken up for sure, but with not a scratch on him!

In the 1970s I saw Jack, who was then in the Motion Picture Retirement Home, and while talking to him I brought up the motorcycle episode. He still remembered it.

Rex, King of the Wild Horses

*A*bout that time Mr. Levoy brought in another man to help me. His name was Leonard Kunody. He later became an assistant director with whom I worked many times over the years. After I turned over the office duties to him (and I made sure to show him about the swinging drain on the water bottle) I was sent out to the set to be a "gofer." Today I would have been called a second assistant director. The serial was called *The Law of the Wild*. It featured Rex, "King of the Wild Horses," and Rin Tin Tin, Jr. The directors were Mandy Schaefer and B. Reeves Eason (Breezy to everybody). Mandy I knew well. He was Bert Clark's best friend; my sister and Audrey, Mandy's wife, palled around together. After Mandy and Bert finished a serial they would come down to Coronado to relax. I swam and played tennis with them, so I knew Mandy by his first name. Breezy Eason was something else: a small, wiry man with the same weatherbeaten face that all outdoor directors end up with. Today I have the same beat up face that Breezy had.

Directors are busy people. They are the hub of the production wheel; every move of the crew is made to help them make their schedule. On a serial, one hundred setups a day was the norm. Someone once asked me what it took to become a director. "Good headlights on your car, because you come to work in the dark and go home in the dark, and a good bladder, because you don't ever have time to go potty" was my answer.

I quickly discovered that the set was run by the first assistant. In this case he was a ruddy-faced, rather clumsy man with big feet and clothes that seemed too big for him. His name was George Webster and he ran the set with an iron hand. His assistant was a dapper, neat Frenchman named Louis Germonprez. Louie was a very polite, gentle person. I can close my eyes and see him at day's end, standing on an apple box in the middle of the crew. His speech was always the same: "My people will be at the studio at 5:30 A.M. ready to go to work. My actors will leave the studio at 6:00 A.M. in makeup and cowboy outfits!" Most of the actors put on their own makeup in the early days; only the girls

22

and the leading man had the luxury of a makeup man and hair dresser, and then only sometimes. Mascot Pictures, money-wise, was still not far from poverty row. This was the name given to the buildings around Sunset and Gower, where most of the independent producers had offices and where most of them were starving to death.

I didn't realize it at the time, but George and Louie had devised the way a picture was broken down into a shooting schedule that is standard practice in the entire picture industry today. There was a big board set up in the office. It had strips of celluloid that could be written on and moved around. Each sequence was put on the strip, with the scene numbers and the actors who worked in the sequence, also including anything special, like horses, props, special effects, special wardrobe or makeup.

This enabled them to look at the board and move the strips around so that all of the same sequences could be grouped together. Then all of the scenes with the same actors would be grouped together. In this way they could hold the number of days the actors worked to a minimum. Most actors were hired by the day. Once you moved into a set, all the scenes in that set were shot before you moved out. You might be shooting sequences in all twelve or fifteen episodes in the same day. There was no such thing as shooting in continuity, like shooting scene one, and then scene two. You might start the first day by shooting the end of the episode.

I clearly remember one time during the first days of shooting on a new picture. It was early in the morning, and I stood in the middle of the still dark set, the overhead lights on the stage casting a dim yellow glow on the set walls. The whole stage was cold. I asked the assistant to bring the actors out of makeup so we could give the cameraman a rehearsal. He would light the stand-ins while makeup put the finishing touches on the actors. A young girl was the first on the set. She was about eighteen, and I'd cast her just the day before. Then a young boy came through the stage door. After saying good morning, I beckoned them both to come onto the set. I pointed to a door and told the boy, "You come through that door and stop when you see her sitting in the chair." I pointed to the young lady. "When you see him, jump up, stand only a moment looking at him, and then the two of you run across the room and fall into each other's arms and give each other a big kiss." That was the end of the picture. The girl looked at me for a moment and said in a very small voice, "Can I meet him first?" That's how far out of continuity most pictures are shot.

The motion picture set has a language all its own. I quickly learned the jargon for the industry. A gaffer is the head electrician and works directly under the cameraman. The best boy is his right-hand man, and he looks after the equipment, has the proper lights on the set and prerigs the lights on the parallels, which are catwalks above the set walls. The grips also work for the cameraman. They push the dollies and set the gobo stands, single pipes attached to heavy three-legged bases that hold the various pieces of wood or flags to take light off a part of the set, or block off light where the soundman's microphone might move through the scene and cast a shadow on the back wall. They might also hold a silk screen over a light to soften it, usually for a feminine face. The apple box is a four-sided oblong box that can be used as a base for a low light, or you can stand on it instead of a ladder, or just sit on it. The apple box is one of the handiest tools on the set.

Then there is the barney, a fitted cover that was put over the camera, usually on the exteriors, to shut out the sound of the camera so the sound man won't pick up its whining noise. Some of the lights had strange names. The baby was a small light the cameraman used to reflect into the eyes to give them life. The Mama Dietz was a big broad light, usually used under the camera to light the entire set. It was named after Ralph Dietz's wife. Ralph had a light rental business in Hollywood, and he invented a lot of the lighting equipment still used today. Having met Mama Dietz, then looking at the big broad light, what else could you call it? It took me awhile to get used to the gaffer yelling to his electricians, "Kill the baby and hit Mama Dietz."

The Law of the Wild had been shooting several weeks when I joined the crew. There was a polo field facing Ventura Boulevard a few blocks from the studio with a barn area in the rear. The cast, besides Rex and Rin Tin Tin, Jr., included Ben Turpin, the cross-eyed comic out of Sennett's Keystone Kops. Bob Custer and Lucille Browne were the leads, and Ernie Adams, a small man, was cast as a crooked jockey. Connie was still keeping script notes, and Mandy Schaefer was directing the first day. At least I knew two people. The script girl was named Ella Arnold. She was a small redhead, and having a redheaded sister, I was immediately drawn to her. The scripts were the size of a big Sears Roebuck catalog, and extremely heavy. Whenever I could, when the setup moved, I'd grab her chair and the script and move it for her to the next setup. I made a friend in one day that was to last a lifetime.

I was fascinated by the big horse called Rex. He was sixteen hands tall, a perfectly proportioned Morgan stallion. The trainer never left him alone unless he was locked into his own trailer. I soon learned why. The trainer, Swede Lindell, had found Rex in a boys' school in Flagstaff, Arizona. The horse was "whip trained." This does not mean he beat the horse to get him to do his tricks. Go to the circus, and you'll always see the ringmaster put the horses through their paces with a whip. He uses the whip to cue them through their routines. Swede soon found that when he'd crack the whip at Rex, he would charge and try to bite the whip. He knew that this was an unusual trait for a horse, so instead of breaking him of the habit, he encouraged it. Rex would charge Swede with teeth bared and take a vicious bite at the whip. Rex also found that he could run ordinary people away if he charged them. He really became "Rex, King of the Wild Horses" on that afternoon.

Swede was working Rex at liberty, which means there were no wires or ropes, and this time there was no bridle or saddle either. Rex was to come around the corner of the barn and charge the camera. Swede was just out of camera range behind the camera. They had walked Rex through the shot once with Swede calling him, but Swede was in front of the camera then. Now the assistant trainer on another horse put a rope on Rex and led him back around the corner of the barn. They rolled the camera. Swede stepped in back of the camera, cracked the whip and yelled, "Turn him loose!"

Rex came charging around the corner of the barn. Swede cracked the whip again and Rex charged the camera with teeth bared. Swede held the whip in both hands as a signal for him to stop, but there was no stopping Rex. He reared and spun away from Swede, knocking over a couple of reflectors. Somebody yelled, "Rex is loose!" and the crew scrambled for cover wherever they could find it—an open stall, a car, or behind a tree. Some of the actors were playing cards on a furniture pad in the shade. They looked up as Rex charged them, and then they scattered like a bunch of chickens.

Rex took off after Ernie Adams. Ernie was a small man but a good athlete. He dove under a Buick touring car that was parked in the aisle between the stalls with the horse in hot pursuit. Rex dropped to his knees, turned his head sideways, and with teeth bared, tried to bite Ernie, who was under the car. Swede ran up, cracked the whip, and Rex stood up and calmly walked to him. I had been standing behind the camera and when I looked around, the place was deserted. Even Mandy Schaefer, the director, had run into a stall and slammed the door. I had been around horses all my life, and I'd never seen anything like the show Rex put on that day. I decided then and there that if Rex was loose, I wouldn't be standing with my back to a wall.

I made a picture in 1955 where a horse went wild and tried to kill anything that moved. I described the scene to Glen Randall, who had a trained horse that we were to use, and he said, "I can put that trick on my horse," and he did. The picture's name was *Stranger at My Door* and the sequence that was put on the screen is every bit as wild as the one I witnessed that afternoon.

The second morning of the picture, I was told to pick up Louie Voccalis and bring him out to location. Louie had two beautiful German Shepherd dogs that doubled for Rin Tin Tin, Jr. He and his dogs lived in the old gatehouse at the studio during production. The house was built into the big cement wall that ran along the front of the studio on Radford Avenue. I picked up Louie and his dogs in the Chevrolet touring car that was being used as the heavies' car in the picture. Louie was a short, wide, red-raced man who had a large scar around his entire neck. He told me he had been a motorcycle officer on the police force before he had an accident and nearly lost his head. One look at the scar and you knew he didn't make up the story.

He had trained dogs as a hobby, and now it was his living. I soon found out why Rin Tin Tin, Jr. needed a double. Those two dogs of Louie's could do anything—and in one take. Rin Tin Tin, Jr. was owned and trained by Lee Duncan, a handsome grey-haired gentleman with a soft-spoken voice. The original Rin Tin Tin may have been a great dog. I never knew him. Junior was a beauty, but they only used him for close-ups. The running, jumping, and fighting were done by Louie's dogs. They were the best trained dogs with which I have ever had the privilege of working. When Rex worked with Rin Tin Tin, Jr., it was always Rex's double and Rin Tin Tin's double. Then they were both isolated for the close shots.

The next day was Breezy Eason's day to direct, and I met him for the first time. Bert and Breezy had worked together and were friends. When Connie introduced me to Breezy, he smiled and said, "Well, you sure as hell aren't as pretty as your sister." I thought to myself, "So this is what a legend in the picture business looks like." I worked with him many times and it was from him that I learned how to shoot action and how to get the best out of the stunt people.

Ben Turpin was born cross-eyed, and somehow Sennett thought that was funny. He had starred Ben in comedies of his own and as a Keystone Kop. Actually, Ben was nearly blind. Ben was a small man and had a lot of experience in front of the camera. Now he was getting old, and I imagine he was put in the cast because Levine thought he still brought some name value to the people who bought the serials.

Breezy was explaining the scene to Ben and acting out the part as he showed Ben what to do. The scene was set on the outside of a stall in the middle of a long runway of stalls. All the stalls had dutch doors—you could open and close either the top or bottom door separately. On this particular stall, the top door was open and the bottom one was closed. The hasp on the door had a pin through it that locked it and Rex could be seen standing in the back of the stall. Breezy said, "You're sneaking up to the stall so no one can see you." Breezy hugged the wall and inched toward the open door. "You reach for the pin to unlock the stall door." Breezy reached for the pin, Rex lunged for Breezy, and his teeth snapped together inches from Breezy's face. The big horse's chest slammed into the locked door. It stopped his charge and made a noise like a clap of thunder. Breezy never even flinched. He turned to Ben and said, "That's all there is to it." Ben hadn't moved. He said to Breezy, "Do you want me to pull the pin?" Breezy smiled at him and put a hand on his shoulder. "No," he said, "I'll let the double pull the pin!"

Ben had been in the business a long time, and he was a real trouper. The camera rolled, Ben slid along the wall, reached at arm's length toward the pin and Rex lunged at him with his teeth bared. Rex hit the stall door again, only this time the hasp flew off and the door crashed open. Ben turned and ran. With his poor eyesight, he didn't see the reflector that was set up at a low angle. He ran right up the reflector and flew into the air at the top. His legs were still running when he hit the ground on his belly. It was a scene straight out of a Keystone Kop slapstick comedy, but no one laughed.

If Ben had waited a second longer he would have seen Swede step into the stall opening and drive Rex back into the stall with the whip. Breezy ran to Ben and picked him up. Ben was shaken but not hurt. Ben said, "Breezy, if you need another take on that, call the double!" Then he laughed, and Breezy laughed, and then the whole crew laughed. I learned something from that scene that helped me when I later became a director: never put an actor at risk if you can use a stuntman.

Larry Wickland

*W*hen *The Law of the Wild* finished I went back into the Santa Monica Boulevard office and waited for the next serial to start. I remember reading parts of the script as I mimeographed the pages. With my recent experiences on the sets, the scripts made more sense to me. There were headings at the top of each scene: "INT CAVE," or "INT RATTLERS HIDEOUT," where "INT" meant interior; "EXT RAILROAD TRACK," or "EXT ROADS," where "EXT" meant exterior. There were scenes marked "LS," meaning long shot, taking in the entire set or countryside, "MED SHOT," meaning a little closer to the people or subject being photographed, "CUP," meaning close-up, which speaks for itself, or "INSERT," which can be a newspaper headline, feet walking along, a hand pinning on a star, or a big close shot to sell a point to the audience or "MOS," shot without sound. I asked why it shouldn't be "SWS." The answer was that it means "mitt out sound."

It was Saturday afternoon, and a man whom I had seen on the set but never met came into the mimeograph room. I greeted him as he came through the door. I didn't know it then, but this man would change my entire life. His name was Larry Wickland, and he was a tall, spry man with ill-fitting clothes. He was quiet and, I learned later, very artistic. He had been a set designer and had worked for the major studios doing miniature work. He was hired to make the miniatures on the serial I was mimeographing, which was called *Mystery Mountain*. The miniatures were mostly trains running through the mountains or running in and out of tunnels that ran through the mountains.

Mr. Wickland asked me if I would go out the next day and pick up a truck full of fresh juniper. The place he wanted it cut was Mint Canyon. This canyon had a highway that ran through it from San Fernando Valley to Palmdale. He explained that the juniper in the miniatures alongside the small trains looked like big trees to the camera. He also told me that if I got caught cutting juniper I might end up in jail. I laughed. He didn't smile, but informed me to call him if that happened and he would come get me out. I laughed again and told him that sounded like a fair deal. I drove up to Mint Canyon in a flatbed truck early Sunday morning and found a dirt side road. There was practically no traffic in those days, but today a freeway has replaced that dirt road. I filled the truck with juniper, covered it with a canvas tarp and got back to the studio before noon with no problems.

Larry was at the studio and came out to inspect the cargo. He congratulated me on a good job and helped me unload. Larry asked me what I was doing the rest of the day. It seemed he was an ardent sailor and invited me to go sailing. It didn't take long for Larry to find out that I was a pretty good sailor myself. Living in Coronado, I had raced Star Boats since I was a kid. The boat we used was a forty-foot catch rig that belonged to a writer named Ron Davidson. The boat was moored in San Pedro, and after we got out of the breakwater Larry decided to put up all the sails we carried. There was a pretty good breeze blowing and we tacked up to Santa Monica against the wind. Then we turned to make the run for home.

When we started to take the sails down, Larry bent over to put them in the sail bag. He suddenly grabbed his back and fell onto the deck of the cockpit. I grabbed and pulled him up onto the bench that ran along the sides, and I could see that he was in pain. He told me he had a back problem and his disc had slipped out of place. I looked up at the breakwater, at the sails that hadn't been taken down, and at Larry, who couldn't move. I thought, "He thinks *he* is the only one with a problem!" I'll never know for sure how I got those sails down—all but the jib—or how I managed to sail into the mooring slip without wrecking the boat, but there wasn't even a scratch on it when I docked. I carried Larry to the car and got him to his chiropractor, who snapped his back into place again. After that I took him to his home and left him. It had been some day.

When I picked Larry up the next morning he was fine, and on the way to the studio he said, "A hell of a day yesterday—thanks." A few days later he came to me and asked me to be at the studio at four the next morning to pick up some box lunches and a bundle from wardrobe that would be at the gate. I was to meet him at a railroad trestle about twenty miles above Santa Barbara. The serial hadn't started production yet, but he wanted to be sure he had the process plates and the few scenes he needed for the first couple of days of shooting. He gave me a map and directions and said he would meet me there.

When I got to the trestle a truck was already parked as close as possible to the tracks and three carpenters were putting planks inside the tracks that ran across a short but deep ravine. The trestle was a couple of hundred feet long, and the ravine was *very deep*. The chief carpenter's name was Ezra Paul. Ezra was six foot six, a tall Swede who always wore white, farmer-type overalls and was a genius at building oddball constructions, from car ramps to chutes on the top of cliffs for dumping horses into the water. He was a production designer's dream.

I had picked up donuts and coffee on my way out and everyone stopped work and gathered around the car. Larry told me he had hired horses from a nearby ranch and now I could see a lone Mexican riding toward us leading another saddled horse. There was to be a cowboy coming up from Hollywood in his own car, and he was going to run the horse across the bridge in front of a train. Larry had made arrangements with the railroad for a train to stop on the far side of the trestle so he could give the engineer instructions on what he was supposed to do. Then the train was to continue on its way. It only gave Larry about ten minutes to get the shots he wanted.

The cameraman and his assistant arrived and unloaded the cameras from the back of their cars. The cameras were set up and everyone went to work. I helped the carpenters put up a small eight-inch railing on the inside of the tracks. Now the trestle looked like a narrow bridge and it wasn't long before everything was ready to roll. Two things were missing: the cowboy who was going to ride the horse over the trestle and the train. The train wasn't due for another half hour. Larry kept looking at his watch and then at the dirt road that the cowboy's car would have to come down to get to our location.

I walked down to where the Mexican with the two horses was resting in the shade at the bottom of the trestle. Larry had already tried to talk to him, but his English wasn't very good and Larry's Spanish was worse. Fortunately, I spoke fair Spanish. Coronado was right next to the California-Mexico border and I knew a lot of Mexican kids when I was growing up. This fellow knew that a man was going to ride a horse over the trestle, and it didn't seem to bother him. I asked him if he thought it would be good to take the horses over the trestle a couple of times to get them used to it. He looked up at the trestle, then said to me, "Es no bueno por nada," which means "not good for anything." I asked him if it would be all right if I walked them over it. He nodded, got up and pulled the cinch straps tight and handed me the reins of the other horse.

We led the horses up the hill to the top of the trestle. The horse that I led seemed very calm, but he was old. When I started to lead him across the trestle, he hesitated a moment and then followed me across on the two by sixes that the carpenters had nailed down to the railroad ties. I looked back and the Mexican was following me across the trestle. On the other side I looked at him and shrugged. He shrugged back—no big deal—so we both mounted up. The old horse felt good under me. He was steady and well broke, and had probably chased cows through these deep canyons all his life. I reined him back and pointed him at the trestle. He didn't even hesitate this time, but walked steadily across the boards. I didn't like the ringing sound of his steel shoes on the boards. At a fast gallop they could be slippery.

Larry was waiting for us when we reached the other side again. He looked at his watch one more time. We had about fifteen minutes before the train was due to arrive, and there was still no cowboy in sight. Larry asked me to see if the Mexican would ride the horse across the trestle in front of the train. The rider looked to the ground three hundred feet down and wanted to know how fast he was expected to go. I made the motion with my hands of a horse at a fast gallop. The rider seemed to talk for five minutes. I translated for Larry in two words: "no way!"

There was a silence that settled over all the carpenters and camera crew that had been listening. All this work would be for nothing. I turned to the Mexican and asked if he'd pull the shoes off the horse I had walked across the trestle. He agreed and I asked Ezra, the chief carpenter, if he would loan the fellow a pair of pliers, side cutters and a hammer. Ezra would do more than that. He had been raised on a farm in the old country and he would be happy to pull the shoes off. Ezra picked up the horse's hoof like an old pro, and said in his thick Swedish accent, "But if the cowboy doesn't show up," and then he looked at me. I nodded and he turned back to the horse, shaking his head.

I walked over to the wardrobe I had brought from the studio and started to change into it. Larry walked up to me. "Do you know what you're doing?" I remember the concern he had on his face. I pulled on the pants and shirt and turned to him. "If I didn't think I could do it, do you think I'd be dumb enough to try?" He still didn't like the idea much, but I put on the black cape, mask and hat that comprised the wardrobe, pulling the hat down over my ears so it wouldn't fly off. Then I walked over to the horse as Ezra finished pulling the shoes. I mounted the old boy and rode across the trestle, turned and galloped him slowly back to where the group was standing.

We could see the train coming down the track. It stopped about a quarter of a mile from the trestle. Larry and I went up to the engine, told the engineer what we wanted them to do, and then I galloped the horse across the trestle in front of the train. There were two cameras grinding on the shot. One was a long shot of the horse and rider running across the trestle to show the height. The other camera was buried in the center of the track and the train ran over it. This shot would be used as a process plate. Later in the process stage, Yakima Canutt would fall a horse in front of the process screen just as the train ran over the camera to give the illusion of the train running over the horse and rider for one of the serial's episode endings.

Larry and I helped the carpenters pull the two by sixes off the trestle and load them on a truck. The camera crew was long gone. I was throwing the empty boxes from lunch in the back of the car and Larry came up to me. He picked up the wardrobe I had brought out and threw it in the front seat, then turned to me and thanked me for helping him out. I told him I got a kick out of it. Larry offered to pay me what the cowboy would have been paid. I shook my head saying, "I'd appreciate it if you never told anybody. I don't want to get in dutch with the cowboys. Tell the studio that the Mexican did it." Larry nodded and said that Al Levoy would either fire him or wring his neck if he ever found out what I had done. The lost cowboy never did show up.

The serial went into production a few days later. *Mystery Mountain* starred Ken Maynard who had been almost as popular as Tom Mix a few years before. My memories of Ken Maynard are not good. He brought five beautiful palomino horses on the set. Tarzan was his lead horse, and the other four were doubles. One day in a fit of temper, he ran one of Tarzan's doubles at a tree with his spurs dug deep into the horse's flanks. As the horse tried to shy away from the tree, Maynard stepped off the horse, jerking the reins with him, thereby pulling the horse's head into the tree with a sickening thud that knocked the poor animal to the ground. Another time I saw him beat one of his horses until it screamed. These actions upset me so much that I stayed away from the set and spent most of the time with Larry working on the miniatures. It was this kind of cruelty that eventually brought an SPCA representative onto the set at all times.

On that picture I met another cowboy who was to turn out to be a big star. Nat Levine had signed a radio singing cowboy to a term contract with his sidekicks Smiley Burnett and Frankie Marvin. The cowboy's name was Gene Autry. I remember the first scene he was in. He was supposed to come by the camera fast. I was standing in back of the camera. Gene came by, barely missing the camera, and scattered the crew in all directions while they tried to save their lives. I hadn't heard him sing yet, and I thought to myself, I hope he sings better than he rides!

The next serial was going to star Gene Autry. It was called *The Phantom Empire*. The serial was being shot in Bronson Canyon located in Griffith Park in the Hollywood Hills. It once was an old rock quarry that supplied the material that built the streetcar tracks on Hollywood and Santa Monica boulevards. There is a tunnel that goes nowhere and ends up still inside the quarry pit. It is big enough to drive a truck through and has probably been used as a background in a thousand old westerns. *The Phantom Empire* was being shot inside the tunnel.

It had been raining and there were big puddles everywhere. Breezy Eason was directing. There were five or six horses standing with their backs to the camera and Gene's double, Kenny Cooper, was going to make a "Crouper" mount on one of them, spin the horse and gallop out of the tunnel. Kenny made a practice run to see if the horse would stand still for him. He ran at the horse, jumped at the rear end of the horse, and putting his hands on the horse's rump, vaulted into the saddle. Kenny had been World Champion All-Around Cowboy, and the way he did the mount made it look so easy that it seemed anyone could do it.

Gene was dressed in a very fancy white cowboy outfit like those you see the western singers use in their stage shows. He said to Breezy, "I can do that." Breezy looked at him and said, "Fine, let's make it. Roll 'em!" The cameras rolled and Breezy said "action." Gene ran at the horse, jumped, and put his hands on the horse's rump. However, Gene's jump was about half as high as it should have been. His belly hit the horse just above the tail, and Gene fell backwards and landed on his butt. There was a big splash in the puddle that the horse was standing in, and the white suit changed to a horse-manure brown. I still hadn't heard Gene Autry sing. In later years Slim Pickens said to me, "I don't know why Gene's always singing 'I'm Back in the Saddle Again' when his butt's never really been near one."

The Phantom Empire had a lot of miniatures and matte shots written into it. This was my introduction to Jack Coyle, who Larry brought in to assist him. Jack had extensive experience in miniature work and was an old friend of Larry's. I spent most of the time during the shooting of *Phantom Empire* running errands and picking up material that went into the making of the miniatures. There were a couple of kids about my age, Babe and Ted Lydecker, who were also working in the shop. In the following years they both would have a major impact on the quality of serials.

Mascot was going great guns. Levine had moved his operations onto the Mack Sennett lot in January of 1935 with a five-year lease at one thousand two hundred dollars monthly with an option of first refusal to match any bonafide offer to buy it.

Just after Mascot moved to the Sennett lot Al Levoy called me into his office and asked me what I wanted to do. He was still my boss. I had been to the Consolidated Labs picking up and delivering film many times and knew a lot of people who worked there. I told him I would like to learn the laboratory business. He thought about it a moment and shook his head. "If you want to know the picture business, go into the cutting room and learn to be a film editor. If you can edit films, you can go as far in this business as your ability will allow," he told me.

I talked with Larry, and he thought it would be a good move. I also talked with my brother-in-law. Bert had not been connected to the serials for quite some time. With increasing costs and the move to the new lot, Bert had gone back to writing and producing features. Bert's advice to me was the same as Larry's, so I moved from gofer to cutter.

The cutting rooms were not new to me. I had been in and out of them many times as a gofer. Before the move to the Sennett lot, the Mascot cutting rooms had been located in the Consolidated Film Laboratory in Hollywood, and the work force was very small but very good. Earl Turner worked with an assistant, Les Orlebeck. Helene Turner (no relation) was a small, good-looking woman in her late thirties. Joe Lewis was a handsome, curly-headed man with a ready smile in his late twenties and an excellent film editor. And there was Bertha, the negative cutter.

Upon moving to the Sennett lot, Mascot began using the cutting rooms which were already there and this is where I did my first work in film editing. I was assigned to be an assistant cutter to Helene, who had come out of the silent era and was good at her job. It was very unusual in those days to find a woman editor. There were women in the editorial department, but they were mostly in the negative cutting rooms. Helene had the patience of Job as she led me through the technicalities of learning to break down a thousand foot reel of film, reassemble it in continuity, and sync up the sound track with the picture. She taught me to run the reels through the numbering machine, which allowed the cutter to keep the picture and the track in sync once the slates had been cut off. I also learned how to order the fades, wipes, and dissolves from the laboratory. If Helene got behind schedule, she would let me cut a sequence or two, then she would look at it, tell me where I could do better, and let me go back and fix it myself. When the cutting rooms were very busy I would sometimes lay in sound effects or music to help out. It was a madhouse at times, trying to keep up with release schedules.

The first picture I worked on was a serial, *The Miracle Rider*, with Tom Mix and Tony, his "wonder horse." Just a few years back Mix had been one of the most popular, highly paid stars in the picture business. I went on the set every morning to pick up the script notes so that I could assemble the "dailies" and check to make sure none of the film had been lost in the lab. Tom Mix had been one of my favorite Saturday afternoon cowboys, and it surprised me that he wasn't six foot six. He seemed to be about my size, five foot ten, even in his cowboy boots, and was so thin that a gust of wind could blow him away. He had a slight speech impediment, and when he would say "Miracle Rider" it sounded garbled, like he couldn't move his tongue. Someone told me that a woman in San Diego had shot him in the jaw, but I don't know if that was fact or fiction.

There were a lot of independent producers making pictures in competition with Mascot. They were all working on the proverbial shoestring and the same film laboratory did all of their developing and printing. It was Consolidated Film Industries and it was owned by Herbert J. Yates, a small, bald, stocky red-faced Scotsman from New York. He did most of the independents' lab work on credit. Without him, the studios—even Levine—would not have been able to raise enough money to buy the negative raw stock from Eastman Kodak, which always had a cash-and-carry policy for everyone.

Beginning in late 1934 and continuing into early 1935, Yates had been developing an idea to band six independents together to form one new company. The theory was that they could save money if they merged all their operations and distributed through one exchange to sell their pictures all over the United States, cutting rental and personnel by about eighty percent. The six companies that Yates targeted as an alliance were Monogram, Liberty, Majestic, Mascot, Chesterfield, and Invincible. After long discussions Monogram, Liberty, and Majestic agreed, and Yates decided to call the new company Republic Pictures, named after his first film laboratory. Two Monogram executives took over important posts in the new combine, with Ray Johnston becoming the president of distribution and Trem Carr acting as vice president of production. The official papers were signed in March and April.

Levine at first rejected the overtures to come in with the new group, and he even took out trade-paper advertising to declare that Mascot would remain on its own. But Yates doggedly pursued Mascot, and a few months later Levine finally agreed to pitch in with the new group. Chesterfield and Invincible continued to decline the invitation to join, and within a year both went out of business.

Everything was now moving at a rapid pace. With Yates bankrolling the new alliance, Republic Pictures Corporation was set up as the distributor primarily using Monogram franchise exchanges. Republic Productions was named the producer, and film output eventually became centered on the Sennett Studios which Mascot had under lease. For two thousand five hundred dollars monthly, Levine sublet the lot to Republic. A few years later Republic purchased the studio outright.

When Mascot joined Republic Levine took over as production head. Internal disagreements caused both Johnston and Carr to resign by year's end.

Republic's main office was in New York where taxes were lower than in California, and Consolidated Film Industries, which made all the release prints, was located next door in Fort Lee, New Jersey. The office in New York City was located at 1776 Broadway, a symbolically great address for the patriotic Yates who already used the American bald eagle as part of Consolidated's logo. The first Republic logo was a shield with "Republic Pictures" slanted across it, but soon thereafter a further touch of Americana appeared when it was supplanted by the Independence Hall tower that housed the Liberty Bell.

A few years later I recall Yates inviting all the directors and producers into the projection room to give their opinion on what was to be a new logo. When the picture came on the screen the bell tower had been replaced by a shield, but the eagle was still sitting on top of it. It made a handsome logo. The one part of the design that made it stand out was the broad black stripe that ran diagonally across the shield. The lights came back on and Yates stood up and asked everyone what they thought about it. Everyone seemed to agree with Yates that it was impressive and much better than the old one. Everyone but me. I said, "It stinks." Yates snapped his head around and looked at me; so did everyone else. "Mr. Yates, if we put that logo on our pictures we will be the laughing stock of this town," I said. "That black band across a shield is called the *Bar Sinister*. The bastard side of the royal families could use the family coat of arms, but it had to have the Bar Sinister or black band across it. Now I don't feel that Republic is the bastard side of the picture business." The proverbial pin could have been heard dropping in the projection room, and it would have sounded like a clap of thunder.

With the new Republic set-up and all the new pictures going into production, the cutting rooms had to expand. Joe Lewis was one busy boss. It was his job to oversee the editing of all the pictures. After a reel was edited, it was turned over to Roy Granville, who ran the sound effects department. Roy knew more about film than anyone I have ever known. He was a master at laying in the effects. When he was finished with the reel it would be turned over to Jerry Roberts who would lay in all the music. Most of the music was rented from the Abe Meyer Synchronization Service. It was bootlegged from Europe where it had been recorded by their big symphony orchestras.

The dubbing room, where all of the dialogue effects and music are blended into one track, was still at the Ralph Like Studio, which was located not far from where Hollywood and Sunset boulevards came together. There were several small studios in that area left over from the silent days. I think Ralph Like had taken over the old Charlie Ray Studio. All of the sound equipment had been rented from Ralph, and it was all bootlegged equipment. There were two types of sound that were patented at that time. One was by Western Electric and the other was by RCA. Western Electric's was "variable density" and RCA's was "variable area." Both were photographed on film and appeared in a long line that ran down one side of the film, about a quarter of an inch wide. The variable density had bars (striations) that ran across the track, and they got darker and lighter with the variation of sound vibrations they picked up. The variable area showed up on the film as a jagged line that ran up and down the track, and it got thicker and thinner as it picked up the vibrations.

Ralph Like sound was the Western Electric type. Being bootlegged, it was not as good as RCA but it was a lot cheaper. If you used Western Electric, besides having to rent their trucks, you had to pay royalties; with Ralph Like sound you only had to rent the trucks and equipment. Western Electric, of course, knew about the bootlegged equipment, but never stopped him from infringing. I don't know why that was so, but we discussed it many times and came up with the theory that Western Electric was afraid of an antitrust suit.

Shortly after Republic was formed, Joe Lewis quit as head of the cutting room. We were sorry to see him go since we all felt he was the head of our team, but he wanted to become a director. He followed his dream and became a damn good director. The main title card would read, "Directed by Joseph H. Lewis."

The studio replaced Joe with Murray Seldene. Murray and I had a personality clash, and I realized I could never be happy working with him. I went up to the front office and told Al Levoy I was going to quit and go back to school. I still remember him leaning back in his big leather chair and shaking his head. "You can't quit. We have too much invested in you. How old are you, anyway?" I told him I was nineteen. He nodded his head knowingly. "Look," he said, "go back out on the set and keep script for awhile. Your cutting room experience should make it easy for you. When you have cooled off, you can go back into the cutting rooms." When I left the cutting room I thought that I had also left Murray Seldene behind me, but Murray stayed at Republic as head of the cutting room for the next twenty years. Our paths crossed many times. By mutual agreement, we traveled in different lanes.

I looked up my old friend Larry Wickland. He was still working in the miniature department and designing sets. He had also been promoted to production supervisor along with Barney Sarecky on the serial that was about to go into production. It starred Clyde Beatty, the world famous animal trainer, and was called *Darkest Africa*. They hadn't hired a script clerk yet, and Larry told me to pick up a script and go see Barney. I had known Barney for a long time; he had been a regular at Mascot long before I came to work for them, and said I could share his office. Barney had been a script clerk on a lot of serials. He showed me the easy way to break down the wardrobe plot and told me the things to watch out for that might give me trouble.

Because of my cutting room experience, I knew I could bully my way through any of the technical parts. This was the first time I had been on the set every minute of the production. The two directors were Breezy Eason and Joe Kane. Breezy, of course, I knew, and Joe I had met in the cutting room. He was the editor on *Little Men*, one of the early features that Mascot had produced. Joe was a tall, gangly man who was very quiet and seemed to me to be shy. He had no sense of humor. He too stayed at Republic for the next twenty years, and when Republic folded he still didn't have a sense of humor.

Darkest Africa—The First Serial Under the Republic Banner

C lyde Beatty was a fascinating man—short, stocky, and good-looking. His arms—from handling the chairs and whips that his profession called for—looked like Popeye's after he had eaten a can of spinach. He was as quick as the lions and tigers that he trained and knew them forward and backward. He had to have more guts than they did because that is what it took to get into the ring with those big cats. He was quiet but friendly. He brought a few animals with him and kept them in cages on one of the small stages. Workers, carpenters, and electricians could walk onto the stage and the cats would never pay any attention to them. If the animals were asleep, they would not even raise their heads when the big doors were opened and closed. But the second Beatty stepped through the door, every animal came alive, and with a roar would start pacing the cages. Those animals had been raised in the wild, captured, and then trained as adults. The training had in no way domesticated them.

Beatty's act in the circus was one of the most hair-raising wild acts that ever hit the big top. The billboards said, "See one hundred lions and tigers in a cage at one time!" I don't know how many Beatty actually used, but the ring was full of very large cats. The ring had seats attached to the bars. The animal seats ran clear to the top of the cage. The handlers, using sticks to prod the cats through a chute that led into the ring from the animals' cages, would open a sliding door and allow one cat at a time into the caged ring. Beatty met them with a whip in one hand and a wooden chair in the other. He would yell "seat" and crack the whip at the animal. The cats knew where their own seats were and Beatty would work them up around the cage to the seat that belonged to them. Some of the cats had to be forced. They snarled and roared as he popped the whip and poked the chair in their faces. I asked him why the chair, and his answer made sense: "It has four legs that stick out at a cat. If you use just a single stick the cat can focus on it and knock it away. With four coming at him, he gets confused and backs away."

By the time Beatty got them all on their seats, he was surrounded by the big cats who never took their eyes off him. One mistake now and there would be the biggest and bloodiest cat fight in history. Lions and tigers do *not* like one another.

A few of the animals were specifically trained for certain tricks. Beatty would bring them off their seats one at a time, make them roll over, sit up, jump through flaming hoops, or walk a tightrope. For the grand finale, he would stand in the middle of the ring, wave the whip in a circular motion and all of the cats would sit up. Beatty would take a bow and throw the whip and chair to one side and start for the safety gate. Just then one of the lions on the far side of the ring would suddenly jump from his seat. Beatty would look back, see him, and run for the gate with the lion in hot pursuit. Beatty would always get through the gate just in time and slam it in the lion's face. The lion would come to a roaring halt. That brought the crowd screaming to their feet. Beatty would wait a few seconds, then slowly open the gate and stand face to face with the lion. The crowd, still standing, would freeze. Beatty pointed his finger at the lion and slowly advanced on him. They would stand eye to eye for a long moment. Then the lion would turn and run back to his seat. It was one hell of an act. I asked Beatty what would happen if the lion caught him before he could get out of the gate, and his answer was, "He would probably knock me down and give me a big kiss. He's the only lion in the cage that was raised in the kitchen."

Darkest Africa also had a young boy named Manuel King starring in it. They said he was eleven years old, but to me he looked and acted like eleven going on forty. They hired him because he had an animal act with lions and tigers that had been playing at fairs and in vaudeville. I never saw the act, but in one sequence he and Beatty had to drive off a pack of lions with just sticks. The kid worked the big cats alongside of Beatty, with the same professional approach that Beatty always showed when he was in the big cage.

His father was always on the set with Manuel and had trained the lion act that Manuel starred in. These big cats were tough and always ready to go on the attack. When the boy was working them, his dad stood, chair in hand, ready to charge through the safety gate at the first sign of danger. Mr. King did not want his son to come out second best to one of the big cats as he had. Mr. King had only one arm.

The script called for Beatty to wrestle a tiger in a pit. The set was built inside a sound stage and had three high walls that had been plastered to look like dirt. The fourth side was open so that the camera was on the floor of the small pit. The tiger had been trained to wrestle and had been rented from the Goebel

Clyde Beatty, Manuel King and Crash Corrigan in his ape suit.

Animal Farm in nearby Thousand Oaks. It had been declawed, but when it snarled even I could tell the teeth weren't false.

Beatty had never seen the tiger before that morning. The trainer went onto the set, and on command the tiger reared up and put his front legs over the trainer's shoulders. The trainer pushed the tiger backwards, and he and the cat went to the ground and rolled around.

I looked at Beatty. His face was a study of concentration as he studied the action in the pit. The wrestling match finished and the trainer came out to Beatty and said that was all there was to it. Beatty crouched and moved slowly and in a loud command he said "hup hup!" Beatty kept advancing, and the tiger kept backing up until its rear end hit the wall. Beatty kept giving the command "hup hup" as he moved closer to the tiger. The cat finally reared up on its hind legs and Beatty closed in on him.

I didn't realize until then how much strength this little man possessed. The tiger probably outweighed him by at least one hundred pounds, and Beatty moved fast as he ducked between its front legs. Beatty took the full weight of the cat as its legs draped over his shoulders. Beatty pushed the tiger backwards and locked one leg around the tiger's back legs. The cat went over and down on his back with Beatty on top. The tiger opened his jaws and locked them over the top of Beatty's head. Everyone on the set gasped. Beatty was faster than the tiger. Before the big cat could close its jaws, Beatty somehow got a hand in the cat's mouth and jammed his fist down the tiger's throat! The tiger coughed and Beatty rolled free. The trainer stepped in between the cat and Beatty with a chair, and Beatty, cat-like, came out of the set. The tiger had put two holes in his scalp that had to be stitched up. The next day Beatty again went into the cage with the tiger, and this time the wrestling match went as planned. I had never seen a picture crew, all of whom had seen stunt people risk their lives and had themselves dared fate in this wild and crazy business, hold another in such high respect as they did this quiet and friendly man.

The story line for *Darkest Africa* was about a lost city in the middle of the jungle. The writers put in everything, including the kitchen sink. I could believe all the lions and tigers, the lost diamond mine, white goddess, and costumes that looked like they came from Mars, but the kitchen sink lost me. The "flying bat men," who were dressed like Roman soldiers, had spears, but also had wings attached to their backs. The wings did not flap, but that didn't keep them from flying, even in formation. Larry Wickland had built life-sized balsa wood figures with wings and outstretched arms. On location at Iverson Ranch, the figures slid down piano wire, and they looked absolutely real as they came down from the high rocks over some extras running on the ground in the same spread-armed position, ready to take off.

The captain of the batmen was Ray "Crash" Corrigan. He was big and had muscles and he was fairly good looking. His claim to fame was that he had played Apollo in MGM's *Night Life of the Gods*. There was also a gorilla in the picture. Inside the gorilla suit was Crash Corrigan. He had made the suit himself and it was one of the best lifelike imitations I have ever seen.

On location at Lake Sherwood, the prop men had rigged hanging ropes that looked like vines. Crash, in his ape suit, was to swing from tree to tree. The trees were big sturdy spreading oaks, and the swings were designed so that Crash could stand on one limb and swing to another and land standing up. Although the person on the swing was never over six feet off the ground at any time, a low camera setup would make it seem like he was up in the treetops. Breezy Eason was the director. He made the swing and showed Crash what to do. Crash put on his ape suit and climbed up a ladder to the limb. The prop man handed him the headpiece.

After adjusting the headpiece, Crash grabbed the rope and took off. With his full weight on the rope, Crash lost his grip with one hand on the downward swing and on the upward swing his other hand gave way and he came crashing down to earth in a cloud of dust. Breezy turned to me and said, "With all those bulging muscles you'd think he would have enough strength to hold on." Then he added with a laugh, "That's what I'd call a real fart knocker!" As we ran to

Clyde Beatty fights one of the flying batmen. Compare this flying, and sliding down a wire, with one of Captain Marvel flying in chapter 15.

pick up the actor, Breezy and I wondered if this wasn't how Ray got the nickname Crash. The next take we did, the prop man tied Crash on the rope like a trunk on the top of a stagecoach, and we went swinging along to the next scene.

A few weeks after we finished filming *Darkest Africa*, Breezy began to prepare to direct a Gene Autry picture, *Red River Valley*. Gene had caught the public eye and it looked like he might end up as a big star. Breezy slapped me on the back and said, "Get a script. I'm taking you with me. We leave Monday for Yuma [Arizona] to use a little mine train that hauled rock to the dam they built a couple of years ago." So off we went.

It was the third day of production. Mandy Schaefer was the film's producer. Everything appeared to be in order; the little engine and the ore cars were picturesque and practical.

The story line had the heavies trying to stop the train by placing a wagon across the tracks. I can close my eyes and see it all again: The little train, smoke pouring from the engine's funny stack, barreling down the track toward the wagon, then the cowcatcher throwing the wagon in the air. And in slow motion we watched as a wheel came off the wagon and flew high into the air. The cameramen stepped back away from the camera and the heavy wheel landed on it dead center with the accompanying sound effect of a helluva crash.

Silence followed the noise as we all looked at the camera—or what had been a camera. Now all eyes turned to Mandy Schaefer. To save money Mandy had left the second camera at the studio. It would be the next day before another one could be sent from the studio. Mandy was famous for saving a buck. Now he stood in shock. The budget on the picture was as "shot to hell" as the camera. It was conference time with the crew in a circle around the camera which still had a large broken wheel sitting on top of it.

It so happened that David O. Selznick had a major motion picture—*The Garden of Allah*—in preproduction shooting nearby in the sand dunes. An old friend who had worked at Mascot was directing the second action unit. We all knew Otto Brower, so Breezy and Mandy hopped in a car and took off for the sand dunes that were about ten miles away. In half an hour they were back with a loaned camera, and I'm sure that Mandy thanked Allah.

The next day we were working on top of the dam that the little train had helped build. The top of the dam was about forty feet from the water. Breezy always wore white silk shirts and pants in the summertime. It was sort of a trademark. He was showing a stuntman who was going to fall off the top of the dam how he wanted it done. He said, "You take the bullet," Breezy grabbed his stomach and bent over, "then you stagger back to the edge of the dam." He staggered back to the edge of the dam and disappeared. Before we could run to the edge, there was a loud splash. When we looked down there was no sign of Breezy, only ripples from the splash. In a moment he bobbed to the surface, looked up and yelled, "But wait 'til the camera is running!"

A stuntman told me a story about Breezy. He wanted a Running W horse fall at the edge of a creek. The stuntman refused. He wanted to move it back a few feet so he could land on solid ground. Breezy got mad, put on the double's clothes and did the stunt himself. It was a spectacular horse fall, but he wound up with a broken arm. Over the many years that I stood behind the camera, I often thought about Breezy. I found myself using the same techniques that he had to make an action sequence come to reality.

When we returned to the studio, Larry Wickland told me that he was being promoted to supervisor for the next serial. That meant that he had everything directly on his shoulders. The front office gave him the title for a film and it was up to him to hire writers and get a story ready to fit that title, then be responsible to see that the picture was made for the money that the front office had budgeted for the project.

I asked him what happened to Barney Sarecky, the man who had worked so long for Mascot Pictures and had supervised production on the last two serials. Larry said that Universal Studios had started to make serials in competition with Republic and had hired him at a lot more money. He also said that Universal had hired John Rathmell and another writer, and he was looking for someone to replace them. This was early 1936.

Bob Livingston fights with Russian heavies in *The Vigilantes Are Coming.*

When I asked him what the new story was about, he said he would like to make a Zorro type of picture set in early California. I had been a nut on California missions since I'd been a kid. My sister Julie probably knew more about their history than the Catholic priests who watched over them. The two of us spent many hours wandering through the San Diego backcountry and exploring the many missions in the area. Some of them were abandoned and in ruins in those days, but since that time many of them have been restored. I told Larry about the missions and he said, "Let's go."

We spent three or four days wandering around the San Diego backcountry and Larry decided to bring a silent skeleton crew down and shoot a bunch of footage and chases around one old mission we found on the Pala Indian Reservation near Escondido. We could also hire the Indians and their horses a lot cheaper than the Hollywood cowboys.

We stopped at a roadside plaque to see what it said. The paint had peeled off years before and the only readable words said something about the Russians. On the way home Larry and I talked about the history of the Russians trying to take over California and make it part of the Russian empire. We both decided that we'd better hit the nearest library. Our combined knowledge about the subject was "poorly."

He hired Maury Geraghty and a kid named Winston Miller to write the serial. When I read the script I was delighted. No kitchen sink, no everything but—this story made sense. Sure, it was like Zorro. Sure it was like Robin Hood. Sure it had the black-hatted heavy, only this time he was dressed like a Russian soldier. The serial was titled *The Vigilantes Are Coming*.

Larry hired an actor who was just coming from a contract at MGM. Bob Livingston was one handsome young man, a good actor and a fine horseman, and he learned to handle a sword like an old fencing master. He also cast Big Boy Williams and Ray Hatton as his sidekicks. Two new directors also were hired, Mack Wright and Ray Taylor. Mack was a tall, handsome, gray-haired gentleman. Ray Taylor was short and thin, and seemed to run everywhere.

I asked Larry why he hadn't hired Breezy, and he told me he was working at Warner Bros., shooting the action sequences on *The Charge of the Light Brigade*. When I saw that picture I felt proud that I knew Breezy. The film's action sequences are the best ever put on film. I could see Breezy's touch in every horse fall and every explosion.

I went along with a second silent unit to the backcountry of San Diego. The skeleton crew consisted of a wardrobe man, a prop man, two grips, one cameraman and an assistant. We hired the Indians and their horses. When they were on the ground they looked funny in the Cossack costumes we had brought along, but on their horses they became believable. Larry was the director and I became his assistant and script clerk. I believe I was the only script clerk in history to lead Indians in cossack uniforms in chases and over the old broken down walls that surrounded the vacant crumbling missions, always taking time out to give slate numbers and make script notes.

The Old Order 5 Changeth

I headed for Larry's office to get my next assignment. When I opened the door I saw that there was another man sitting in the office with Larry. I said, "Sorry," and started to close the door. Larry waved at me to come in. As I closed the door behind me Larry introduced me to Sol Siegel and said that he was the new producer. Sol was a nice looking man, a little on the heavy side, with light sandy hair. He was from New York and I believe he came out of the record business. I immediately assumed he was here to learn the picture business.

Larry handed me a script and I glanced at the title. It read, *Robinson Crusoe of Clipper Island.* Larry had been working with some new writers to get the script together. He asked me if I'd like to go with him on a location scouting trip to the Santa Cruz Islands, about twenty miles off the coast just opposite Santa Barbara. He already knew the answer would be yes. I looked at Sol Siegel and knew that he wouldn't be going along. His fair skin indicated that the only water he had ever seen was from the Staten Island ferry.

In those days the Santa Cruz Islands were privately owned. Today they are a government-owned bird sanctuary and wildlife refuge. Larry had gotten permission from the owners to photograph the location. We rented a sailboat in Santa Barbara and crossed the channel, anchored the boat in Valdez Cove and spent the next three days exploring. It fit the script perfectly, with coves full of sea lions, high cliffs, and arches along the beaches with water pounding under them at high tide.

The small fishing boat was so loaded with camping equipment, camera gear, miniatures and cook stoves that the decks were nearly awash. The boat sank lower in the water every time one of the crew stepped aboard. We sat on top of the equipment whenever we could find a spot big enough. We had a camera crew of three, two grips, one dog trainer, one double dog for Buck the Saint Bernard, two acting doubles, one cook, Larry and me. As we chugged out of the breakwater and headed out into the Santa Barbara Channel, I looked

Lobby card for *Robinson Crusoe of Clipper Island*.

back at the large rowboat that we were dragging behind, with another one following, tied to its stern. I looked ahead and thanked the good Lord for giving us a beautiful day, with an ocean like glass and long lazy swells.

The captain pulled in as close as he dared to the lazy surf rolling in Valdez Cove. Most of us swam ashore, including the dog trainer and the double dog. The water was warm and so was the weather. It didn't take as long to unload the boat as it had to load it. We set up a camp and started to roll the camera after we ate a box lunch that we had brought along.

We had brought along a large miniature flying boat with a wing span of maybe ten feet. It was a perfect replica of the big clipper airplanes that flew over the oceans before jet aircraft was invented. At the end of World War II, I flew home from Hawaii in one that was identical to our replica. It had a circular stairway from the passenger compartment to the cockpit. The passenger windows were at water level when we started our take-off run and ten miles later the pilot lifted the plane off the water into the air. The trip took seventeen hours. The fuel was stored in the pontoon, and when we landed the passenger windows were about forty feet above the water. That is how much fuel the plane had used from Hawaii to San Francisco.

This was my first experience of shooting a "combination miniature." The camera was set up in the large rowboat, and we were perhaps two hundred feet from shore. The little miniature was floating close to the rowboat. The camera was shooting over the miniature toward the shore. On the shore the two doubles ran down the beach, launched the small rowboat through the surf and rowed toward the miniature. The camera speed was cranked up from the normal of twenty-four frames a second to forty-eight frames to take any jerky motion out of the small airplane bobbing on the ocean swells.

Next we shot a process plate of the shoreline, with the water in the foreground. This was used on the process stage to simulate an open door inside the airplane. The rowboat on wheels would be pulled into the space between the set and the picture on the process screen and the two men would climb out of the boat into the airplane. Most of the material we were to shoot was long shots of a few doubles running the beaches, and the lead's double and the double for Buck the Saint Bernard dog being chased down the beaches.

Valdez Cove—where the camp was set up—was famous during the prohibition years for being the base of the rumrunners who ran booze between the islands and Santa Barbara. This had only been a couple of years before, so after dinner every night we all went digging in the many caves that had been formed over hundreds of years by the pounding surf to look for any booze that might have been hidden and forgotten. We dug and dug, but when we set sail for home we all admitted it was the driest camp we had ever been in.

The dog trainer's name was Carl Spitz. Carl was German and had only been in the United States a few years. He had a heavy accent, and he said that Hitler had driven him out of his homeland. This was the first time I'd ever heard the name Hitler. Around the campfire at night, Carl told us about the man and what he was doing to Germany. It wasn't too many years before the world was hearing the same stories that Carl told around the campfire.

Carl was an excellent dog trainer, and Buck, his Saint Bernard, had just starred in *Call of the Wild* with Clark Gable. He had only brought his double on this trip. "Cappy" turned out to be the best trained dog I ever worked with.

About the fourth day, Cappy's feet were so sore from running over the rough rocks and shells on the beaches that he left a trail of blood after each scene, but still he would work. We didn't have a wardrobe man, but we did have sewing equipment. Carl and I cut out the tongues of everyone's shoes. I had learned to make sails and repair them when I lived in Coronado, and those skills allowed me to make Cappy some very fancy booties that protected his feet from the rocks. Carl, Cappy, and I became good friends, a friendship that lasted for many years.

Larry came to me early in the morning on the third day. He nodded for me to follow him away from camp. Something was bothering the hell out of him. In a moment it was bothering the hell out of me too. He stopped, looked back to camp, shook his head and in a low voice said, "The cook's got a dose of clap." My "Oh boy! Oh boy!" didn't help. Larry asked, "Shall I tell the crew?" I said, "Hell yes, but let's get him out of here right now." Larry looked at the fishing boat that had brought us here. "We've got to get another cook. Can you keep the crew working while I go to Santa Barbara and find someone to replace him?" I said, "I think so, Larry, if there is no miniature work." We walked back to where the cook was serving breakfast, picked up a script and looked at the day's work. There were some miniature shots planned, but we crossed them off and substituted some process plate work instead.

In an hour Larry and the cook headed for the mainland in the fishing boat with the captain at the helm. As the boat got smaller I prayed that no one would get hurt while our only means of transportation to the mainland was not standing by.

One of the stuntmen we had brought along to double Ray Mala was Loren Riebe. Loren had been a trapeze artist in the circus. He could do it all. He was a great tumbler and acrobat. He was the only man I've ever known who could walk up to a doorway and reach up, grab the frame with his fingertips and do a one-arm lever. This means he could pull his body up parallel to the floor with legs straight out and hold that position for a minute or two. We had struck up a friendship swimming together every evening. That friendship would remain until his untimely death in an airplane accident in the late 1950s.

Larry didn't get back that afternoon. When we finished shooting, Loren and I climbed the cliff in back of the cove to see if we could see any signs of the fishing boat coming back. We walked along the top of the cliff. When we looked down, the surf was breaking about one hundred feet from the base of the cliff. I guessed the cliff was about two hundred fifty feet above the surf, Loren thought about a hundred and fifty. He knew that there was a scene where Mala dove off a cliff to get away from the heavies. We talked about it for a few minutes, threw some rocks to see how far out they landed, marked the spot as best we could and made our way down to the beach below.

Loren Riebe's dive off the cliff. It was used as a main title background. It takes guts to take off from the top of a cliff when there is only dry beach when you look down.

The tide was almost full in and the breakers behind the crest were rolling almost to the base of the cliff. When they rolled back, the sand was exposed on the beach. We waded out to the spot Loren thought the dive would carry him. We were about waist deep in water, but when the next wave swept over us and then settled down before it started out to sea, there was about fifteen feet of water.

The fishing boat with Larry and the new cook got back just at dusk. We all helped unload some fresh fruit and other supplies and I told Larry what I had shot that day, and about Loren and the dive.

Just before high tide the next morning, we set the camera up on the beach below. Loren climbed to the top of the cliff and started to throw rocks at the surf below. He had to time his dive so that the wave would be full in when he hit the water. He waved at us to roll the camera, and a moment later took off from the cliff. When he jumped there was no water under him, only sand. His arms came out in a perfect swan dive. He seemed to float down and the wave seemed to speed up to be under him when he hit the water. He landed, hardly making a splash. I ran to the beach and dove into the water just to make sure he hadn't hit the bottom, but he surfaced before I got there. The dive was used in the main title to open the picture. It was a beauty!

The picture went into production a couple of weeks after we got back from Santa Cruz. It had Ray Taylor and Mack Wright as directors. Mack had come up from an assistant director. I had worked with him before.

Ray Mala was the lead. He was half Eskimo and had starred in *Eskimo*. It was a semidocumentary picture made by MGM and was a big moneymaker. The leading lady was Mamo Clark, who was Clark Gable's girl in *Mutiny on the*

Bounty. Rex, the horse, was not the same horse we worked with on *Rex, King of the Wild Horses*, but was a new horse that never had the fire that the old stallion Rex was born with. Buck the Saint Bernard finished out the cast.

The shooting went smoothly until the last week of the picture. We were working in the old rock quarry in Bronson Canyon. The floor of the old quarry is covered with sharp jagged rocks. Ray Taylor was directing. Loren Riebe, riding Rex, was to come in on a gallop and pick Mala up and throw him up behind him and gallop up the hill. This is not a difficult stunt, but there was no saddle on the horse. I watched as Ray set up the shot with Mala and Loren. I went to Mala and told him to let his double do the stunt. Mala was a good athlete and as game as they come. He said, "I can handle it."

He couldn't. Loren came in on a full gallop, reached down with his right hand and caught Mala's arm. The momentum of the horse threw Mala onto the back of the horse—almost. Mala slipped off the horse and landed in the rocks on his back. We sent him to the hospital. His back wasn't broken, but he could hardly walk for the rest of the picture. To this day I blame Ray Taylor. He should never have asked Mala to try the pickup while the double was standing and watching.

The day before the picture was to finish we were working in the big tin shed in the cave set. The cameraman had two open arcs, and the grips were shaking some branches with leaves on them in front of the lights to cast a shadow that looked like the reflection of a big fire. This was supposed to be a volcano starting to erupt. Situations like this were the only times that arcs were ever operated without the glass lens in front because the arc, like a welder's arc, throws off a bright light that will sunburn your eyes.

John Piccori was playing a high priest and worked in front of the arcs all day. The next morning his wife brought him to the studio hospital. He had what the old vaudeville actors who used to work in front of the arc footlights called "klieg eyes." His eyes were sunburned. The only way to cure it was to slice potatoes very thin and make a poultice to cover the eyes. The potatoes would turn black in just a few minutes, and the whole process was very painful. We doubled him for the long shots, but for the close-ups they led him in front of the camera, rolled it, and pulled off the poultice. He would read his lines and the doctor would slap the poultice back on. This was making commercial pictures at its worst: not even a blind actor in pain could stop the studio from finishing a picture on time.

Larry asked me if I would go back into the cutting room and help cut a few episodes. They couldn't find another cutter and there was a release date to meet, so again I joined that beautiful lady, Helene Turner, who had taught me so much when I was her assistant. Larry promised he'd keep Murray Seldeen off my back, and I'd keep script on the next serial.

It was quite a change going from the noisy set, with the dead run pace of commercial production that was never slowed by heat or cold, to the quiet and relaxed cutting rooms. I renewed my friendship with Roy Granville, the sound editor, and Jerry Roberts, the music editor.

In the normal way any picture is edited (or cut), the cutter puts all the pieces together the way he feels makes for the best picture. Then a cutting session is set up with the producer and director to show them the first cut. This is a stop and go session where anyone can stop the picture at any point to discuss any problem. The cutter takes notes and makes the changes. On the serials usually there were only two cutting sessions. The third was to check the composite answer print before all of the theater prints were run off a lavender dupe negative. The original negative was stored away and only used to replace a worn out dupe negative.

Before *Robinson Crusoe* was finished, Larry knew he was over budget. The serials were sold to the exhibitors by the episode for fifteen or twenty dollars each. He decided that if he could find a way to make two extra episodes by reusing the film that had already been shot, he could make up the deficit. He assigned Barry Shipman, a young writer on the serials, to see if it could be done, and the retrospect episodes were born. *Robinson Crusoe* was written for twelve episodes. When it was released it had fourteen.

A retrospect episode was where someone says, "Remember the volcano exploding?" Then the sequence of the volcano is lifted from an earlier episode. A dupe negative is made from the entire sequence and inserted into the new episode. It is like seeing a rerun on television. Barry wrote the new episodes from the old script, along with two new episode endings and "takeouts." A takeout was the way the hero got out of the death-defying predicament in which he was trapped at the end of the previous episode.

The few additional scenes needed for the new episodes were shot on the last day of regular filming, so they did not cost anything. The only trouble was that the directors had changed the script on the set and Barry didn't know it. When I tried to put the episodes together in the cutting room, they just didn't make sense. Larry, Helene and I tried every possible way to correct the oversight. We decided to shoot a couple of inserts of hands, rocks, smoke—anything that was in the scene—and use a voice-over to tie the story together. That didn't work either, but that's the way the episodes were finally released. In later serials there was usually one retrospect episode. They were a little improved, but not much. They still stunk.

Roy loved horses as much as I did. There was a stable across the creek bed that ran through the studio back lot. It was run by John Goodwin, who was also a horse trainer and dealer. Roy found a small buckskin that had belonged to a professional calf roper, and I found a big sorrel that looked like he might wind up as a jumper, and we bought them. Every evening after work we'd saddle up and ride for an hour or so in the long summer twilight.

One evening Roy had to work late, so I went for a ride by myself. At the time only the main streets of Studio City were paved and there were very few houses. You could ride for miles and never see a car. In the distance I saw a girl on a little white chunky horse who was riding in the same direction that I was. The horse was walking and she turned to see who was catching up to her at a slow canter. I pulled up beside her and pulled down to a walk. After we greeted each other, she grinned at me and said, "Can he run?" I shrugged, "I don't know." "Let's find out," she said, and took off in a dead run. A moment later I took off after her. I chased her for two blocks before I knew that I didn't have a chance against this pretty girl who sat in her saddle like a cowboy.

She pulled up laughing. "That answers that question. He can't." I sat looking at her. She was a real beauty, and I liked her. She turned and started to walk to cool her horse and I fell in beside her. Her name was Maxine Jones. A few blocks away she stopped in front of an iron gate. Behind it was a big house that you could see through the walnut trees. She stepped off her horse to open the gate. "I live here. Maybe we can race again sometime." I smiled and said, "I sure hope so." I watched as she closed the gate and led her little horse up the driveway. She turned and waved. As I turned the horse back toward the stable, I looked at the name on the rural mailbox out on the street. It read B. Jones.

We did race again and again. It seemed like we were destined to meet. Both of us seemed to enjoy the long evening walks. The "B" in front of the Jones name stood for Buck. Maxine's father was Buck Jones, one of the biggest cowboy stars of the early westerns. Maxine came by her riding ability honestly. Her mother was a champion trick rider, and she'd been sitting on a horse before she could walk.

I had met Maxine's mother, but not Buck until one moonlit night when Maxine and I were slowly walking home. We had been out since about 6:00, and it was now about 11:00. We moved off the road to let a car pass, but it didn't. Instead it pulled up so that its headlights were shining on us. A head stuck out the window and a deep, heavy, authoritative voice bellowed at us, "Get your ass home!" I had just met Buck Jones.

Maxine told me a wonderful true story. When she was about five years old her father bought out a wild west show and took it on the road. Her mother worked in it as a trick rider, and she rode in the grand parade. The rains came that summer, and the people stayed home rather than face the mud. The wild west show went broke when it hit the Midwest, and went into bankruptcy. Everything in the show had to be sold off by the sheriff to pay the creditors.

Silver, Buck's famous horse, was included with the items to go under the auctioneer's hammer. Buck hired a local attorney who told him there was an old law still on the books that said, "when a man goes into bankruptcy, the sheriff must leave him a horse and a gun." Buck checked with the sheriff who confirmed it. Buck knew that a "horse" would never include Silver, who was as famous with the fans as Buck.

The night before the auction they painted the real Silver—who was snow white—black and substituted another white horse in his stall. Early the next morning the sheriff came and Buck asked if it was all right to leave. With the sheriff's permission he strapped on his gunbelt, threw Maxine up on the painted Silver, and with Maxine's mother leading Silver they headed for another state.

I saw a lot of Maxine the next few weeks. We went out to dinner, and rode all the amusement rides at the Santa Monica pier. We both loved the roller coaster. I decided that just maybe I might spent the rest of my life with her. I didn't know about Noah Beery, Jr.—Pidge to everyone. He had been on location and had returned to pick up his friendship with Maxine. Old John Goodwin who ran the stable told me that they had been going together a long time. They were married a short time later.

I worked with Pidge many times in later years and still call him a good friend today. I was kidding him one day, "If I'd have met her first, I might have beaten you out." By this time they had been divorced for a few years and he looked at me, and in his own homey way drawled, "Just your good luck."

Thirty years later I attended one of those nostalgia film festivals at the Ambassador Hotel that was screening some of the old serials. There were a lot of the old leading men and women that I had worked with, and it was great to renew acquaintances. We all gathered around a big table to have lunch when someone tapped me on the shoulder. I turned to see who it was and two soft hands took hold of my face, and someone on the other end of the hands planted a big kiss smack dab on my mouth, then stepped back and said, "Remember?"

A tall, slender, beautiful woman stood looking down at me. As I stood up I glanced at the people at the table. They were all grinning. They knew I didn't remember the now smiling face that I studied. There was something very familiar about it, but I drew a blank. She puckered her lips. "Want to try it again? Maybe it will bring back some memories." I looked at the group at the table. They were all smiling but I knew I wasn't going to get any help from them. She said, "Let's go ride a roller coaster." A big light shined in my head. Now I knew. "Or a horse race?" I asked. It was Maxine Jones.

Maxine passed away in the late eighties. I'll never forget the pretty girl sitting on the little white horse.

A lobby card for Dick Tracy.

Larry brought me a script for the next serial, *Dick Tracy* and asked me if I'd like to go to San Francisco with him to photograph the opening of the new Oakland Bay Bridge that had just been completed. It was an eight-mile span, an engineering marvel that connected Oakland to San Francisco.

The end of the first episode of *Dick Tracy* had the bridge being destroyed by sound waves coming from an airplane called "The Wing." Dick Tracy had a speech near the end that summed up how the heavies were going to achieve this: "Enrico Caruso's voice could shatter a wine glass by finding the wave length of a crystal glass." The heavies had a machine that could send out sound waves focused on the bridge. They would shake it to the ground. Many years later the army experimented with sonic booms to do the same thing, and the army came out with a plane that looked just like the wing that the Lydecker brothers from our miniature department had dreamed up for the serial.

The small crew took off for San Francisco the day before the big opening ceremony and ribbon-cutting was to take place. We needed some shots of the empty bridge and the cars starting out over it. In the script, after Tracy finds out about the sound waves, he says, "If we can load the bridge with cars and trucks, it will change the length of the sound waves—like the glass Caruso could break empty, but full of wine the glass would be safe."

We photographed the empty bridge. I don't think it has ever been empty since. Our camera car led the parade and all of the dignitaries over the bridge. All of the footage was used in the serial. To me it was one of the best and most logical of all of the hundreds of episodes I've watched.

Larry had picked a young actor named Ralph Byrd for the role of Dick Tracy. He looked like the character Chester Gould drew in his *Dick Tracy* comic strip that Republic had bought to put on film. His jutting jaw and piercing eyes, with a trim, practical, athletic body, didn't match the comic strip exactly, but over the years Gould slowly changed his cartoon character to look like Ralph. Ray Taylor and Alan James were the directors. The serial went into production in late November, 1936.

After the first week, we started to fall behind schedule. There was a twenty-four day shooting schedule, and we were to finish just before Christmas. If we had to carry the crew over the Christmas holidays, it would be a real budget buster. The delay wasn't the director's fault. It was caused by bad weather, and a script that had sequences that were more time consuming production-wise than most of the previous serials.

Larry asked me if I thought the kid who was keeping script notes could handle my job for the next couple of days. His name was Buddy Springsteen. With that arranged, I directed a second unit on location, with some chases, a sequence at the Van Nuys City Hall Building, and some process pickup shots. The serial finished on time. It was Christmas Eve, and all we had left to do was walk from one stage to the next to join the noisy Christmas party that Republic always gave for its employees.

Again the cutters were behind schedule and struggling to meet release dates that had already been set up by the exhibitors. Consequently, it was back to the cutting room for me to help out. I cut together the sequences that I had directed. There were about five hundred feet of edited film, a total of a little over five minutes. I looked at the trim, a basket of film that had been shot but not used. There was a lot more than five hundred feet, since the basket was full. It would go into the salvage barrel to be processed to take out the silver in the emulsion. It was worth practically nothing.

I took a few minutes to measure each scene and the trims left over from them. The long shots had the most waste. They were only used to establish where the scene took place and who was in it. Later, when I became a director, I remembered that afternoon in the cutting room.

Rider of the Painted Stallion

*I*t was four weeks before Larry called me into his office again. He was the associate producer on a new serial entitled *The Painted Stallion*. He gave me a script and asked me if I'd like to go to Utah with him to scout locations. We took off the next morning and spent the next few days wandering through some beautiful country. It was January and cold, with hip-deep snow covering most of the places we scouted.

Larry finally settled on St. George, a small town with one street and one hotel owned by Jockey Hale, who helped us contact the Indian reservation agent. The hotel had enough rooms for our crew if everybody doubled up, but there was only one bathroom on each floor. It was going to be a rough trip.

St. George is about a hundred and fifty miles from Las Vegas, Nevada. The nearest railroad station was at Moapa, Nevada, about fifty miles from St. George. Larry decided that it would be cheaper to rent cars and busses in St. George rather than bring them from the studio. We would come by train and Jockey Hale would do all of the advance work. Larry decided to tell everybody that it was going to be a tough location, so they could make up their own minds whether they wanted to weather the storm or not.

We were scheduled to return to St. George during the first week of February to commence principal photography on *The Painted Stallion*. As we were preparing to leave, another bombshell rocked the studio. Nat Levine resigned. Yates had now bought out the last of the men who had pooled their companies to form Republic Pictures. With the buyout there was supposedly a stipulation that Levine would not go back into independent production for two years. (I'm not sure about the time, but that was the rumor.) Yates must have had this in mind when he got them all together in the first place. Now he had it all: the studio, the exchanges, and the personnel to make his own pictures and keep his laboratory moving ahead to number one. I will say one thing for him. He screwed a lot of very smart men.

Soon thereafter Bert Clark, my brother-in-law, resigned and moved to

Paramount as a producer-writer. But the one that hurt the most was losing Al Levoy who had been steering my career with his sound advice. He left with Levine. I felt I'd lost my best friend.

Levine's office was then taken over by Sol Siegel's brother Moe. He was now the head of the studio. M.J. Siegel looked so much like Babe Ruth that when he traveled he was asked to autograph baseballs. He didn't carry a bat but the studio soon found out he wouldn't hesitate to tell you that you were out. Despite this distraction, my focus returned to getting *The Painted Stallion* underway.

The crew, actors and stunt people loaded the train early in the morning. We were to get to Moapa around 5:00 that afternoon. The trucks and equipment had left for the location a few days earlier. Alan James, who was to direct on the first day, had gone ahead with Larry to pick his location for the first day's shooting.

The train creaked and rumbled, and the coach car was uncomfortable. After a few hours, somebody broke out a bottle and we all had a drink. By mid-afternoon, nobody was feeling any pain. Ray Taylor had brought his son, who was about ten years old, with him. It seems that Ray had a drinking problem and Ray's wife had sent the boy along, apparently to try to keep him sober. By the time we got to Moapa, Ray was loaded.

Larry was waiting for us at the train station with a couple of cars and a small bus. The wind was howling and it was freezing cold when the train stopped. We all crowded into the small station, which consisted of one room with a big potbellied stove in the middle. The stationmaster knew we were coming and, trying to be nice, he had built a red hot fire in the stove. The place was as hot as hell.

Apparently Ray's son was trying to get him to come with him to the car waiting outside. Ray objected to being pulled, and he pushed the kid roughly away. The boy hit the wall and fell. I didn't see that, but the next thing I knew, Lee Lukather, the lead grip, grabbed Ray by the front of his coat. I thought Lee was going to hit Ray, so I grabbed Lee around the neck and we both went down. We got up facing each other. Lee and I were friends, having lived together at Santa Cruz Island and worked on two or three serials together. I said, "Sorry, I thought you were going to hit him." Lee looked at Ray, holding onto a chair to stand up, and said, "Thanks. I might have."

Larry came through the crowd, wanting to know what was wrong. Yakima Canutt pushed his way through the crowd as well. Yak was the stuntman on the picture, and all of us had worked with him and liked him. He had worked with Ray on many pictures. He offered to take Ray, and asked Larry which car to use. Larry said he could take any of the cars, but to take the boy along with them. Yakima took Ray's arm and easily pulled him outside. Larry looked at me, then at Lee. Nobody said a word. The assistant director then came up and suggested, "Let's get the hell out of here. It's a long drive to St. George."

When we arrived in St. George, we all settled into the cramped hotel. At dinnertime we got the shock of our lives—Utah was dry. It didn't mean anything to me, but half of the crew mumbled something that sounded like "sorry I came."

I was sound asleep when the racket of someone pounding on a door woke me up. Then I heard voices. I was bunking with Bud Springsteen, the other script clerk, who was keeping the script notes for the cutting room. We both sat up in bed a moment, and then I got up and threw on a robe. Looking out in the hall, I saw Ray Taylor pounding on the door of the girl we had brought along to double the leading lady. Her name was Babe DeFreest, and she was a champion horsewoman. We had all worked with her before.

Ray was drunk, and again Yak came down the hall. "Damn you, Ray," he said. "When I put you to bed you promised you'd stay there!" Ray looked at him and told him to mind his own business. Yak took him by the arm and growled, "This is my business." Then he looked at me and said, "Give me a hand." Yak dragged him down the hall into the only bathroom on the floor. Inside was a great big bathtub, which Yak told me to run full of cold water. As the tub filled, Ray fought to get away from Yak. Needless to say, Ray's language wouldn't pass the censorship board.

Ray was in his pajamas, and we picked him up and dumped him into the cold water. After we got him back in bed, I walked to Babe's room and knocked on the door. She peeked out, then opened it. She stood smiling at me as I asked if she was scared. She moved to a chair and picked it up over her head and held it like a club. "Hell no. Why didn't you let him come in? I was ready to greet him!" she said, shaking the chair.

The picture started filming the next day with Alan James directing. On the second day Ray took over. He was sober, but in bad shape. That night at dinner there was a vacant seat next to Larry. He asked how the day had gone, and I told him it was okay. We both decided that the crisis was over and that Ray would be all right from there on out.

The weather so far had been good. This was February, and in Utah we all knew anything could happen with the weather. That night it turned freezing cold. The next morning everyone wore heavy coats and stocking caps. Ray had a big sheepskin coat with the collar turned up. He got out of the car and gave the first setup to the cameraman. The prop man brought him a chair and set it up next to the camera. The first scene Ray was to direct was a run-through of Yakima doubling the leading man. He was to come from the background and make an exit close to the camera.

Ray said "roll it." The camera man replied "speed," and the assistant director yelled, "Come on, Yak." Yak spurred the horse and they came on a dead run, just missing the camera. Then Ray got up from his chair and started to walk across the barren landscape. I noticed that he hadn't said "print it," so I looked at the cameraman and said, "I guess it's a print."

When a director walks away from a scene the crew always follows. It is a regular routine on any picture. The crew knows the director is going to pick the next camera setup. So the crew picked up the reflectors, the assistant camera-man shouldered the camera, and the sound truck wrapped up its cables. Every-one followed Ray.

About three hundred yards from the first setup there was one small sage-brush poking its head up about three feet above the barren landscape. Ray stepped in back of it and ducked out of sight. As the crew moved toward the spot, all we could see was the big fleece-lined coat collar showing above the sparse brush. Ray was still squatted down when we caught up to him.

He pulled a pint bottle from the inside of his big sheepskin, pulled out the cork, and took a big slug from the bottle. Carefully putting the cork back in, he put it back inside his coat. By now the whole crew had circled him, watch-ing.

As he stood up, Larry pushed his way into the circle, stood a few moments looking at him, then turned to Lee Lukather, who was standing next to him. He said in a quiet voice, "Lee, put him in a car and send him home." Lee's jaw took a grim set as he answered, "It'll be a pleasure." He walked over, took Ray's arm, and said, "Come on." He pulled him toward the parked equipment. Ray never said one word; apparently that wasn't the first nip he'd had that morning.

We watched as the car pulled out. Now all of the thirty or more crew members turned to Larry. With no director, what now? We were three hundred miles from home. Larry walked over to me and said, "You know I can't take over directing and keep the company running, too. There isn't anyone else that's ever read the script. Can you take over?"

I looked at the crew. Their deeply lined faces from working in the sun and wind gave testament to the fact that they were all professionals. They had prob-ably made more pictures than I'd ever seen in my baby-faced twenty-one years of life. Now they all stood looking at me. I knew all of them pretty well, and I was sure they were all my friends. I turned back to Larry. "Okay," I said, "but get another director up here as fast as you can. I don't want to be a director, Larry. I want to go back into the cutting rooms where I belong."

I finished the day's work and we went back to the warm hotel earlier than usual. I had made some new friends, that was for sure. I immediately looked up Alan James. He knew what had happened and asked me if he could help in any way. I told him they were going to get another director here, so I'd only have one more day.

There will probably never be another stuntman who can compare to Yakima Canutt. He had been a world champion cowboy several times and where horses were concerned he could do it all. He invented all the gadgets that made stunt work easier. One of his clever devices was a step that attached to the saddle so that he had leverage to transfer to another moving object, like a wagon or train. Another was the "shotgun," a spring-loaded device used to separate the tongue of a running wagon from the horses, thus cutting the horses loose. It also included a shock cord attached to the wagon bed, which caused the wheels to cramp and turn the wagon over on the precise spot that was most advantageous for the camera.

He had also designed a blindfold to put on a horse so that the horse could not see him drop off a rock or wall onto its back. A blindfolded horse will stand still. If you're dropping off a ten-foot wall onto a horse's back and he moves, there is no way you're going to hit the saddle with your feet to break the speed of the drop, then slide into the saddle. The blindfold was made up of two round pieces of leather with eyes painted on them. A straight pin was run through two loops between the eyes to hold them together. The blindfold was then tied behind the horse's ears to hold it in place. A string was tied to the straight pin and run over the horse's head between the ears and tied to the reins on the horse's neck. When Yak hit the saddle and picked up the reins, the string pulled the pin and the blindfold dropped off so that the horse could see and Yak could gallop him out of the scene.

The night before Yak got married we gave him a stag party. We had one of those gadgets made up in very fancy lace. We even had the eyes painted on it. We thought it would make him more comfortable to use something he was used to on his wedding night.

My first day of planned shooting had some stunt work that involved Yak. He was going to turn over a small buckboard pulled by two horses. We had brought the buckboard with the trick shotgun tongue from the studio where the welder in the special effects department had assembled it under Yak's watchful eye. The horses and harness were rented from local ranchers.

I asked Yak where I should put the camera. He said that the running team coming straight at the camera would be the best angle because the team would be past the camera, giving a clear view of the wagon turning over to the audience.

The cameraman moved the camera back further from the stunt than I wanted it. When I complained he said that he had a close-up lens that would give the same effect as putting the camera in the spot I'd picked, but that this way there was no chance that the team, when it was running loose, would hit the camera. Yak measured the airplane cable that was to pull the safety off the pelican hook that held the tongue in place. He drove several steel stakes in the ground to secure the end of the cable, and hooked the other end of the cable to the wagon. Then he carefully laid the cable out so that the team wouldn't get tangled in it. He put a small piece of white paper on the ground to mark the spot where he was to jump off the wagon. He was ready.

This was the first stunt that I was responsible for. I had seen many of them shot, had seen stuntmen sent to the hospital and horses hurt and put away on the set, but it was like watching a rodeo or a football game from the stands. You feel sorry, but you don't feel responsible for the injuries, and you don't usually know the injured. This was different. I knew Yak, knew his wife Audrey, and knew he had a couple of kids.

The horses were supposed to run about two hundred feet before the wagon was to break loose. I looked at Yak as he climbed onto the wagon seat and picked up the reins. A wrangler stood in front of the team, holding them. He would wave to me when Yak was set, and when I yelled, "Come on!" he would turn them loose, falling to the ground behind a sagebrush to hide from the camera. I said a little prayer and turned to look at the cameraman. He said, "We're ready." The wrangler waved his hat. I could hear the camera roll, and when somebody yelled "speed" I turned and yelled, "Come on, Yak!"

Yak had a whip in his hand and used it on the team, then threw it away. The team took off on a dead run. I watched as it closed on the spot where Yak was to jump. About twenty feet before it hit the turnover spot, one of the traces (the parts of the harness that attach the horses to the wagon) broke. The sudden release of the weight of the wagon on that side jerked one horse into the other, knocking him to his knees. Yak jerked on the reins and pulled him to his feet. The tongue broke and the team pulled loose from the wagon, jerking Yak off the seat and into the path of the wagon. The wagon rolled over on top of him, and the team came straight at the camera.

We all scrambled to get out of the way. The team just missed the camera, and before the dust had settled, I was on a run to Yak, who was still on the ground. The wagon lay on its side next to him. Before I got there, Yak got to his feet. I stopped in front of him. He looked at me a moment, then turned his head and let go of a big stream of tobacco juice. He walked over to the wagon and looked at the broken trace. "That's the last time I'll ever use a bunch of rotten local equipment!" he said. Yak kicked the trace hanging from the wagon. It was backed up by one of the wheels, and when his foot came in contact with the wheel, he hopped around on the other foot for a moment or two. *His* language would not have passed the censorship board. When the wagon rolled over Yakima it hadn't hurt him, but his kick to the wheel left him limping for a couple of days.

No director had shown up from Hollywood when we got back to the hotel that afternoon. I couldn't find Larry then, but that night I asked him

In *Zorro's Fighting Legion,* Yakima Canutt is coming off a wall onto a horse. If you'll look at the horse's head you can see the blindfold over his eyes and string that holds it over his ears and under his chin.

when the new director was going to arrive. He said they were still trying to find one, but that they hadn't had any luck yet.

The camera crew consisted of Bill Nobles, the first cameraman, Eddie Lyons, the operator, and Monty Steadman, the assistant. There was another assistant, but he was an extra. The other three were a team. All of them had been in the business for a long time and had come up from the silent days with the

This is the baby face that said good morning to a crew that were all twice my age. I knew how John Ford's second lieutenants felt when they were sent to lead Sargent Victor McLaglan's squad.

hand-cranked cameras. Monty had been a middleweight boxing champion in the army during World War I. His sister had been a star in the silent days— Vera Steadman.

They were standing in front of the hotel before dinner, bemoaning the fact that the whiskey bottle was empty. Next door to the hotel there was a drugstore. It had the usual soda and ice cream fountain. I suggested to them that they go see the local town doctor and get a prescription. No good—they'd already tried it. He was a Mormon.

We decided to try the druggist. We picked Eddie up by the arms and legs and carried his moaning body into the drugstore and laid him on the floor. The druggist came from behind the soda fountain, looked at the moaning Eddie, and asked what was wrong. We told him he needed whiskey. It was the only thing that could pull him through. He walked to the front door and looked up and down the street, then came back. He stepped over Eddie and disappeared into the back of the store. In a moment he was back, hiding something under his white coat. He kneeled down to Eddie and slipped a bottle under his sweater, stood, and said, "The prescription will cost you three dollars."

Billy Nobles said he hoped there was more of that medicine available, just in case. The druggist said, "I like to take a nip, too. If you run out, there's plenty more. Just be sure that when you come in, somebody has on a loose sweater. I'm short of wrapping paper." We went back to the room and toasted the pharmacist for saving our lives.

Billy gave me my first lesson in photography. About the fourth day of shooting, I stood looking at a setup for a few lines of dialogue. He took me by my shoulders and turned me ninety degrees. I looked at him. "What's that for?" He answered, "It's obvious that they're not going to bring in another director. You're doing a better job than Alan, and you're making the schedule earlier and easier than any director we've had since Breezy, so if I'm going to be stuck with you, I'd better teach you a little bit about the camera end of the business."

He turned me back ninety degrees to the camera setup I had just picked. "If you feel the heat of the sun on the back of your neck, that's called flat light. Turn until the sun is hitting the side of your face, and makes you squint. That's called cross light. I know it's tough looking into the sun, but if you have flat light during the dialogue, the shadow of the mike is going to be on the actor's faces, and I'll have to take time to break out a scrim to take the sun off their faces. Then I'll have to break out another reflector to put some light back onto their faces. It's time we're talking about."

I looked at his weather-beaten face, and then at the weather-beaten faces of the crew. The sun had beat the hell out of them all. I slowly walked around in back of them. "Billy," I said, "how come the back of your necks are as wrinkled and beat up as your faces?" He shook his head and explained, "It's because I didn't get the damn directors early enough in life to train them."

I realized that Larry didn't intend to get another director to replace me, so I settled into the every-other-day routine of directing. There was one sequence of an Indian attack on the wagon train. It was scheduled on one of my shooting days. Larry hired about a hundred Indians and their horses from the Ute Indian reservation for two or three days. I picked the location and the whole tribe moved nearby and set up an Indian village. About twenty tepees appeared out of nowhere. From the ranchers around St. George, Larry found enough wagons and people to man them to make up a good-sized wagon train.

The story was about breaking a wagon trail from Independence, Missouri, to Santa Fe, New Mexico. Historically there was a Santa Fe Trail in use around the early 1820s. This was the story of breaking the first trail. The studio had bought *The Painted Stallion* title from a magazine story. Somewhere along the line, the writers forgot to include a painted stallion in the story, so out of desperation they invented a blonde girl on a pinto stallion. At least that was my way of thinking.

She was supposed to be the only survivor of a wagon train massacre, and she had been brought up by the Indians. She lived in a cave with a mountain

Bottom row: Hoot Gibson, Sammy McKim, Crash Corrigan, Oscar and Elmer. The man in back of Hoot Gibson is Hal Taliaffero.

lion that she could talk to, and in the story she felt it was her duty to help the wagon train break the trail. Both the Mexicans and the Indians thought she was a blonde goddess. Just in case the audience didn't feel that was enough, the writers threw in a trick arrow that whistled when sent in to warn someone of danger. Larry picked a budding young actress who had been a Wampas baby star. (According to Halliwell's *Filmgoer's Companion* [1985], WAMPAS stood for Western Association of Motion Picture Advertisers which were a group of publicity executives who gave annual certificates to promising female starlets from 1922 to 1934. Among those awarded were Bessie Love, Laura La Plante, Clara Bow, Mary Astor, Joan Crawford, Delores del Rio, Janet Gaynor, Lupe Velez, Jean Arthur, Loretta Young, Joan Blondell, Anita Louise, and Ginger Rogers.) Her name was Jean Carmean, but for this picture she changed it to Julia Thayer. In her Indian buckskins and chief's feathered headdress, she was a beauty.

The wagon train, led by the famous old silent star Hoot Gibson, came thundering across the prairie chased by Larry's Indians. They formed up in a big circle and the Indians started circling the circle. That was a cut. Now the camera moved closer and the prop man gave the local men some ammunition to shoot at the Indians in the next scene. He also gave the Indians some rubber-tipped arrows to shoot at the local people as they circled the wagon train.

Yakima and Duke Taylor, another of the stuntmen we had brought from Hollywood, dug up a couple of spots to soften the hard ground to be sure there were no hidden rocks where they were supposedly shot off their horses in front of the camera. I had talked to the Indian chief, who spoke broken English, and he said his braves were ready. The camera rolled, the Indians started to circle the wagon train, and the townspeople let go of a barrage of rifle fire that sounded like the battle of the Marne.

Some horses tied to the wagons broke loose and stampeded through the enclosed circle. Dust started to obliterate everything. I was waiting for Yak and Duke to make their falls when an Indian took a fall right in front of the camera. It was the most realistic fall I'd ever seen, and for a moment I thought it was one of our stuntmen. It wasn't. Yak and Duke came by and each one hit his dug up spot as they fell. The Indian who fell never moved after he hit the ground.

I waved a white flag, which was the cut signal. I knew that no one would hear a shouted "cut" over the rifle fire and the sound of running horses. Yak and Duke stood up and walked toward the wagons. The rifle fire stopped and things seemed to get awfully quiet. I looked at the Indian who had fallen. He was still motionless on the ground, and the other Indians started to gather around him. The assistant director yelled for the first aid man we always brought along, and we ran over and pushed our way through the Indians. The chief was kneeling beside the fallen man. I said, "first aid," pointing to the first aid man. When that didn't register with the chief, I said, "doctor."

The first aid man kneeled on the other side of the man. The Indian's shirt was bloody. The first aid man tore the buttons off and exposed a chest dripping with blood. He wiped the blood away and with a pair of tweezers pulled out a small rock that had stopped when it hit a rib. A bandage stopped the bleeding, and smelling salts revived him. The wardrobe man gave him a new shirt, and he got back up on his horse and it was all over, or so I thought.

The chief pointed a finger at me. "Where boss man?" I looked at the assistant, then pointed to myself. "Me." The chief shook his head. "Chief boss man." The assistant said, "Larry hired them." I looked at the hundred Indians all looking at me. Boy, oh boy, oh boy! "Go get Larry fast!" As the assistant took off, the chief mounted his pony and leaned down at me. I thought from his height he might be checking out my scalp. "Mormons," he said, then continued with something in Ute that sounded like he was tracing their ancestors, put a period on it as he spit, turned and rode off. His braves followed him to the top of a small hill about a quarter mile away. They stopped and turned back, facing us, and quietly sat on their horses.

The prop man was talking to the first aid man. He motioned for me to join the group. He had the small rock that had been pulled from the Indian's chest. "Look," he said, as he dropped the rock down the barrel of the old fashioned long rifle. Then he held up a blank that the townspeople had been using. "It's the same as a real bullet!"

Rifles and pistols were a way of life to these ranchers. They knew that if you dropped a rock down a barrel, the blank cartridge would propel it out like a bullet. I looked around at their innocent faces. One of them would brag around the fireplace tonight, "I got me an Indian today."

We were shooting some close shots that didn't require any gunfire, and still the Indians sat waiting. Ted Towey, the wardrobe man, came up to me. "If they take off with my wardrobe, there won't be any more Indians in this picture. They're wearing every last stitch in the truck." I laughed as I studied his red, Irish face. "Hell, Ted, go take it away from them." He looked at the Indians sitting in a John Ford "ready-for-battle" position, mumbled "smart ass" and turned back toward his wardrobe truck.

Finally the boss man showed up. The assistant had told him what had happened, and I showed him the rock and the blank cartridge. Larry hadn't told me about the trouble he'd had getting the Indians and townspeople to work together. It seems that a few months before there had been a big fight in town and an Indian had been killed. The feelings between the two groups rivaled the actual feelings in the early West.

We talked to Jockey Hale. He was sorry it had happened, but brushed it off as just an accident. I turned to Larry and said, "Come on." He took off across the prairie. I followed him. Now the Indians seemed much closer than they had before. Larry turned to me and said, "They all look grim as hell," and I agreed. "Larry, this seems like the longest walk I've ever taken." Larry turned to me and said, "Kind of like the last mile?" We decided that a peace sign might keep us from getting scalped. As we got about a hundred feet from them we both held up both hands. The chief raised one hand and slid off his horse and met us.

He squatted down. We squatted down. I expected the peace pipe treatment, but the old boy started to talk and talk and talk. After about a half hour of this, we had everything settled. The boy who was shot got an extra five dollars in pay. They would come back and ride around the wagon train and shoot arrows at the wagons, but no more gunfire from the wagons at them. With a hundred Indians following us, I turned to Larry. "What if an Indian pulls the rubber tips off an arrow and it goes into a townsman?" Larry thought a moment and then said, "Keep the cameras running, because you'll see the shit hit the fan!"

I worked the next three days straight because Larry was afraid that Alan might not understand how serious this fight might become if anyone else got hurt. We finished our ten days of shooting and boarded the train for home. On location, Sunday was just another shooting day. It had been a rough trip. We had suffered through two days of rain with our trucks stuck up to their running boards in the red mud. We had filmed in the rain, and the wind blew almost every day at gale force. It was a quiet ride home for one beat up crew.

We hadn't worked with the principal people on location. It was mostly long shots, chases, and stunt work. We had doubled all of the leads, so now we had to work back over every sequence, shooting close shots of the leading people to match with the long shots.

The famous old western star, Hoot Gibson, was playing the wagon master. Crash Corrigan, of the monkey suit, was the leading man. There was a kid in the show, Sammy McKim. Sammy was about twelve years old, a great kid and a good actor. There were five McKim kids who worked in pictures. They were managed by their grandfather, a wonderful grey-haired man who looked like a picture of a riverboat captain.

Sammy, at twelve, was a talented artist. When he grew up he worked at Disney's for years as one of their top artists. Every year at Christmas I always got a hand-drawn Christmas card with cartoon characters of Grandpa and the five kids drawn by Sammy. It read "Merry Christmas and happy new year from the McKim family," and (in parenthesis) "now available."

The back lot at Republic had a few acres of trees in the river bottom through which a small creek ran on its way to the Los Angeles River. I picked a spot on the edge of the trees to shoot a couple of sequences to match into the material that we had shot in the rain on location. When we had filmed the sequence on location, we had shot in the daylight with a filter on the camera to make it look like night. It involved some movement of the wagon train. Now to match into it we were shooting at night with the big rain towers over which we had full control. It was a time-consuming operation and my first rain sequence.

As I studied the script, I realized that if I used the normal procedure of moving the camera for every shot, I'd never even come close to making the schedule. Night shooting involved big arc lights. It takes three men to move them on dry ground, and after the first scene when we opened the rain-making towers with hundreds of gallons of water spraying out of them, the ground would be a muddy mess.

Again I went to Billy Nobles, the cameraman, to ask him a question. "Which would be faster: to move the wagons or the lights?" He looked at me and scowled, "Now how in the hell are you going to shoot a sequence without moving the camera?" I scowled back at him. "By using the same technique we use on the process stage. The background is black no matter where we move the camera. We can make the entire sequence without moving one arc. The only time you'll have to move a light will be when the small lights are needed to light the actors' faces." I went on to explain that we could move the wagons so that they faced the camera or we could move them so we could only see their sides, or so we were shooting into the back end. Moving the wagons would be easy. They would all be pulled by horses.

Billy was skeptical. He thought that to make it work we'd have to shoot in all the sequences when the wagons were facing us, then again in the same sequences when they had been turned to the side, repeating the procedure when the tail ends of the wagon faced the cameras. He figured we would be so far out of continuity that we'd never be able to cut it together. I had already thought that part out. "If we do it the old way, it's going to be a long night. This way we should go home by midnight. I'll have every move laid out on paper so everyone understands each move." Billy smiled, which was unusual for him. "You've got a weird mind. Let's go for it."

It was a cold, wet, miserable night, but we wrapped up all the sequences by midnight. The next day when we looked at the film, no one in the projection room guessed that the camera had never moved from its original spot.

Hoot Gibson (Hooter to everyone) was easy to work with. He was a real professional, knew his dialogue, and was never late on the set. You'd never know that at one time he was one of the biggest stars in Hollywood.

We had a scene where he came into his small bedroom to go to bed, and as he started to undress, a whistling arrow came through a window and stuck into the wall. The arrow had a note on it. I said to him, "Hooter, in this scene you come in the door, close it after you, hang your hat on the bedpost, take your gunbelt off and hang it on the chair by the bed. Then sit down on the bed and start to take off your boots, and I'll send the whistling arrow into the wall."

Hooter shook his head. "You mean, come in and close the door, take off the gunbelt, hang it on the chair, then start to take off my boots." He'd never questioned any of the directions I'd given him before. "Come on now, Hooter. You don't go to bed with your hat on, do you?" He smiled, "I do," and with a gesture he took off his hat. His bald head reflected the lights on the set.

Julia Thayer had a scene in her cave where she walked up to her pet mountain lion and gave him an order in her Indian language. We were in the big cave set and the trainer had put the mountain lion on a flat rock. He sat there looking down on her. She looked at me. "I'm afraid of him." I walked over to the mountain lion and reached up and petted him. "See, Julie, he's as tame as a house cat, only bigger. Come on over and pet him." She thought about it a moment. I reached up and petted him again. Then she slowly moved over beside me and gingerly reached up to pet him. He licked her hand. She smiled and scratched his ears, turned to me and said, "He's as tame as a kitten." She moved over to the dressing table where the makeup man touched up her makeup and the wardrobe girl put the big Indian-feathered headdress on her head. She turned to me. "Ready."

I rolled the camera and she came through the cave entrance, stopped a moment, then moved over and stood in front of the mountain lion sitting on the big rock. She raised her arm and pointed to the lion to give him a command and "whapp"—the movement of his big front paw was so fast that it was a blur as it wiped the feathered headdress from her head. She fell backwards and screamed, then grabbed her head. The lion never moved off the top of the rock.

Julie sat up as I kneeled beside her. I looked at her head—no blood. When things calmed down on the set we talked about the incident. The wardrobe girl had put a couple of hairpins through the headpiece into her hair to hold it on. When she screamed all that happened was she lost a few strands of hair when the headpiece was knocked off.

When she was petting the mountain lion she didn't have the feathered headpiece on. I'd forgotten that we'd been teasing the lion with a live chicken to get some expression out of it earlier in the day. Needless to say, the next time a scene like that came up, it was the double girl who gave the lion her orders.

The picture wrapped up and the following day Larry, Alan and I went into the projection room to see the final rushes. We were all tired. It had been a rough go. I asked Larry if he wanted me to go back into the cutting room. He shook his head. "Manny Goldstein wants to see you." Manny had taken my friend Al Levoy's spot in the organization. Needless to say, he wasn't my favorite person. I asked Larry what he wanted me for, and Larry laughed, "Now I know you don't like him, but before you get your Polack temper up, cool off and go see him."

I walked up to his office, wondering if I had done something wrong. I knew his secretary from my errand-running days. She said he had somebody with him, but invited me to sit down and wait. She said he'd only be a minute. I stood in front of her desk a moment, then moved to the door. "I'll be back tomorrow," and walked out.

I went to our little coffee shop by the generator room. There were no stools, and they only had coffee and donuts. When I turned from the window with my coffee, Manny was standing in front of me. We exchanged good mornings and I stepped aside so he could get a cup of coffee. "Why didn't you wait for me? My girl told you I'd only be a minute." I took a sip of my coffee and asked what he wanted, ignoring his question. He invited me to return to his office, and that he would tell me there.

As we walked back to his office, he asked me if Al Levoy was a good friend of mine. I told him he was, and there was silence between us. I took a close look at him as he sat behind his desk. He was in his mid-forties, with a face that

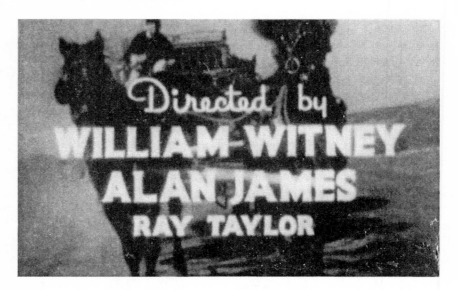

I see my name on the screen for the first time as a director. We had to remake the main title over; they had spelled my name "Whitney." In later life I've had paychecks spelled wrong and the IRS has come back on me numerous times claiming I never filed an income tax return. I always had the same answer for them; try "Witney."

looked like he'd beat little kids. He asked me if I felt he had pushed Al out of his job because of the change in management. I just stared at him, as I felt the hair standing up on the nape of my neck. The last time this had happened I wound up in jail and the judge the next morning asked me if I'd had an altercation the night before. I wasn't sure what the word meant, but I did know there had been one hell of a fight. I felt I was about to get into another.

I stood standing in front of his desk. "Why don't you just tell me what the hell you want?" He smiled at me. "Are you Irish? You've got one hell of a temper." Again the hair on the back of my neck bristled. "I'm Polish and Welsh." I turned to go, but he said to wait a minute. I looked back at him and he reached into his desk. I thought he was going to pull out a gun. Instead he pulled out a bunch of papers and held them out to me. "We're offering you a director's contract," he said.

The contracts in those days were a little one-sided in favor of the studio. They were for seven years. The law said that more than that was slavery. They had six-month options and were for twenty out of twenty-six weeks, which meant that they could lay you off for six weeks without pay in any twenty-six week period.

I'm not sure about any of these figures. It's been a long time ago, but I think I was making forty-five dollars a week as a cutter. It seems like starvation wages today, but in the late thirties, coffee was five cents a cup and a drink at the bar cost fifteen cents. A forty-cent lunch was a luxury. This new contract called for seventy-five dollars a week. The unions and guilds hadn't come into reality at this time.

I told Manny that I'd have to get some advice before I could sign it. Larry said to go for it. My brother-in-law, Bert, said go. My mother said that I should go back to school.

In my own mind, I'd already decided that the excitement of making a picture was for me. I signed the contract in March 1937. I was twenty-one years old. I kept signing contracts until 1956, when the studio folded.

Now instead of going back to the cutting rooms, I had the privilege of sitting in with the writers. I had more regular hours, and could spend more time with my horses. Things were looking up. Like the song that went with President Roosevelt's election, and the theme of pulling out of the depression that had devastated the country since 1928: *Happy days were here again*!

I was busy as hell. There were cutting sessions on the serial, story sessions with Larry and the writers, and the next serial was to be called *SOS Coast Guard*. From what I knew about the story, at least it made sense. There were no ghost riders, and no whistling arrows.

I Lose a Friend and Gain One

I came into the office one morning and looked at the writers and the secretary, all sitting around like a bunch of zombies. No one even said good morning. I asked where Larry was, and one of the writers said he was gone. I asked where and he said to work for Sol Lesser as a production manager.

Larry had never said anything to me, but I knew he was upset when Sol Siegel was given the job as associate producer on the next serial. I was naturally upset. I'd lost a good friend. It wasn't until later that I realized people move around in the picture business. When a picture is finished friends part and may not see each other for a long time, but when you work with them again you pick up your friendship right where you left it. Everyone seemed to speak the same language. I looked forward to working with Larry again.

Sol Siegel took over the associate producer's job of working with the writers. Larry had actually been holding down two jobs. As the associate producer he was responsible for the entire picture. As production supervisor (today that would be called a unit manager), he took care of the money, lined up the sets in advance and acted as the director's right-hand man.

They hired Bob Beche, who had been keeping script on the early Nat Levine serials and the features, as production supervisor. Bob was a knowledgeable, bright man with a terrific sense of humor that was a little on the dirty side maybe, but he was well liked by everyone. As the story progressed episode by episode, I could see it was going to be another rough one. The basic story was about a man who had a gas that could disintegrate anything it touched. The coast guard was trying to find the gas and destroy it before he got it into the country.

Alan James was going to be the other director. Sol hired Bela Lugosi, who had played the original Dracula, to play the heavy, and Ralph Byrd, who had played Dick Tracy, to be the leading man. The leading lady's spot hadn't been set when Sol asked me to go down to San Pedro and check out a freighter that had run aground on Point Firmin a few months earlier. The end of episode one was on a freighter that contained the gas and has hit a reef. The leading man, some heavies and the girl who played a reporter were trapped in the hold as the freighter is slipping off the reef into deep water. A studio car and driver took me down to Point Firmin. I stood on the cliff and looked down at the freighter. It was lying on its side and a lazy surf was breaking over it. I asked the driver to keep an eye on me in case I got into trouble. I was going to swim out to it to see what we'd need in case we decided to use it in the picture. I had brought my swim trunks and a sweat suit. I swam around the ship. It was a big, rusty, empty hulk. Everything that could be salvaged had been stripped off.

I had a hell of a time climbing onboard. The seaweed and moss made it so slippery you couldn't stand up. There was no way we could use it. When I got back to the car, the driver asked, "What did you do to your head?" I felt my forehead and looked at the blood on my hand. "I scraped it on a low hatchway." I pulled up my sweatshirt and wiped off the blood, then forgot it.

I opened the door to Sol's office. Sol was seated behind his desk talking to a girl who was seated with her back to me. Alan James and Bob Beche had pulled up chairs next to Sol. I apologized for intruding and started to back out, but Sol stopped me. Well, I knew he wanted to know about the freighter. I was still standing in the open door. "It's no good. It's an empty old hulk," I told him. Sol again waved me in. "Come in and meet your leading lady," he said.

Now the girl turned toward me. "Maxine Doyle, this is Bill Witney, the other director." She looked at me in my beat-up old sweat pants, with my hair uncombed, and my baby face smeared with blood across the forehead. Then she turned and looked at Alan James. He was in his late forties, handsome, with a sport coat and white shirt, open at the neck. She laughed, "I'll bet!" and turned back to Sol. Bob was a born heckler. "Don't look much like a director, does he?" She never even turned back to look at me. "He sure doesn't."

I could feel my face turn red. I knew that if I stuck around Bob wouldn't let up needling me. "Glad to meet you," I said, and backed out the door and closed it. My thoughts as I stood for a moment on the opposite side of the door were, "This might be an interesting picture with a smart ass leading lady."

I had seen Maxine on the lot a few times. She had played the lead in an Autrey picture, *Roundup Time in Texas*, and the entire cast had come up with klieg eyes. She also had the lead in a "Three Mesquiteer" western, *Come On Cowboys*. I had never really taken a good look at her.

A few days later Alan and I went to the wardrobe department to check her wardrobe. She smiled at me and said hello. I nodded back and let Alan do all the talking. When we were about to leave she looked closely at me. "Your name is Bill?" I nodded. "I thought you were the same person I met in the office. I could tell by the scab on your head."

Ralph Byrd and Maxine Doyle.

Outside again, Alan shook his head. "She has a knack for saying the wrong thing at the wrong time." I laughed as well. "She sure as hell does!"

I was the director on the first day of shooting. The back lot had a big pool that the Lydeckers had built to shoot miniature boat scenes. They were going to use it on the miniatures in the first episode of the freighter in a storm at sea and then the ship sliding off the reef into deep water. The Lydecker brothers and I had designed the hold of a ship, built in the middle of the pool. The water was waist deep when the pool was full. It was also rigged so that the entire set would slowly drop four feet, simulating the ship sinking into deep water.

It was early morning and a chill was in the air. Bill Nobles worked on lighting the set for a half hour before he said "ready."

The first scene consisted of the doubles falling into the ship's hold from above. There were four of them: the girl, the lead and a couple of heavies. The drop to the water was about eight feet. Then the lead and the heavies got into a fight. There were floating balsa wood boxes to use as props to throw at each other. We shot all the long shots of the fight with the doubles, and I asked the assistant to call makeup and send the leads to the set.

The car arrived a few minutes later and Ralph got out of the back seat and opened the door for Maxine. I said good morning to both of them, then took a good look at Maxine. She looked like she had just stepped out of a bandbox. Her hair was immaculately set; every curl was in place. Her pink slacks suit was new, with every crease showing like a marine at inspection. I turned and looked at the dirty water that I was about to ask her to get into. We had darkened the water with dye, so it would look oily. It also looked dirty, and probably was. I thought to myself, "my turn."

I took her by the arm and led her to the edge of the pool. "You've read the script. This is the end of episode one, where the ship slips off the reef. You and Ralph have fallen into the hold and Ralph is fighting with the heavies. Get into the water. It's only waist deep. When the stuntmen start to fight, just stay out of the way." She looked at the water. "Where are the stairs?" I told her that all we had was a ladder, and pointed to it. "Or you can just jump in." She looked at the ladder. "If I jump in, I'll get my hair wet!" This was getting more interesting by the minute.

She walked to the ladder that a prop man in waders was holding for her, and gingerly put one foot in the water. "It's cold." I was waiting to field this one. "Republic is a small studio. It's not like Warners, where you were a star. We can't afford to heat the water like you're used to." Man, the look she gave me was a study of concentrated hate. She climbed down the ladder, slowly getting into the water with a minimum of gasps. I walked over to the stuntmen. "I told her to keep out of your way. Splash hell out of her and work her over to the camera. Be sure she's facing it. I'll drop the set."

The camera rolled and the fight was on. They kept throwing boxes over her head and falling into her. I thought, "She's pretty damn athletic." She was scrambling, but keeping out of their way. By that time her hair was a mess. She screamed a couple of times. The stuntmen put her exactly where I wanted her and I gave the signal to drop the set. She looked up at the top of the set falling slowly toward her, and let out an academy award winning scream that any serial leading lady or horror movie lead would have been proud of. I yelled "cut" and the stuntmen stopped fighting.

Maxine's hands were still in the air to protect herself from the falling set. The set had stopped falling about three feet over her head. I was only a few feet from her, behind the camera. "That's great," I said and held out both hands. "Let me give you a hand." She waded through the waist-deep water to the edge of the pool. I reached down, grabbed her wrists and lifted her out of the water to a standing position. She looked like a wet cat. With her hair scraggly, she was a mess. She was breathing heavily and she coughed up some water. "Max, that was a hell of a scene," I said.

She had a right hand as fast as the mountain lion's. She slapped my face and almost tore my head off. When the bells stopped ringing I asked a simple question. "What was that for?" Her voice was low and sounded like Humphrey

Bogart pronouncing a death sentence on one of his gangsters. She glared at me. "For not telling me the set was going to fall." Then between clenched jaws and with an even lower voice, she continued, "And don't call me Max. If you want to shorten my name, it's Mackie." I thought to myself that she was right. Max sounded like a fighter whose name was famous at the time, Slapsy Maxsy Rosenbloom. I'll bet he wished he had as good a right hand as she had. She turned and walked toward the portable dressing room. The wet slacks clung to her body. It was a pretty damn good-looking one, too.

That night at dinner I told my mother about the incident, thinking I'd get a laugh out of her. Instead I got a lecture that started with "Shame on you" and ended with, "I'd have done the same thing."

The feud got even worse over the next ten days. She only spoke to me when she had to. When I'd tell her what I wanted her to do in a scene, she'd listen, looking me straight in the eyes. (I noticed her eyes were as clear and blue as a mountain lake.) Then she'd nod and go into the scene.

Billy Nobles caught me early one morning sitting in a chair and pulled another chair up next to mine. I asked what was wrong, and he fiddled with the dark glass that always hung around his neck. He used it to balance the light on the people's faces with the background. "This feud you've got going with Maxine is getting on everyone's nerves. We used to have a lot of laughter on the set. Have you noticed how quiet it is? Why don't you see if you can work out a truce of some kind with her? I have a feeling she's unhappy about the way things are going." I laughed, "And get my bell rung again?" Billy laughed, too. "Well, watch her right hand." I shook my head. "Ten to one her left is as fast as the right."

Billy went back to finish lighting the set. I knew he was right and I was wrong. Maxine came on the set, got a cup of coffee and sat down in a chair with her name painted on the back. I pulled my chair over to her. "Mind if I sit down?" I held up both hands like Larry and I had done to the Indians. "I'd like to talk to you but first I wonder if you'd mind sitting on both your hands." She looked at me with a big grin. "No guts." I nodded. "No guts." She put her coffee cup on the floor and tucked both hands under her fanny. I sat down. "How about having lunch with me today and let's see if we can be friends." She pulled her hands out from under her and extended one of them to me. As I shook it she said, "You've got a deal."

The handshake and the deal lasted for the next thirty-six years, through thick and thin, laughter and tragedy. The set returned to its old noisy self.

Maxine had been in show business since she was twelve. Born in San Francisco, she and her sister, who was six years her senior, had both been in dancing school since they could walk. It was the same school attended by the Gale quadruplets and also, I believe, by Loretta Young. Maxine specialized in acrobatics and tap dancing. Her father, John Joseph O'Doyle, was born in County Cork, Ireland. Her mother was German.

Her father was an insurance adjuster for Fireman's Fund Insurance Company, and he died of a sudden heart attack when Maxine was eleven. She was raised in the Catholic religion, but something happened between her mother and the church. After her husband's funeral, Maxine's mother never set foot in a Catholic church again.

Her sister, Bernice, Billie to everyone, was eighteen when their father died. She was a good dancer and pretty as a picture with her blue eyes and freckles. With no money coming in and a small sister to raise, she went to work in a San Francisco nightclub as part of the floor show. When Maxine was twelve, Billie got her a job in the show by lying about her age. It wasn't long before she was doing a solo headline act. She could dance, that was for sure.

Vaudeville was still very popular and the Fanchon-Marco Revues moved around all over the United States. They put together small units that kept the same people together and, as agents, kept them booked at least a year ahead. They came into the nightclub, saw the show, and signed Billie and Maxine to a contract. Maxine was still a minor, so they hired Maxine's mother as a wardrobe lady to chaperone her, and all three of them hit the vaudeville trail. They did three or four shows a day, then moved on to the next small town. They didn't need two headliners, so they moved Billie to another unit, which left Maxine as the star of her unit.

After a few years on the road, Maxine's mother was ready to give it up. The constant moving, sleeping on trains and in strange hotels had worn both of them down. Maxine got a job as mistress of ceremonies at the Earl Theatre in Washington, D.C. She stayed there four years. The Earl Theatre belonged to Warner Bros. Studio. Someone in the casting department thought she could become a star, and they signed her to a contract.

She starred in *Six Day Bike Rider* with Joe E. Brown, *Babbit* with Guy Kibbee, and MGM borrowed her for *Student Tour* with Jimmy Durante and Phil Regan. The picture wasn't very good. It wasn't her fault, but her career slowed down and she started to do independent pictures. She had made two westerns for Republic when she came to work on the serials.

In Washington she had been dating the radio personality, Arthur Godfrey, for several years. I asked her why they never got married. She thought about it a moment and said, "I chose a motion picture career instead."

Bela Lugosi had a heavy accent, Hungarian I think, and he was hard to understand. He was a quiet man, and basically a good actor. He had a set of eyes that seemed to change color from blue to black, and came to work in the first cashmere suit I'd ever seen.

It was a simple scene. He looked out the window and was to turn to his

Dick Alexander and Bela Lugosi. These two old pros were a young director's dream come true.

henchmen and say, "Quick, out the back door," and everybody would run out the back door. It was almost 8:00 at night. I think we were on the tenth take. It still came out, "Qvik, out zee back yad." It sounded like yard. I said, "Bela, it's door—door!" I walked to the door and opened and closed it. "Door, Bela, door!" We tried it again and again it came out "yad" as they ran out the back door. When he came back through the door he looked at me. "I've got zee mental block," he said.

He did have a sense of humor. We were working at an old pier in

Hueneme. There were produce packing houses and a Mexican settlement nearby. Bela was sitting in a chair, and a bunch of Mexican kids circled him, but not too closely. They jabbered and pointed to him. The only English you could understand was "Dracula." He pointed to one of the kids and made a gesture with his finger to come closer. No one moved. He stood and narrowed his eyes down to slits. "Let me see your throat, little boy." In two seconds all of the kids had stampeded around the corner of the building.

I don't know about other directors, but if someone asks me who is the most important member of the crew, I'd have to say the prop man. In those days the term "special effects" hadn't been coined. The prop man set the explosions and helped the stuntmen rig a swing from roof to roof. If you wanted a pie thrown or someone eating half an apple, he could go to his prop box, pull out one of the many drawers, and presto, a half-eaten wooden apple would appear.

Roy Wade, our prop man, was indispensable if you wanted to make your schedule. We were set up on the end of the pier in Santa Barbara. The episode ending was of a speed boat exploding. I told Roy that I wanted a good one, not one of his usual puffs. Roy was a mumbler. You could never quite understand what he was saying, but this time it sounded like, "Damn director's trying to get someone killed."

I watched as he put a large mortar on the ground. It was like a big dishpan, only made of thick welded steel. They usually carried two or three of them. The shape of the sides either pushed the explosion straight up, or (if they were slanted) the explosion spread out like a mushroom. He put two packets of black powder tightly wrapped with friction tape and an electric igniter in the bottom. He looked at me. I said, "No puff, Roy." He mumbled again, and this time it sounded like, "Good one, good one. He says good one." He placed two more packs in the mortar, then covered the powder with fullers earth, which is the material that face powder is made from. He topped this with some balsa pieces.

The grips put the mortar in the back end of the big Cris Craft and Roy hooked it up to a battery in the cockpit in back of the driver. He was going to set it off when it came by the end of the pier. He got into the cockpit and covered himself with a brown tarp. The stuntman driving the boat gunned the motor and went out to sea, turned around and came toward the pier at full speed. When it came by the end of the pier, we were looking straight down into the boat when Roy set off the explosion. It blasted the camera, hiding the boat with white dust. It was just what I wanted. When the dust settled I looked for the speed boat. The mortar blast shouldn't have hurt the boat, as all the force of the explosion had gone up—or that's what it had always done. That's what the mortar was for, to send the force up, not down.

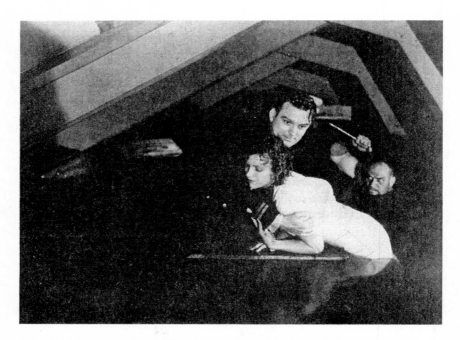

Ralph Byrd, Maxine Doyle and Dick Alexander in the ship's hold as it sinks into deep water to end episode one of *SOS Coast Guard*. When we finished the water sequence she looked like a wet puppy.

The boat was still moving, not very far from the pier, but it was moving in the wrong direction. It was going down, sinking fast. The stuntman was already in the water. My first thought was about Roy. I knew he couldn't swim. We hadn't even thought about a life jacket. I pulled my wallet out of my pocket, tossed it on the ground, and dove off the pier, yelling, "Somebody help!" Lee Lukather followed me and one of the stuntmen hit the water as well. As we got to the boat it sank, but Lee and I had a good hold on Roy. He was really mumbling now, but this time everyone could understand it. He was tracing a certain director's ancestry with language that would never pass the censorship board. The blast was too much for the wooden bottom on the boat. It had blown the big iron mortar right through it into deep water. We pulled the boat out but never did find the mortar.

When the serial finished I asked Maxine if she'd go to dinner with me. When she got in the car I asked, "Chinese? Mexican? Steaks?" She told me she'd never had Chinese food, never tried Mexican food. She was a typical Irishman—meat and potatoes. I persuaded her to try Chinese food. I knew a Chinese actor who sometimes worked for us. He owned a restaurant above a theater where Hollywood and Sunset boulevards come together. It also had a back room with a crap table. I knew we'd get the red carpet treatment. It was excellent, and she loved the food. After dinner we went into the back room and she learned how to shoot craps. It was an expensive dinner for me, but we both had a good time.

Ralph Byrd and I had struck up a friendship while shooting the *Dick Tracy* serial and it had gotten stronger working on *SOS Coast Guard*. He knew that I was dating Maxine and invited us over to dinner at his home in Hollywood. Maxine and I had met his beautiful wife, actress Virginia Carroll. She had come to Santa Barbara and stayed with him during the week we were shooting on location. She and Maxine had gone shopping together on the several days that Maxine had off, and they liked each other. Virginia was *slightly* pregnant—like right now! That night was the start of a close, lasting friendship.

After we finished *SOS Coast Guard*, Larry's old friend Jack Coyle came to me and asked if I'd like to make a western between serials. He'd asked the serial producer, Sol Siegel, and had gotten an okay to talk to me. The next serial wouldn't be starting for two months and the script wasn't ready. I read his script and it was a good one. The title was *The Trigger Trio*. It was one of the Three Mesquiteers series with Crash Corrigan, Bob Livingston and Max Terhune.

We left the next day to scout locations at Kernville. I'd worked there once when I was keeping script. Kernville had one great big old wooden hotel, and if it could talk, it could tell the history of western pictures. It was in the hills in the pine tree country, with Bakersfield on one side and the Mojave Desert on the other. There was a river that ran down into Bakersfield and the weather was hot. I think every western star must have worked there at least ten times.

We were back at the studio the next day. There was a dog in the picture that had a lot to do. I asked Jack if he'd cast the dog, and when he said no I suggested we use Buck, the Saint Bernard that had done such a good job for us in *Robinson Crusoe of Clipper Island*. I was thinking of that wonderful dog, Cappy.

The next couple of days we finished the casting, including Buck. I lucked out. I got my entire serial crew assigned to the picture. I told Roy Wade to have a set of miniature hobbles made up, the same kind we used on the horse in a "Running W" fall. There was a scene where the dog gets shot and I wanted to use the same Running W technique on the dog. He looked at me, said okay, and as he walked off he mumbled something that sounded like, "He's nuts."

There was an Indian reservation near Kernville and whenever a picture company went there on location we collected everybody's clothes that they did not want and took them with us to give to the wonderful old priest who looked after the tribe. I knew he'd be down the first evening to say hello. He loved his martinis. The only bar in town was around the corner from the hotel. The sign over the door of the old frame building read "Bar," and under it: *No Indians Allowed.* We would send the father back to the reservation loaded with clothes and with martinis.

We took the lead horses and their doubles from the studio. The rest of the stock we rented from Irving Wofford, who also ran the location for us and supplied the local cowboys we used. Irving had a large ranch in Kernville and I believe his family settled on it in the late 1800s. He was a short, heavy-set, red-faced man who had a reputation for being tough. There were stories that he had once killed a man in a gunfight; I never asked him.

The trucks and horses had arrived the day before we were to start. The crew and actors left the studio early in the morning and arrived in time to have a catered lunch on location. We started the picture right after lunch. It was hot as hell. I worked with the actors and doubles until about 5:00 in the afternoon, and when it started to cool off, I sent Bob, Crash and Max back to the hotel and started to work with Buck and the double dog, Cappy. My old friend from *Robinson Crusoe of Clipper Island,* Carl Spitz, was the trainer. I knew the dogs would work better in the cool of the late afternoon. I wanted to be able to shoot over a rifle barrel that followed the dog as it ran toward home to get help for one of the leads who had been trapped by a falling tree. The rifle fires and we see the dog fall.

We put the hobbles on Cappy and ran a thin piece of fishing line through the rings sewn into them, tied off one end to the bottom of a belt tied around his middle. When the line was tightened it formed a W, pulling both of his legs up into his stomach which was a natural lie-down position for any animal.

Carl had had the hobbles for several days and Cappy was used to running in them. We sat Cappy down on the spot where I wanted him to fall. We had carefully dug it up so it was like sifted sand. Carl took the fishing line back to a stake driven into the ground and tied it off hard and fast. He walked Cappy, dragging the line back past the stake to the end of the line and sat him down. I pulled the line to one side so that Cappy wouldn't run over it and get tangled up. The camera was set up so that it could shoot over the cowboy's shoulder as he tracked the dog through the rifle's sights. The dug up ground was marked with a small white piece of paper. The cowboy was to shoot when the paper came into his sights. Carl told the dog to stay and walked back over the route that Cappy would run, hiding from the camera behind a tree, and we were ready. Carl called Cappy. The camera moved as the cowboy tracked the dog through the rifle sights. When he picked up the white paper, the rifle fired and Cappy went down in a cloud of dust.

Cappy got up and shook himself and when I walked up to him and kneeled down to take off the hobbles, he nuzzled my ear. I don't think I've ever felt so guilty in my life. I told Carl, "A thousand to one you'll never get him to run again with those hobbles on." I scratched Cappy's ears. The fall hadn't hurt him. I turned and handed the hobbles to Roy. He took them and turned away, mumbling. It sounded like, "I'd have bit his damn head off."

It was almost dark when our car pulled up in front of the hotel. As I got out of the car Buck Jones, who had been shooting a picture the last week and only had one more day to go, got out of a chair and walked down the walk toward me. I had talked to him the night before, and he'd told me that his daughter and Pidge Berry were going to have a baby. He said, "Billy, you'd better go down to the doctor's office. Your leading man's been hurt. I asked which one. We had three leads. "Bob Livingston." My heart sank. The story was built around him. "How bad?" Buck said, "I don't know. He went swimming this afternoon in the river and hit his head on the bottom." I thanked him and walked the block to the doctor's office.

Crash Corrigan and Max were sitting in the outer reception room. I asked what happened and they told me that they had all decided to go swimming and cool off. They had walked down to the river, and Ray and Max went to the beach. Bob, who was an excellent swimmer and diver, dove off the bridge and hit the bottom, hurting his head. It didn't sound too bad. I knocked on the inner door and a voice said to come in. I opened the door and Bob was strapped face down over a barrel. A nurse had just finished shaving his head and the doctor was starting to sew about half of his scalp back on. He was under a full anesthetic.

The doctor asked who I was. After I told him he said he'd already called for an ambulance from Bakersfield. I asked about the barrel. He said he wasn't too worried about his head, but his back might be broken. I asked if he had talked to anyone at the studio. He said they had just brought him in a few minutes before and he hadn't talked to anyone yet.

As I walked back to the hotel, I saw the assistant getting out of the last car in from location and told him what had happened. Jack Coyle was still at the studio; he was to come up the next day. We decided it was better if I called Jack and let him make the decisions. Jack wanted to know how much I'd have to shoot over if we replaced Bob with another actor. I told him if we dressed him in Bob's outfits, practically nothing. He decided to make a few changes in the script to make the new man a brother or a cousin and go ahead with the picture. He'd have another actor to replace Bob in Kernville by late that night.

I hung up the phone and called Maxine. She was a good friend of Bob's wife. I never did know her real name, but to everyone she was Buggle. I told Maxine to tell her to head for the Bakersfield hospital. I had checked, and there was only one. Crash and Max and I walked down to the river to see if we could reconstruct what had happened. They showed me the spot on the bridge where Bob had gone off. I looked at the water rushing down the river. It sure looked deep enough to me, but he dove upstream. It was a dumb decision. The minute you hit the water the fast rushing water would take your head and drive it straight down to the bottom. It was a long time before Bob would be able to make another picture. His back was not broken, but it sure as hell didn't do it any good.

When anyone talks about replacing an actor who's been hurt, I think about a remark Monte Hale made to me. He once fell off a horse and broke his arm during filming. I saw him a couple of days later at the studio, and he told me, "Billy, they had me replaced before I hit the ground."

It was still dark when I came down to breakfast. Jack Coyle, who had arrived that morning, sat facing me. There was another man at the table with his back to me. As I walked around to an empty chair, Jack said, "You know Ralph Byrd." Ralph stuck his hand out to me, and I started to ask him what he was doing in Kernville when I realized he was the replacement for Bob. As I shook hands, I thought, "Oh, no!" I knew Ralph had never been around horses.

Ralph shook my hand. "They tried to get every available actor in Hollywood. I'm the only one who could fit into Bob's clothes." The only thing I could think to say was, "How's Virginia?" He grinned. "Getting bigger and bigger. I hope she holds out 'til I get home." I thought to myself, "So do I."

The big moment in the picture was a cross-country race between the heavy and the character Ralph was to play, and I'd planned some pretty rough terrain for the race. If Ralph got hurt, I was sure Virginia would shoot me on sight. Jack had had a writer make the changes in the script and had brought them up with him—no problems, just a name change that the script man would have to watch like a hawk.

I rearranged the schedule so Ralph would have the morning off. Yakima Canutt was the stuntman on the picture, and I asked him to give Ralph a riding lesson. At lunch Yak told me that Ralph had a lot of athletic ability and seemed to get along well with the horse he had picked for him.

Yak was doubling Ralph and in the script was a Running W horse fall. Just before the camera rolled, Ralph went up to Yak and retied his neckerchief and reblocked his hat to match his own, and placed it on his head exactly the way he wore it. When he was finished, Yak spit out a stream of tobacco and said that he was ready. Ralph walked back to the camera. I told him he was wasting his time. He said, "It may not be important to you, but it is to me."

Yak climbed on the horse and I yelled, "Action!" Yak reached up with both hands and pulled the hat down over his ears. The horse took off and when he hit the cable, went down in a cloud of dust. I turned to Ralph. He was smiling. "I see what you mean." I explained to him that it was a sort of trade-mark with Yak. Show me fifty stunts and I can pick out the ones that Yak did by the way the hat is pulled down over his ears. We decided that was because a cowboy hero never lost his hat. Yak wanted to make sure he didn't have to do the stunt over again.

I got Ralph home to Virginia in good shape—a little saddle sore maybe. The baby was born a few days later, a pretty little girl they named Carroll.

John 8English

I met Jack English shortly after finishing *The Trigger Trio*. He was to replace Alan James as the other director on the next serial. I judged Jack to be in his early thirties, a good-looking man. He was from Canada, about my height, but I don't think he weighed one-twenty carrying a suitcase full of lead. He had black hair and a small neat mustache. He had worked at MGM as a cutter on some of the Irving Thalberg pictures. At that time Thalberg was in his early thirties and was considered a genius. He made several blockbuster pictures and had never made a bad one.

Jack wanted to be a director. He felt he'd never get a chance at MGM, where there was a stable of contract directors who were the best in the business, so he quit. He had been directing pictures for the poverty row producers since then. He asked me why they were replacing Alan James. I thought about it and explained, "He's been having trouble making the schedules. Alan is along in years, but I don't think that's the reason. Republic is a young organization. Bob Beche, the production manager, is in his early thirties. Sol Siegel, the producer, is about the same. I think they are looking ahead into the future."

There is one other thing that I think brought it to a head. There was a scene in the last serial where the lead watches the heavies take off in a truck. By the time he gets into his car, the truck has vanished. There was an insert as the truck took off of a bottle marked "acid" tipping over and the acid spilling off the truck bed. When it hit the ground, the acid fumed like smoke. The lead notices this and follows the trail of fuming acid and at one point the lead lost the acid trail. When he picks it up again he gets out of his car and his eyes follow the smoking trail around a corner.

In the script there was no dialogue indicated. Alan put in a line: "The trail's getting hot." When we had a cutting session on the episode we all laughed. There was a discussion about it and we decided to leave it in. Moe Siegel usually looked at the finished print before it was shipped. When that line of dialogue came on the screen, Siegel pressed the button and the episode stopped. The house lights came on, and he glared at all of us. "What are you trying to do, kid the serials?" I told him I thought it was funny, and he glared at me. He pushed the button to finish the episode. When the lights came on again he turned to his brother Sol, who was the producer, and told him to come up to his office with him.

They redubbed the episode and took the line out. Now redubbing the episode cost money. It meant that the negative had to be recut and a new print made of that reel. It had never happened before to a studio where every dollar meant survival. As I explained all of this to Jack, he listened intently, then asked, "Moe Siegel is head of the studio, isn't he?" I nodded and said, "Haven't you met the old son of a bitch?" He shook his head. "You will," I said.

The next serial was entitled *Zorro Rides Again*. It had a lot of action and a lot of miniatures. The basic story was about trying to link up Mexico and California by rail. Jack and I scouted all the locations we might use. I introduced him to Howard "Babe" Lydecker, the man who ran the miniature department.

When we finally got the finished script a few days before we were to start I asked Jack what he thought about it. His only comment was "Wild!" I asked him if he noticed how many things Zorro pulled out from under his cape. We counted guns, whips, knives, ropes and a board. We both wondered how he was ever going to get this on his horse. Jack suggested we add one more thing—a bottle of booze, because the jams he got himself into he could sure have used a slug or two to calm his nerves.

I asked the assistant director to put me down for the first day of shooting. I figured I could tell the crew about Jack and maybe make his first day a little easier.

They had picked an actor named John Carroll, who had been under contract to RKO, to play Zorro. On first glance he had it all: tall, handsome, moved well, and had a great singing voice. I wondered why RKO ever let him go. He had starred in a picture called *Hi Gaucho*, which had been very successful. I later heard the story which answered my question.

He had been bugging the head of the studio to do another picture. There were no pictures on their schedule that he fit into at the moment. One day he went into the head office and demanded a release from his contract. The boss said, "John, you're unhappy here, aren't you?" John had a southern accent. He was from Louisiana. He blustered, "I've made a great picture. You've let me sit for six weeks. You're wasting my great talent." He apparently went on and on. The boss pressed a button and over the intercom told his secretary to bring in John's contract. A few moments later she brought in the contract. The boss tore it up and handed him his contract.

So that's how we got the jerk. After several days of shooting I told him that when we got back to the studio to come into Sol Siegel's office. I told Sol about the problems Jack and I were having with him. When he came into the office I walked up to him. "John, I asked you into Sol's office so he could referee the fight.

John English and I struck up a close friendship that would last until his death in the early sixties. He was my only son's godfather.

Now, you son of a bitch, I'm going to give you the first punch." The first punch
never came. I walked out of the office. Sol told me that after I left he waded into
him. Things got better for a few days, then he went back to his old ways.

We were at the old Iverson Ranch. Roy Wade had set up a muzzle loader cannon on top of a rock. He was trying to explain to John where he should stand and
how to fire it. John said, in his southern accent, "Roy, down where we come from

John Carroll as Zorro and Duncan Renaldo as his faithful servant look at a picture of Zorro's great grandfather who was the original Zorro.

we have race riots. I've fired cannons like this at the black mobs many times." He continued on and on. Roy looked at me. "Come on off the rock, Roy. Quit mumbling and let him fire it." His mumbling sounded like, "Gonna kick back and knock the dumb bastard off the rock." John fired the cannon. It kicked back and knocked him off the rock, right on his ass. The crew stood around watching him, but nobody offered to pick him up.

One early morning we were working on the back lot and John was late. He was in the first scene, so we all stood around drinking coffee. A big Cadillac with John at the wheel drove up to the set and stopped. John got out, reached back into the front seat and pulled a girl out of the car and slapped her. He was married to Steffi Duna, a petite Mexican actress, at the time. Lee Lukather, the always righteous grip, started for the car. I grabbed him by the seat of the pants. "That's a no no, Lee. Stay out of a family squabble." Roy Wade mumbled what sounded like, "Turn him loose, Billy." If you get the impression that I didn't think much of John, you should have heard Jack English give a half-hour dissertation on him.

On the better side of the balance wheel, it was a pleasure to work again with a wonderful man with whom I worked on *The Painted Stallion*, and would work with many more times over the years. Duncan Renaldo was one handsome gentleman, best remembered for his television role as the Cisco Kid. He was playing Zorro's faithful servant, who took care of El Rey, his horse, and always seemed to be around to get Zorro out of trouble. He looked like a Spanish gentleman, though he claimed he was born in the United States. His slight accent led many people to believe he was born outside the United States, a fact that derailed his career.

During the filming of a picture called *Trader Horn*, Duncan was cast opposite a girl named Edwina Booth. Rumor had it that the director was playing hanky panky with her. He thought Duncan was doing the same. The picture was made in Africa, and everything that could go wrong did. When the picture was over, everyone came back to the good old U.S.A except Duncan. The director said he wasn't a citizen and had entered the country illegally. It took Duncan several years and a hell of a lot of money to prove he belonged here. By the time he got back, people had forgotten that he was a budding star when he left to go to Africa. He never was able to pick up where he left off.

We grayed his hair for the part of Zorro's faithful servant and took the heels off his boots so that he would be shorter than Carroll. If we hadn't done that, standing beside Carroll, he would have made him look like an ugly duckling. Jack got along fine with the crew. He had no trouble making the tough, impossible schedules and made a lot of new friends, including me.

I was never satisfied with the way movie fights were shot. Three or four stuntmen on a set would get into it, with some breakaway balsa chairs with which to hit each other. The stuntmen staged the fights, and they stunk. When I was cutting the serials I had a hell of a time cutting away from a punch that missed by a foot, yet the man who was punched staggered back or went over a table backwards.

A good punch has to be shot either over the puncher's shoulder, or over the shoulder of the man taking the punch. The first can miss by a foot if the other man snaps his head back as the blow passes his chin. The fights always seemed to be okay for the first punch. Then the stuntmen were always out of place for the next punch. By the time three or four minutes had passed, the stuntmen were out of breath, scattered all over the set and seemed to be staggering around waiting for someone to hit them.

A friend of mine was working as a grip on a picture at Warner Bros. We were going to have lunch together. I arrived at Warners early and decided to go on the set to see him. He was working on a Busby Berkeley picture. Busby was a dance choreographer turned director. When I arrived he was rehearsing about forty girls, all in their own rehearsal clothes, but in full makeup. I watched as he started the girls, to playback music, in a perfect circle, giving one high kick. They broke up into groups and several dance steps later formed a line and did several high kicks. He rehearsed them until the point at which, when they formed the line, you could have shot a bullet down the line and not hit anyone. They were great.

The assistant told them to take a break and get dressed. While they were catching their breath, putting on their costumes and having their makeup touched up, he shot a close-up of one of the leads doing the same dance steps that the other girls had done. The girls came back to the set, costumes pressed and clean, makeup perfect. He rehearsed them one more time and then rolled the camera. The whole scene took maybe forty-five seconds. The dance number in the picture probably ran five minutes.

After lunch I went back on the set and stayed all afternoon, watching him rehearse, break, close-up. On the way home I stopped at our local watering hole. Jack English was sitting at the bar, and I crawled up on a stool next to him. I told him where I'd been and what I'd seen—and that I thought we should use the same technique on our fights. As an ex-cutter, he agreed, and on the next picture we started to choreograph our own fights. Each cut might be only fifteen seconds: a punch, cut, a fall over a chair, cut, a charge into someone and over a desk, cut. Each time you saw "cut" in the lines above represents a close-up of one of the leads.

The stunt people caught on fast. It made their work easier. A fall over a table could be done with precision and without the chance of being off balance as they hit the table. A fall off a balcony could be done safer because when they fell they knew their takeoff point was exactly where it should be, and after the fall there was no scramble to get up and continue the fight. And after a few walk-throughs, everyone knew exactly where they should be at all times. There was no more wandering around the set looking for someone to hit them so they could fall down.

Later on we used another technique where the actors worked in slow motion. They could actually smash their fist into a nose and press it flat. We would bring it back to normal by shooting the camera at sixteen or eighteen frames a second rather than the normal twenty-four. Every time we had a fight on top of a cliff, we used this technique to make sure a slip didn't actually send the stunt people over the edge.

Driving to work one morning it occurred to me that the first option on my contract was coming up in a few days, and the studio had not contacted me about it. I had made two serials and one feature western. That night over dinner I talked it over with Maxine. She had been under contract to four or five companies since she was fourteen. She thought about it a few minutes. "They do this to you for one of three reasons. They figure if they wait 'til the last minute, you'll get nervous about losing your job and they can make a deal with you to rewrite the contract with no raise." I had a twenty-five dollar raise coming. "Or they want to extend your contract, or they don't intend to pick it up."

If I'd had an agent, he could have gone in and asked. Maxine asked why I didn't get an agent. I said, "To hell with that. They take ten percent of your salary—for what?" I already had a contract.

I remember an old show business story. Two agents are sitting in an audience watching their client work on the stage. He dances, he sings, he does pratfalls, he tumbles until he's exhausted. One of the agents turns to the other. "Look at that guy, getting ninety percent of our dough!" Jack Fier had been on the serials as an assistant producer for a short time and I liked him. Columbia Pictures had just started making serials in competition to Republic and Jack had moved from Republic to Columbia. The day before my option was up, I called him in the morning to ask him if he might be interested in hiring me. He couldn't believe that Republic would let me go after spending so much time bringing me up. Yes, he would be interested in hiring me at Columbia.

After I hung up the phone, it wasn't five minutes before Moe's secretary called me and said he wanted to see me immediately. I could feel the hair standing up on the back of my neck. It took a half hour for it to lie down again. I walked down to see what Moe wanted. His secretary said, "Bill Witney's here." I knew her well, and she grinned at me. His voice came over the intercom. "Send him in." She clicked it off, still grinning. "He's a wee bit upset that you kept him waiting. I've called you three times in the last half hour." I grinned back at her. "I took a walk to cool off." As I opened the door to his office she said, "Hang in there." I hoped she didn't mean it literally.

Moe Siegel was behind his big desk, and sitting with him at the end of the desk was Manny Goldstein, the man who had given me the contract originally. I thought to myself, "Crap, two against one." Moe nodded to a chair sitting across from him. "Sit down." I stepped up in back of the chair and put my hands on it. "What is it you want?" Moe's face turned red. "What right have you to call Columbia and try to get another job? You're under contract to us."

I realized immediately that the boss network in the entire picture business all hung together. I would remember this in the future. "Not after tomorrow I won't be." Moe looked at Manny. "Who said we weren't picking up your option?" I shook my head. "Nobody, but you both had to know at least two weeks ago that you were or were not going to pick it up, and you should have had the courtesy to tell me. I don't feel I want to work for a company that doesn't have any feeling for the people who put in fourteen-hour days, including Saturdays and Sundays, for them."

Moe looked down at the pad on his desk, his face as sour as yesterday's milk. Manny looked at him like "say something." I stood silently behind the chair. There was a complete silence in the office. I finally said, "Will that be all?" Moe looked up from the desk. "That's all." I turned to leave and Manny said, "Wait a minute. I'll go with you."

We walked down the hall in silence. When we came to the door of his office I asked him, "Manny, you don't have to answer this question: were you thinking about asking me to stay on at the same seventy-five a week?" His ugly face smiled. "We were until you made that little speech. I was too embarrassed, and I guess you caught Moe by surprise. He couldn't think of anything to say." I put out my hand. He shook it. "Thanks, Manny. I suspect that under that tough-looking exterior there is a heart of gold, but as for your explanation about Moe—bullshit!"

I had been dating Maxine for nearly two months. She lived with her mother in a bungalow court in Hollywood. Her mother and I had formed a mutual admiration society. I'd rented a small house on Fairfax Avenue just below Sunset, and talked my mother into keeping house for me. She had a lot of friends as it seems she played bridge day and night. She and Maxine had also formed a mutual admiration society. My sister Pickie and her husband, Bert, joined the club.

Maxine was a good horsewoman. She had learned to ride when she lived in Washington, D.C. on the trails that run through Rock Creek Park. On the trails she met senators, presidents and congressmen who recognized her from the theater. She was known as the "thank you" girl. It seems on her first opening night she was so nervous that her voice cracked. The "thank" came out okay, but the "you" was pitched two octaves higher. The audience laughed. Her boss told her to use that same inflection from then on. I'd saddle up Roy Granville's horse and my own and we'd spend hours exploring the Hollywood Hills above Laurel Canyon. Maxine had learned to ride on an English saddle.

She was the leading lady on an Autry western. There was a scene where she was to ride down the western street. Joe Kane was directing. She came down the street posting in the western saddle. Joe yelled "cut" and walked up to her. He said, "I thought you could ride. Stop bouncing up and down!"

The picture was set in an African location and the sun didn't come out from behind the clouds during the entire production. The crew changed the title of the picture from *The Old Corral* to *The Dark Corral*.

Gene and Maxine had a song to sing around the campfire at night. It was shot outside and the cameraman pulled the lenses off the front of the big arcs and used the branch of a tree waving in front of it. The shadows of the shaking leaves gave the impression of a fire flickering on their faces. The next morning she woke up blind. She knew immediately what was wrong—her eyes were sunburned from the open arcs. She called the studio and told them to send a driver to pick her up.

When she got to the studio, the driver took her to first aid. When she opened the door to go in, she saw she wasn't the only blind person. Gene and several of the actors were moaning and groaning. Gene was hollering that he was going to sue the studio. He was blind for life—he had a headache, etcetera,

etcetera, etcetera. Maxine said, "For heaven's sake, Gene, why don't you shut up long enough for me to tell you what's happened. You're not hurt that bad. All the old vaudeville people had it happen many times. It's called Klieg eyes."

She turned to the first aid man, who told her they were waiting for the doctor. She told him to send out and get a bag of potatoes. When they arrived, under her guidance he cut them in very thin slices and made poultices and put them over everyone's eyes. Mandy Schaeffer, the producer, came in. He watched as the potatoes turned black and everyone started to get their sight back.

Gene later sued the studio, but not for going blind.

Before making *SOS Coast Guard*, Maxine had worked in a couple of quickie ten-day pictures. We had gone to see one of them from 1935 that was still around and there was a chase sequence over the tops of some buildings in Hollywood. Her character was running over the top of the roofs, and in one scene across a long bouncy plank between the tops of two buildings. I asked her who doubled her. She pointed to herself. I felt my heart stop. "Honey, don't ever do anything crazy like that again. The next time, demand a double!" She laughed. "Double? I'm lucky my paycheck didn't bounce." The name of the picture was *Condemned to Live*. When the reviews came out, the *Hollywood Reporter's* headline read, "Condemned to Live Condemned to Die," period.

The studio was on Radford Avenue. Radford dead-ended into a wash, but there was a dirt road that turned left and ran through a big eucalyptus grove for a few blocks before it crossed Laurel Canyon Boulevard. There were some very nice homes in the tract and I knew several stars lived in the grove. From the studio the road was a shortcut to Laurel Canyon. Late one afternoon Maxine picked me up at the studio and we took the shortcut. There was a small sign on a corner that read "Saint Bernard Puppies for Sale." When we passed the sign I told her about falling in love with Buck's double, Cappy. Neither one of us had ever seen a saint puppy, but I put the car in reverse and backed up to the sign. The address led to a very nice home. The back yard was big with a board fence screening it from view. A young, very pretty, neat blonde opened the door. When I told her we'd never seen a saint puppy, she invited us in. Her name was Elaine. She took us into a beautiful den with dog show trophies and ribbons lining the walls, and said she'd get her husband. She stuck her head out the door and yelled "Dick." Maxine looked at me and said, "Nothing wrong with her lungs."

Dick Walt was six-two and a little on the heavy-set side. He was about my age and looked like he'd been sick. I later found out he was a medical student at the University of Southern California and was recovering from lymphangitis, contracted from a nick on the finger from a scalpel when he was dissecting a corpse that had died of the same disease. He was getting over an operation where all of his lymph glands in the upper parts of his arms had been removed. I also noticed that he stuttered slightly. He was also a salesman. He showed us a pedigree of the puppies, the trophies that the champion parents had won at the shows, and gave us a booklet about his kennels, which were named Rueswald, German for "quiet forest."

Bette Davis, the film star who lived next door, later told me the name didn't fit when all the saints cut loose at night. She told Dick, "I don't mind the dogs barking. It's you yelling 'Shut up' that keeps me awake." Bette was an animal lover and a good friend of Dick and Elaine.

Then he took us out to the kennels. We met the mother of the litter, a beautiful dog. Her name was Marita. Dick had imported her from Bern, Switzerland. Then we met the father, Pluto. Pluto was smaller, with a big head like a Disney cartoon character. They both were as pretty as Buck and much prettier than my friend Cappy. Next came the puppies. They looked like a bunch of cuddly little bears. They surrounded us and Maxine sat down on the grass and they smothered her as she rolled around with them. I couldn't take my eyes off one of them. He didn't have the usual two black ears with the white strip running down his nose. One side of his face was all white. It gave him an entirely different look, like the ugly duckling. The other puppies, after the first greeting, wandered away to explore the yard. The white-eared pup stayed with Maxine until she stood up. Then he sat down on her feet. She picked him up and cuddled him.

Dick and Elaine had been standing by, not saying a word. They let the pups sells themselves. I turned to Maxine. "We'd better get going. We've taken up enough of these nice people's time. I'm glad to meet both of you." Dick and Elaine smiled and Dick said, "Anytime. Come back and see how the pups are doing." We started out the gate through the fence. The puppy tried to follow us. Elaine picked him up. Maxine roughed up his ears. We again said our good-byes and left. I stopped at the stop sign when we came to Laurel Canyon Boulevard. Neither one of us had spoken since we'd gotten into the car. "Let's go back and buy him." It was Maxine voicing my thoughts.

Maxine had an old Pekingese she had bought to keep her mother company when they lived in Washington, D.C. I knew she couldn't take the pup. Maxine had figured it all out in the two blocks that it took us to stop at Laurel Canyon. "You've got a big back yard. And I'm sure your mother would like the company." I sighed. She would if the dog could play bridge. Mom had lived with horses and dogs all her life. She had been an excellent horsewoman when she was young. A few years back we had put away a German Shepherd that was fourteen years old. He had been part of the family. We hadn't had a dog since I'd moved to Hollywood. I turned the car around. Before we got back to the kennel we decided to name him Cappy.

"Look at that tail wag." Cappy was sitting in mom's lap. "Where did you get him?" I knew that if I told her I bought him she'd say, "Just what we need—another dog to look after." So I lied a little. "He was wandering around the street. Even if he's a mutt, I didn't want him to get run over." She put the pup on the floor. "Look at those big feet. If he grows into them he's going to come up to your hips." She had guessed within a couple of inches. She took a deep breath. "Well, we can't put him back in the street to get killed. I'll look in the papers. Any pup this cute, someone is going to advertise for him." I agreed with her. I knew that in a couple of days she'd be in love with him and would fight anybody who tried to take the pup from her. So Cappy joined the family.

When he was about a six-month-old gangly pup, I came home one evening and when I walked into the house I knew Mom was mad at me. She pointed the same finger at me she always used on those occasions. "The new milkman said Cappy is a Saint Bernard." I rubbed his ears. It was fess up time. "The milkman's right, Mom—and he's got a pedigree a mile long." Tears welled into her eyes. "If you'd told me the truth I wouldn't have told all the delivery men and my bridge friends that he was just a big old street mutt. You've made me ruin his reputation."

The Lone Ranger

The next serial was titled *The Lone Ranger*. Sol Siegel was the producer. I liked Sol but he had one bad habit. I was a pretty husky kid and my arms were always big and muscular—my mother called them "Polack arms." Whenever we would meet, Sol would hit me on the arm (when I was a kid they called it a cork) and say howya doin' or good morning. I'd never say anything to him. If I knew it was coming, I would tense my arm, but once in a while he'd catch me when I wasn't expecting it and it stung.

I asked Bob Beche, who had been the production supervisor on the last couple of serials, what I should do about it. He hauled off and corked me on the arm much harder than Sol had ever hit me. I pointed a finger at him. "Bob," I doubled up my fist. He held up one hand and said, "You asked for my advice. I just gave it to you." We both laughed. The next time Sol hit me was early morning and we met in the hallway. After the cork he said, "Good morning." I hit him on the arm with all my weight behind the cork. As he bounced off the far wall, I said good morning with a big smile. The whole problem was solved with one little ol' punch.

Sol had kept Barry Shipman, the writer, on the payroll. He was joined by Franklin Adreon, Jr., and Ron Davidson. They had come up with a great story for *The Lone Ranger* based on the radio show. After the Civil War five Texans return home from the army and find that carpetbaggers have taken over. The Texas Rangers had been disbanded during the war. The five decide to bring the carpetbaggers to justice. One by one through the serial, four of the five Texans were killed off. We dressed all the Texans alike. The only difference was the Lone Ranger's mask. And at one time or the other all five wore it. This was the first time in a serial where you didn't have to cheat the audience to show how the lead miraculously escaped being killed. We could actually knock him off.

Barry, Franklin (Pete), and Ron had come up with a stroke of genius. This group was to stay together until Barry left the studio and Pete left to rejoin the Marines just before the war.

101

I love this picture. I don't think a more handsome group of men were ever assembled together in one picture. They all became friends and worked together as a team. Chief Thunder Cloud is in the middle; from the left are Lane Chandler, Lee Powell, George Letz, Hal Taliaferro, and in the back is Herman Brix.

The studio had decided to spend a little more money than usual. They had bought the Lone Ranger title from George Trendle and Fran Striker, the writers who originated it, and developed it into a top radio show which was currently being broadcast over the entire United States.

Jack and I spent two weeks looking for locations and finally settled on Lone Pine, California, with Mount Whitney in the background. Covered with snow and the brown, odd-shaped rocks of the Alabama Hills jutting out like lone sentinels, it was beautiful. I had worked there when I was keeping script and knew it was a very workable location. The ride from Lone Pine to the location was only about ten minutes. For a commercial picture, it was perfect— no lost time coming to work or getting a tired crew back to the hotel without a long ride. It would give Jack and me more shooting time and maybe a better picture. We knew it was going to be cold. We were scheduled to start the Sunday after Thanksgiving.

I was picked to make film tests of a group of actors a few weeks before we started, to see how the five men we selected for leads stacked up when they were together. Out of the group we picked Hal Taliaferro, who under the name Wally Wales had been, a few years before, a star in his own rights. He had worked for me on *The Painted Stallion* and *The Trigger Trio*, was a good horseman and actor, and never a problem.

Herman Brix, who later became a star under the name Bruce Bennett, had been one of our great Olympic champions in the games that were held in Hitler's Germany in the 1930s. We would be working together many more times, including television. He was a gentleman and a great athlete. Lee Powell was a newcomer who turned out to be a good actor and easy to work with. We picked him to be the lead in the serial we made right after *The Lone Ranger*. Lane Chandler had played the lead in a few westerns. He was a very quiet man, a good horseman, and we would work together many more times.

George Letz was another one of our actors. His brother had worked for us as one of the cowboy extras. He brought George on to the set of *Dick Tracy* and George wound up doing some extra work and standing in for Ralph Byrd. He was big and good looking, a nice kid. He later changed his name to George Montgomery, married Dinah Shore and became a star. He also built the most beautiful western furniture ever made in a factory he founded in Los Angeles.

Jack and I took off for Lone Pine a few days before we were to start. We now had a day-to-day schedule and could pick each day's location. If you had to move all the equipment in the middle of the day, you lost at least an hour's shooting time. So you had to know exactly where to put it in the morning. You asked yourself, "Is it in camera range? Are you going to have to shoot at any time in the direction that it is parked? Is it close enough so that makeup and hairdressers and wardrobe won't hold you up if any of them are needed?"

One afternoon we drove up the Mount Whitney road as far as it would go. The mountain at that time was the tallest in the United States, at fourteen thousand or so feet. At the dead end there was a small valley with a pond. The pond was frozen over. Jack had brought his ice skates along. He put them on and I watched him skate for at least an hour. Of course being from Canada, he'd been skating since he could walk. I still have never had a pair of ice skates on my feet. He jumped and spun, skated backwards. He was good. He was also good and sore the next day.

The crew came up the day before we were to start shooting. Jack and I were staying in the same room. The Dow Hotel was a small wooden building right next to the highway, and everybody had to double up.

We brought the lead horses from Hollywood and stabled them at the Spainhower Ranch. Russ Spainhower was a large man and had homesteaded the ranch years before. He supplied us with the extra horses we needed. Russ was the most honest man I've ever met, and he knew the picture business. Lone Pine had long been a favorite location for the Hollywood studios.

Jack was going to be the director on the first day. It was 2:00 in the morning and the sound of someone retching in the bathroom woke me up. I sat up in bed and turned on the light. I looked over in the other twin bed and found it empty. I knocked on the bathroom door and asked Jack if I could help him. The door opened and Jack shook his head. He was as white as a sheet. I helped him back to bed and threw the covers over him. I went back to bed, but there was no sleep for the rest of the night.

We had a 6:00 call for breakfast. Jack tried to get out of bed. "Stay put, Jack. I'll take over today. I'll send the first aid man in to see you as soon as I can find him." I found him at breakfast and told Bob Beche I was taking over for the day, had breakfast and took off for the location.

Billy Nobles rode out to location in the same car that I was in. He was surprised to see me. When I told him about Jack he laughed. "What did you two do last night, visit Mame's and get loaded?" Mame's was the local whorehouse. It was not your usual house of ill repute; in fact, I'll guarantee you it was the only one like it in the world. It was a big shack about two miles out of town. Mame raised goats. The locals called it the Goat Ranch. She had been there since the gold rush days and was well into her seventies. When the prospectors would come out of the hills they'd head for her place. It was like coming home to see their wife. There were always several girls around. She called them daughters. Mame had a hair lip. When you knocked on the door she'd open it and say in a garbled voice, "Come on in, boys. I'll put on a kettle of water in case somebody wants to diddle a little." If you'd like to know how the phrase sounded coming out of Mame, put your tongue up against your lower teeth, hold it there and repeat the phrase.

Lone Pine Mame was as famous on the desert as Death Valley Scottie, who had built a castle just over the hill in Death Valley. Over the next week almost every one of the crew came down sick, and not from going to Mame's. It hit the town locals just as hard. We called it the "Lone Pine Pip." There was a headline in the trade papers and a swarm of government health people invaded Lone Pine trying to find out the cause. To my knowledge, it's still a mystery.

Billy Nobles and I were among the lucky ones who stood by and watched everyone head for the nearest bathroom, bush or tree—whatever was closest. We attributed our survival to being smart enough to drink the right booze and plenty of it.

Yak Canutt and Ken Cooper were the stuntmen on our picture. These two old buddies had been in the rodeo together when they were both world champion cowboys and were always pulling practical jokes on each other. Yak's entrance into the arena after his introduction as world champion cowboy was a spectacular mount on a horse that was trained to stand in the arena alone. Yak came through the arena gate, ran at him and did a scissor mount, which means

I think that's Herman Brix behind the mask and I'm sure the girl is Lynn Roberts. I'm in the middle where most directors usually find themselves. Again note the size of the script.

he jumped, spread his legs like the bareback riders do in a circus, and landed sitting in the saddle. He wore a cowboy outfit (and, I'm sure, a hat pulled down over his ears) with big bat wing chaps over his levis.

Bat wing chaps got their name because they are big like a bat's wings. Made for heavy brush, they lay back over your legs and over the horse's flanks to protect against the thorns on the chaparral. They are held to your legs by a ring and a clip that fastens together after you strap them around your hips. At one performance while Yak was waiting outside the gate for his introduction by the announcer to finish, Kenny sneaked up behind him and clipped the two bottom clips on each leg together. Yak could run but when he spread his legs apart just before he hit the saddle, it was like having a loose rope tied to each ankle.

While Kenny was telling me this story, Yak was listening. Kenny said, "Clipping the old chaps together gave him plenty of leg room to run. He jumped, spread his legs, and when the clipped together chaps hit the saddle, ol' Yak looked like he was a big spinning wheel. He went under the horse, spun on the other side and nearly wound up standing up on the old horse's back."

As I write this it reminded me of another time. Yak had just built a new house. He was asking everyone on the set if they knew any way to get rid of "lawn moths." They kept leaving brown spots in his new lawn. The very next day, by coincidence, there was a printed sheet in his mailbox. This company absolutely positively guaranteed that they had a product to kill lawn moths. The price was three dollars, and it would be sent COD. Yak sent a letter by return mail. Several days later there was a notice of a COD package to be picked up at the post office, costing eight dollars and forty-eight cents. Yak had his wife pick it up. When he got home it was sitting on the work bench in his garage. He noted how heavy it was. The box had so much tape holding it together that it took him five minutes to open. Inside were two bricks with instructions that read, "To kill lawn moths, catch them, place them on one brick and hit them with the other." Then, to add insult to injury, it said, "Absolutely guaranteed or your money back."

When he went into the house his wife said, "Strange, the letter you mailed to order that lawn moth stuff came back stamped no such address." A big light shined in front of Yak's eyes—Kenny.

We usually carried an SPCA (Society for the Prevention of Cruelty to Animals) representative on our locations. It was always the same old man who had once been a cowboy. The studio paid him on a daily basis. I was surprised when a new man introduced himself to me on the Lone Pine location. Our old friend was ill and he was replacing him for the picture. He was about the same age as our friend, and new to the picture business, but had been in charge of a dog pound.

Our old friend had a way of disappearing when a Running W horse fall or any specialized horse action was about to take place. He'd go to the phone or bathroom. On this day we had a Running W on the schedule. Bob Beche, Yak, Kenny and I had a conference. We weren't sure just how this man would react to seeing a running horse go down end over end. I'd never seen a horse injured in the probably twenty I'd seen performed, but there was always the possibility. Kenny was doubling for one of the leads and was going to do the stunt. He had done at least a hundred of them. He wasn't worried about himself. He was worried about the SPCA man.

Yak went out of his way to heckle him. He told Kenny that the SPCA had told him if there was anything he didn't like or there was any cruelty to the horses, the man responsible could go to jail, something we all had known for the last few years, but Yak just happened to bring it up as a reminder. He also told Kenny that he was glad he wasn't the one doing the stunt because no one knew just how the new man would react to the horse fall.

The Running W had not been banned by the SPCA, but it was frowned on. Bob Beche came up with an idea. He'd ask the SPCA man to get into the back seat of one of the cars with him and go over the action in the script to see

This is a Running W. horse fall. Notice the soft sand that the horse goes down into. That's Yakima Canutt coming off like a ballet dancer. I was happy when the SPCA outlawed the Running W. Yet I never saw a horse injured on any that I set up.

if he had any objections to anything he read that seemed cruel to the horses. He picked an episode that had a stagecoach chase with a six-horse team. The car was parked so that Bob and the SPCA man had their backs to the horse fall location.

We carefully dug up a spot for the horse to fall on. Yak had previously had the stakes that the cable was attached to driven where he and Kenny wanted them and covered with brush. Bob and the man got into the back seat of the car. Yak and Kenny attached the hobbles to the horse's legs. We rolled the camera and Kenny spurred the horse to the dug up spot. The horse went down in a cloud of dust. Kenny rolled free, got up and ran to some rocks as previously planned. It was done.

I always let the camera roll until the horse got up to prove we hadn't hurt him. Usually they hit the ground and were back on their feet shaking the dust off almost instantly. The camera was still rolling. Kenny had run behind the rock and still the horse was down flat on his back with all four feet in the air. His neck was at an odd angle. The camera was still running when Yak ran to the horse and grabbed one of his legs and pulled him over on his side. The horse immediately got to his feet and shook himself. I said cut and thanks at the same time, as I looked up to heaven.

A wrangler ran in and took the horse's reins. Yak walked around on the other side of the horse like he was looking him over. It looked to me like he was checking the cinch on the saddle, and was looking at something over my shoulder. I turned to see what he was looking at and bumped into the SPCA man who brushed past me and went to the horse. I looked at Bob, who was following him. He gave me a little grin and shrugged his shoulders as if to say, "I tried."

I have never seen a Running W performed where the cable didn't break at the point that it is tied to the ring at the bottom of the cinch. When the running horse's momentum plus the weight of the horse come to a stop, the cable snaps and comes singing back in a high arc. Anyone riding behind or even the camera crew are on the alert for the flying cable. Now Kenny came from behind the rock and joined the circle surrounding the horse.

The SPCA man looked at the hobbles on the horse's front legs, then walked around the horse kicking in the dirt. He looked at Kenny. "Where's the cable?" Kenny spit a long stream of tobacco juice. "What cable?" The man hadn't noticed the small frayed ends left on the cinch ring. Now he looked at the wrangler holding the horse. "Walk him." The wrangler looked at Yak. "You heard the man," Yak told him. The wrangler walked the horse about ten feet. He showed no signs of being hurt. He turned him and walked him back.

The SPCA man's face clouded. He walked up to the horse on the side Yak had been standing on and pointed to the cinch. There was a three-foot stick protruding from under the cinch. He pulled the stick out and looked at it. "So that's the way you do it." He waved the stick at Kenny. Kenny said, "Do what?" We were all as puzzled as Kenny. He said, "Make the horse fall. You jam this stick down between his legs and trip him." I almost laughed out loud. Can you imagine a faster way to get yourself killed, being on top of a horse and jamming a stick between his legs? He wouldn't go down, but you sure as hell would.

I looked at Yak. He was nodding like, "That's right." I turned to look at Bob. He was coughing, trying to keep from laughing. The crew thought it was funny. Me too, until I thought about it a moment. That wiped the smile off my face. The SPCA man took hold of Kenny's arm. "You're under arrest for cruelty to animals," he said. He pulled Kenny toward the car he and Bob had been sitting in. Kenny looked at Yak, Bob, and me in disbelief. He turned to the SPCA man. "Listen, I…" The SPCA man said, "You can tell it to the judge in Lone Pine." He pushed Kenny into the car. I turned on Yak. "Damn it to hell, Yak, if you don't clear this up with this dumb bastard, we might not get Kenny out of jail for a couple of days. We need him."

Yak grinned, spat a six-foot stream of tobacco juice and walked to the car as it started to pull out. We couldn't hear what he was saying, but in a couple of minutes Kenny got out of the car and walked to me. "I knew it was a gag. You all knew it was a gag, but did *he* know it was a gag?" The joke was later turned on us. The SPCA man wouldn't give us a seal of approval on the picture when it was released.

Not long after that happened, there was a "For Sale" sign put up on the lot directly across the street from Yak's new house. One night Kenny took the "For Sale" sign down and put up a sign he had made by a professional sign painter. A big sign that read, "Chinese Laundry going in here immediately. Help wanted." The next morning Yak blew his stack, went down and bought the lot, but the laugh was on Kenny in the end. Yak built a house on it and sold the house for a huge profit.

As a film editor I realized the importance of the scenes shot from the camera car. They were called running inserts and could be cut into any chase at any point in the chase. You could work on the same mile strip of insert road and shoot a ten-minute chase with the same background because it was always moving.

Red O'Hare had a camera car rental business and had taken an old simplex truck, cut it down, built low platforms in the front and the back, medium in the middle, and a high one over the cab. These were big lumbering machines, but steady, with no vibration even over rough roads. They were underpowered, to make a running shot of someone riding a horse. The horseman sat his horse alongside the road. The old Simplex started a mile back to get up to thirty miles an hour. When it roared past the horseman, he took off and rode alongside of the camera car at the distance that the director wanted.

It sounds simple, but it took an expert horseman to put the animal where it was supposed to be. After a couple of runs the horses knew from the sound of the roaring engine that they were going to get to run. They'd spin, rear, back up, spin again. It made putting an actor on the horse who didn't ride well downright dangerous. That is one reason we had tested the leading men in *The Lone Ranger*. The insert road in the Alabama rocks was long and smooth and the path that ran alongside had sagebrush on both sides so it didn't look like a road. With the snowcapped peaks of Mount Whitney in the background and the big white horse the Lone Ranger rode, it made a beautiful picture, running alongside at racehorse speeds with the long mane and tail flying in the wind.

I loved the low setup with the horse running directly in front of the camera, coming at you. The action of the legs churning and the dust billowing behind seemed to bring the whole outdoors into the theater. This was a western picture at its best. I always tried to use the running insert on a transfer from a horse to a wagon. It let the camera get close to the action and the fast-moving ground going by led the audience feel the danger of a misstep. I found that dropping down the camera speed from the usual twenty-four frames a second to twenty-two frames when the horse was running at you or away from you gave a little more speed and didn't get jerky. If you dropped the speed any lower, it looked like an old silent movie.

One day a cold wind came right off the snow on Mount Whitney. Horses are weird in the wind. A gentle horse will sometimes buck you off or kick at you. A horse will not run into the wind unless you have a big pair of spurs or a whip. That was the one day we didn't make our schedule. There was a pickup truck with a low canvas top on it over the bed. The wind blew it over on its side. We had to move away from the rocks because small pebbles, thumbnail size, were blowing off the tops. It was like being in a shotgun battle with nowhere to hide.

Overall though, things went smoothly in Lone Pine. But when we finished the location shooting, we still had a lot of exteriors left to shoot. We used Iverson Ranch and the back lot. A new man had joined our old close-knit serial unit. His name was Mack D'Agostino, a good looking Italian, who was friendly and knew his job. Mack was credited as a unit manager but really helped with set design.

The man who had been designing and building our sets was the back lot labor boss. Republic had inherited him from Sennett when they bought the studio. He knew where every flat was stored and the size and shape of it. Our sets were built by assembling a bunch of flats together. They were light plywood nailed to a wooden frame. When the set was finished the flats were taken apart, the paper cleaned off, and stored in a big scene dock to be used another day.

The boss's name was Ralph O'Berg, a big Swede. His idea of designing a set was to take you down on the western street. Once you picked out the bank, storefront or hotel front that you wanted to use, he'd take his foot and draw a line in the dirt, then another line. There was a running patter that went with it. "This is a door." He'd take his foot and cross two lines on the original line. "This is the back room." He'd take the edge of his foot and draw half a box. "This is the kitchen." Another half a box would appear in the dirt and ever-present horse manure on the western street. If there were some road apples in his way, he'd push them aside with his foot, usually into the center of the kitchen. Believe me, Mack D'Agostino was a welcome new member of the serial crew.

When Jack and I took him down to the cave set, we stood staring at the big brown cavern made of plaster of paris. It was a permanent set, built in a big tin shed at the end of western street. It was used in all the westerns and it smelled like a stable that had never been cleaned. Mack suggested taking out the old dirt and putting in decomposed granite. My suggestion was to handle it like Hercules had in Greek mythology: reroute the creek that ran through the back lot so that it would run through the set. Maybe if we were lucky it would wash the whole thing away.

That afternoon Mack brought us a picture of the Carlsbad Caverns and a drawing of what the set would look like using stalactites and stalagmites sticking up from the floor and hanging from the ceiling. I asked if we could afford it. When Mack said he thought so, Jack smiled. "Come on across the street, Mack. We'll buy you a drink. Be-u-ti-fullll!"

I looked at the sketch again. "Which are stalactites and which are stalagmites?" Mack pointed to the drawing. "The ones hanging down are stalactites. The ones rising from the floor are stalagmites." I nodded and said, "When you build them, make me one extra stalagmite with a sharp point. I want to put it on O'Berg's chair." Jack smiled. "That's not where I'd like to put it."

One day when we were shooting on location at the Iverson Ranch, Bob told me that they were sending out some actors late that afternoon for me to test for the voice of the Lone Ranger. We had decided it would be too risky to use the voice of the man who was to be the Lone Ranger. Someone was sure to spot it. When we had picked a mask for the actors to use, it was one that covered his whole face, so we could use any voice because there would be no lip-sync problems with the dialogue. We thought it was a good idea.

Yak, who doubled him throughout the serial, had a terrible time with the mask. Yak always had a chaw of tobacco tucked in one cheek, and at odd times had to get rid of it in the usual five-foot stream. He got so used to wearing the mask that he'd forget to lift the bottom half before ejecting the five-foot stream. It would stop when it hit the mask. When this happened we were glad that the censorship board wasn't on the set.

Late that afternoon five actors got out of a car and the casting director was with them. Each one had a page of dialogue, starting with five yells of "Hi yo Silver. Away!" One by one I stood them up among the rocks, so the sound man could give them a little reverberation or echo. Then they read the dialogue to me. When the casting director introduced me to the last one, whose name was Billy Bletcher, I did a double take. Billy was about five-foot two and probably topped two hundred pounds. I looked at the sound man. He wouldn't look at me, and I knew why: to keep from laughing. When Billy cut loose with "Hi yo Silver. Away!" it practically lifted off his headset and echoed across the valley for what seemed like five minutes. He had a deep voice that was just what we were looking for. Later whenever the Lone Ranger had something to say on the screen, I looked at the tall handsome actor playing the part, but my mind would picture little fat Billy. It ruined my image of the Lone Ranger.

The good story, the stunt work of Yak and Kenny, the Lone Pine location, and Jack and myself being just a little more careful and inventive paid off. *The Lone Ranger* won the Grand Shorts award given by Jay Emanual Publications, which was voted on by the exhibitors who echoed the viewing public. It also made Republic a lot of money and started a trend toward making the serial a better product.

When Republic bought the title from George Trendle, there was rumored to be a clause in the contract that stated after a certain length of time the prints and negatives of the serial were to be destroyed. Today the only prints of *The Lone Ranger* remaining are a few foreign prints with superimposed titles. The quality is bad and the sound worse.

By the way, Lee Powell turned out to be the Lone Ranger.

Republic had always given a party for the entire studio on Christmas Eve. We were still in production on *The Lone Ranger* on a stage next to where the party was being held. It was around 7:00 at night and the party had been in progress since 5:00. We had to ask the orchestra to stop playing when we rolled the camera because the music filtered through the stage walls.

Visitors had come in and out watching us shoot. The crew didn't pay any attention to them. A group of men came through the door and stood in the back of the stage. The stage became so quiet that I turned to find out why. Moe Siegel and Sol, his brother, were standing on either side of a small bald-headed man. I recognized him as Herb Yates. I'd never met him. He stayed mostly in New York and ran the studio and Consolidated Laboratories from his office at 1776 Broadway.

Sol walked over to see me. "The dailies were good—no problems." He indicated Moe and Yates with his thumb. "Mister Yates wants to meet you," and led the way. Mr. Yates put his hand out to me. As I shook it he said, "Glad to meet you, kid." I said, "I'm glad to meet you." He waved his hand toward the set. "Why don't you quit shooting and come join the party?" I laughed. "I should have finished an hour ago, but the music has held us up." He turned to Sol. "Go tell the orchestra to go have a drink until he finishes shooting." He slapped me on the back. "I'll save you a drink." Moe followed him out the door. Bob Beche came up to me, and I told him, "I like him." Bob said, "I do too. Now come on, kid, get this set rolling."

I worked for Yates for the next twenty years. When I was forty, he still called me kid.

That 10 House

S ol Siegel left the serial unit for better and bigger pictures—to name a
couple, *Army Girl* and *Man of Conquest.* Bob Beche took his place. He
was now, like Larry had been, the producer and production supervisor.
They moved the serial offices to a small building on the Mexican street. It was
a church on the outside and offices inside.

When we moved in the first thing we did was check the ceiling. The serial gang in a church! We thought there was a good chance of it falling in on us.

Jack and I had never had an office. If we needed one, we could always find
a vacant one and use it for a few days. The serial secretary was always ready to
help us if we needed any typing done. We were entitled to an office, but we decided that if we had accepted one, we'd have to be in it. To hell with that. Bob
asked us again, "Do you two characters want an office, or do you want to keep
the old one across the street? I might want to get in touch with you sometime."
We both said we'd keep the one across the street. It was the Little Bohemia Bar.

One morning when I checked into the studio, Bob told me that Ralph
Byrd had stopped by the office. He was on the western street next door making a test with a new cowboy. Gene Autry was trying to get out of his contract
and was going to take Republic to court, so they were searching for someone
to replace him in case they lost. Ralph introduced me to Leonard Slye, a good
looking, clean cut kid about my age. Ralph told him that I was a director. He
asked me what I thought of the horse he had picked for his test. There were
five or six horses that had been sent by the stables that rented horses to the studios. He had picked a beautiful palomino. As we stood petting the big stallion,
Leonard told me that the horse had been used a couple of times in pictures.
Did I think it would make any difference if people recognized him? I asked him
what pictures. If it was another western leading man, I'd advise Leonard not to
use him. It turned out to be *The Adventures of Robin Hood*, starring Errol Flynn,
and Olivia deHavilland was the person who rode him. I told him if he could
make as pretty a picture on the big golden horse as she did, he had it made.

Later I asked Ralph how he did on the screen test, and he told me he did great. Ralph and I were both right. Leonard Slye became Roy Rogers on the big palomino named Trigger.

The next serial was called *The Fighting Devil Dogs*. We had already picked the two male leads: Lee Powell, who was the only survivor left of the five Texans and had become the Lone Ranger, and his sidekick was Herman Brix, the Olympic athlete.

Coronado, where I was raised, was next door to North Island Naval Station, so Coronado was a navy and marine town. While each service is a separate organization, they are really a "go-together." The navy mans the ships and the marines fight the land battles. They have always depended on each other when the going got tough.

My sister Julie, the red-headed one, married a marine corps aviator a few years before I came to Hollywood. First Lieutenant Thomas Cleland Green, called Cle, was from the Deep South, fully equipped with a Southern accent, and was an officer and a gentleman. Julie was a beautiful girl, five foot two inches, and a good athlete. She was born in Iowa and got all the brains for the entire Witney family.

When the two of them would get into an argument over the Civil War, it was very interesting. Both of them were students of the war, one from the North, and one from the South. My mother was a member of the Daughters of the American Revolution, and six of her direct ancestors had fought in the Revolution. So Julie felt she had as much of a military background as Cle had. Cle was a graduate of the Citadel Military Academy. The Citadel, he would inform her, fired the first and last shot of the Civil War.

I knew a lot of their friends. Most of them were junior officers and most of them were pilots. Lieutenant Henderson was one of them. He also was from the South. Henderson, at the start of World War II, flew his dive bomber down the stack of a Japanese battleship, killing himself, but sinking the battleship. He spoke rather slowly and nothing seemed to bother him. I can hear him now saying, "If I gotta go, I'm going to take a hell of a lot of those SOBs with me." Henderson Field on Guadalcanal was named in his honor.

I hunted and fished with Cle. Like Bert Clark he was as close to being a father to me as I ever knew. We were close friends until his death in the middle sixties.

This was early 1938, and Cle had been transferred to Marine Corps School, Quantico, Virginia, a few months earlier. The sentiment in the school at Quantico was that we would be in a war within a few years, and that the junior officers of today would be the generals of tomorrow. Already the picture business was starting to make propaganda pictures, hyping the citizens to join one of the services.

My brother-in-law Bert had made a marine corps feature picture for Nat Levine's Mascot Pictures a few years before entitled *The Marines Are Coming*, starring William Haines and Esther Ralston. He had hired a young marine reserve, Franklin "Pete" Adreon, Jr., to be the technical advisor. Pete was a handsome, clean-cut young man who stood tall in the marine uniform. Bert liked him and when he found out he wanted to be a writer, he had talked Larry into giving him a job on the serials. He had worked on the previous *Zorro* picture and *The Lone Ranger*. Pete and Barry and Ron Davidson, who owned the sailboat Larry and I often had sailed, had become a team. Pete was still in the marine corps reserves and would have an impact on my life, as well as Barry's and a lot of other Hollywood personalities when the war came along.

Over the years writing the serials had become a set pattern. Once a year a meeting would be held by the writers, directors, and the front office, who echoed the voices of the distributors who sold them. Out of this meeting would come the titles, the decisions to buy a book, a comic strip, or an idea. I remember one meeting. I suggested we buy a new comic strip, *Prince Valiant*. I explained that it was beautifully drawn and full of action, with an excellent story behind it. Mister Yates asked me what it was about. My answer was King Arthur and the Knights of the Round Table. He held up both hands. "With a war coming on, we don't want anything to do with kings or knights or anything like that." I shut up. He apparently wasn't up on his mythology.

Out of the meeting would come five or six titles. These were tried on the exhibitors and the front office would pick four and the sequence that they were to be made. The writers and the producer were given the title and would huddle and come up with a plot. This was called "the Wienie." What did the heavy want—money, power or revenge? Then they all worked on an outline. A must in every episode was the cliffhanger ending. No two could be alike. There was one by a fall over a cliff, an explosion, a fire, getting crushed or sawed in half by a buzz saw, a drop through a trap door into an octopus pit—I could go on and on—but these were all worked out in advance. Then several of these endings were given to each writer, and he'd go into his office and write the episode.

A meeting was held by the producer every morning to be sure all the episodes and takeouts melded into one story line. The first episode was the most important. It was the one that had to get the audience curious enough to come back the next week. It usually ran a half hour. The other episodes were only fifteen minutes. The main title and the forewords—called overlaps and designed to bring the audience up to date on how the lead got into the predicament—probably ran two or three minutes. These were duped from the previous episode so we only had to shoot them once, using several minutes of film twice. That's what you call getting your money's worth.

The directors didn't have much to say in the way a story was developed.

They were hired a few weeks before production started and accepted the script as it was written. Now with Jack and I under contract and always bitching about the story, Bob Beche said, "Well, come on in and help." We were accepted with open arms by the writers. It still left us with a lot of open time in the afternoons.

Earl Bunn was a stuntman who worked for us on a regular basis. Bunny, as he was called, was probably the only stuntman in the picture business with a wooden leg and one eye. He was one of the most decorated soldiers in World War I. He had every medal except the Congressional Medal of Honor. He lost his leg in the Château-Thierry Battle to save Paris, serving as a machine gunner. He was an excellent car driver and chase man.

The other stuntmen liked him, but weren't too happy to do a fight with him. It wasn't that he couldn't handle the falls and jumps, but sometimes he'd get to throwing that wooden leg around. A whack on the noggin with it sure wouldn't do you any good.

I met Earl on the lot one afternoon and he asked me when Maxine and I were going to get married. When I told him I didn't know, he said, "Well, you are going to someday." Earl had worked on *SOS Coast Guard* and had watched our friendship get warmer over the last seven or eight months. I nodded, "One of these days." He lived in Tarzana, which was about a fifteen-minute drive from the studio. Tarzana was named after the Edgar Rice Burroughs character. Burroughs had bought a bunch of property and built a big home in the adjacent hills. Originally the town was called Runnymead, but he changed it to go with the character who had made him the money to buy the property.

It was really country, with very few houses. Earl said there was a small house for sale on over an acre of property, and that we should go look at it, so Maxine and I did. The house was small with a big living room, one bedroom and bath, and a breakfast room. It was on a corner. The owner was a real estate man who had lost his wife a year earlier. The place was overgrown with weeds and there were so many trees on it, Tarzan could have called it home.

At the very back of the property, set under some towering eucalyptus trees, was a fifty by sixteen building that had been built as a rabbit house. It would make a beautiful horse barn with room for four big stalls with plenty of room for a riding ring between the house and the barn. We went to meet the owner. Al Graves was very thin and had a sallow complexion. He had been gassed in World War I. He told us that the area where the house was built had been a real estate development with the pendants flying and free bus rides out from Hollywood that included a box lunch. This was right after World War I.

He had built the house with a veteran's loan and was disappointed that the area hadn't built up as fast as he thought it should have. His wife loved gardening and had planted all the trees and shrubs. There were twenty different kinds of trees that were twelve years old. The grape arbor had sixteen different kinds of grapes growing all over it, and the big fish pond that had a bridge over it between the garage and the house was outlined with large rocks. He had built the pond and brought in the rocks from the nearby hills.

Then the Great Depression hit. His wife got sick and couldn't keep the garden up. She had passed away a year earlier. He was sorry it was such a mess, but his health wouldn't let him keep the place up. The price was four thousand two hundred dollars—three thousand four hundred dollars to assume Mr. Graves' veterans loan and eight hundred dollars for his equity. He had paid two thousand eight hundred dollars for the lot in 1926.

The rambling rose bush in full bloom over the door sold Maxine, and all the trees sold Cappy, who was now six months old. We decided to buy it. There was only one problem. We didn't have eight hundred dollars to pay the down payment. We both had some money in the bank, but both of us might need it for a rainy day. I came up with the solution. I would sell my horses.

A year before I'd found an American saddlebred colt that had distemper. He was beautifully bred, but because of the distemper, the people who owned him said he'd never grow up to be worth anything. I bought the poor skinny colt for fifty bucks, and boy, were the people wrong. At two years old, he was a beauty. I sold the colt and my other horse for six hundred dollars. When I talked to Al Graves, he said he was happy to see his loss turn into a home for a couple of young people just getting started. I could pay the remaining two hundred dollars off over a period of time.

Maxine said, "We don't make sense. We bought the property so we'd have a place to keep the horses. Now we don't have the horses, so we really don't need the property."

Every weekend we worked like beavers to clean the place up. I never realized how big an acre could be. Mack D'Agostino drew us a picture of a raised fireplace to build in the living room. Mom footed the bill as a wedding present. We each still lived with our mothers. I still couldn't bring myself to the point and pop the question, "Will you marry me?" Maxine was patient and never brought it up.

About a week before we were to start the marine serial, it started to rain. And it rained, and it rained. I drove to work one morning over Laurel Canyon Boulevard. It was one of the few passes that went over the mountains connecting Hollywood and the San Fernando Valley. It was a narrow two lane road with a lot of hairpin curves. It was also awash, with boulders rolling off the steep cliffs into the roadway. It was a mess. When I got to the studio the creek that ran through the back lot was a raging river. Our offices on the back lot were in danger of being washed away. We watched as the jungle where we had photographed so many serials washed downstream toward the ocean.

Word came to us that Billy Nobles's chicken ranch was under water. The studio gave permission to take five trucks and see if we could help our camera-man. We picked up practically everyone who had gotten through to the studio that morning, got rain gear from the wardrobe department and took off through the swollen washes that were between Billy's ranch and the studio. A few times the water was so deep it came into the cab of the truck.

When we got to the ranch it was knee-deep in water. We got all the fur-niture out but watched hopelessly as the chickens flopped around in the water and then drowned. Billy's wife and daughter rode out of the ranch in the truck I was driving. His wife was crying, the little girl was crying, and I was crying. Back at the studio we put them in one of the big star dressing rooms and had hot food brought in. We all went to the wardrobe department and borrowed dry clothes. It was the funniest bunch of people I ever saw—soldiers, sailors, cowboys—but they were all dry.

It was about three o'clock when I remembered the house we'd just bought in Tarzana. I'd loaned my car to one of the grips who wanted to go home and see if his house was still there. I saw Brownie, the telephone operator, walking toward the gate. Brownie and my friend Jerry Roberts had been running around together for about as long as Maxine and I had. We were all friends and saw them often. I asked her if she'd run me out to Tarzana to see if we still had a house. The house was high and dry. I noticed that the fish pond that had been empty was running over. I breathed a big sigh of relief.

The Fighting Devil Dogs started in March 1938. Neither Jack nor I liked the script. It had another one of those masked villains, all dressed in black and wearing a black helmet. On his chest was a zig-zag line that was supposed to represent lightning, and he had a pistol that fired a lightning bolt. Years later they made a picture called *Star Wars* and used a pistol similar to ours. I wonder if the producer ever saw our serial as a kid, because the helmet his heavy wore was almost an exact duplicate of the one we designed for "The Lightning," our villain.

The serial also brought out of the attic the flying wing we had used in *Dick Tracy*. They dusted it off and re-shot a few miniature scenes. It had the heavy firing a rocket that exploded over its target and electrocuted everyone below it. The government hasn't been able to copy that one yet for their arse-nal, but if they had put the Hollywood man who invented all the electrical gad-gets that we used on the sets to work for them, I'm sure it would have become a reality. He had a continual spark that would climb up between two wires six or eight feet, then disappear toward the ceiling. He also had a lot of other gad-gets that were great to watch and left the set full of smoke after every scene.

The last episode did have one good sequence. The man who is suspected of being the heavy ("The Lightning") is brought together with a group of other

A lobby card from *The Fighting Devil Dogs*.

suspects. They are told that the girl can identify him from among the other subjects. The curtains part and the girl is standing between them. As she points a finger at the group, the heavy pulls the lightning pistol and fires at her. The girl disappears and we see it was only her image in a broken mirror. I loved this kind of sequence because the writers only showed signs of genius once in a while.

We finished the serial by the end of March. It had definitely been a real quick cheater and Jack and I were ashamed that we couldn't help make it any better. Everything had gone well. The leads were easy to work with, but even with our best efforts we couldn't make it smell any better.

After the serial was completed, Maxine and I again went back to work on the house we'd bought. The rains had given way to warm spring weather. We had been trying to fix a leak in the fish pond. I asked her to go around to the patio, which was waist high in weeds, and bring me the rake that we'd left there a few days before. She disappeared around the corner of the house and a few seconds later there was a scream. It was even better than the one she gave when the set was falling. I scrambled out of the fish pond and tore around the corner of the house, then stopped and froze. Maxine, still screaming, was holding a big snake by the tail.

I yelled, "For God's sake, drop it!" In one motion she dropped it in the tall weeds and in the next moment was in my arms. I tried to push her away. "Let go. I want to see what kind of a snake it is." She slowly loosened her hold around my waist. I was able to breathe again. I walked over to the spot she had dropped the snake. I didn't tell her, but it looked like it might have been a rattler. It could have been, but it wasn't. A big king snake slid away in the weeds. I looked at her, still frozen to the spot where I'd left her, and saw the rake leaning against the house. I retrieved it and came back to her. "Whatever made you pick it up? Did you want to keep it as a pet?" Her look told me she didn't want to keep it. She took the rake from me and dropped it in the weeds. "I came around the house and saw what I thought was the rake handle hidden in the weeds." She pointed to the rake on the ground. "So I picked it up. I guess I froze because my hand wouldn't open so I could drop the slimy thing. From now on, you go get your own damn rake! Now go kill it." I shook my head. "King snakes do good. They eat mice and gophers." She thought a moment. "I'd rather have mice and gophers!"

Later in the afternoon she was sitting on a rock petting Cappy. I was down in the bottom of the fish pond. I looked up at them—pretty dog, pretty girl. "Maxine, you know what I'm damn tired of?" She looked down at me and asked, "Fixing fish ponds?" "No," I replied. "I'm tired of taking you home nights. Let's get married." She hugged Cappy. "You know what I'm tired of?" she asked. I shook my head. "Waiting for you to ask me."

We had already talked over the fact that if we got married one of us would have to stop working. We had seen too many picture people who both worked break up after a short time. The long hours and working days and nights made them like two ships that pass in the night.

It took us the rest of the afternoon to pack a bag and tell our mothers. They both sent us off with best wishes. It was dark by the time we hit the road to Las Vegas—no big wedding for us. We had spent all our money on the house. When we got to San Bernardino we hit fog, and as we started up the narrow road that wound over El Cajon Pass, it started to get thicker. I pulled over to the side of the road and stopped. I couldn't see the front of the hood. I looked at Maxine. "Let's turn around." She closed her eyes for a minute like she was saying a little prayer. "If we turn around now it might be another year," she said, her voice trailing off. She never finished the sentence.

A truck slowly passed us. Then it pulled over to the side of the road just ahead of us. We watched as an older man with a beard got out and walked back to us in the light from our headlights. I rolled the window down and he stuck his head in the opening. "Fog scare you?" he asked. I nodded. "Follow me. I know this road like the back of me hand. When we get to Victorville there's a little motel outside of town. I'll toot me horn and you can spend the night there. It's the end of me run." He took off before I could thank him.

We followed the red glow of his taillights as closely as we dared. I turned and grinned at Maxine. "When we stopped back there and I asked you a question, did you say a little prayer before you answered?" She grinned. "Why do you ask?" she said. "Because that truck driver said 'me hand' and 'me horn.' He had to be Irish." She slid over to my side of the seat. "My patron saint is Patrick," she replied.

He tooted the horn and we pulled off. The dull glow of a light bulb hung over a motel sign. From the outside it looked like it was right out of *The Grapes of Wrath*. The inside looked like *Tobacco Road*. Maxine said maybe would could find another one—in Victorville! It was a railroad town with one hash joint. She pulled back the burlap shower curtain and quickly dropped it again. It seems she wouldn't be taking a shower in the morning. The double iron bed looked well slept in, and too recently for us. We spent the rest of the night on top of the bed with our clothes still on.

The next morning was still foggy. We had breakfast at the one hash joint in town and it hit the spot. We hadn't taken time for dinner the night before. After breakfast we continued on our trip. The fog finally lifted when we climbed the Baker grade about forty miles from Las Vegas.

Las Vegas was a very small town then with just a couple of hotels. It had thrived while Boulder Dam was being built a few years before, but now it was starving slowly to death. Across from the railroad station was the Sal Sagev Hotel. That's Las Vegas spelled backwards. I made arrangements to be married in their sample room, the one that the salesmen used to display the goods they were trying to sell. The room we were given by the hotel looked to us like the Waldorf Astoria after the one in which we had spent the night before.

We were waiting in the empty sample room when the Justice of the Peace showed up. After he introduced himself he asked where the witness was. "We need a witness?" I asked. Yes, we needed to have a witness. I telephoned the desk and asked them to please send up a bellboy.

While we were waiting Maxine asked, "Can I use this ring for a wedding ring?" She held out her hand to show the justice her diamond ring that my mother had given me to use as an engagement ring. I had given it to her at Christmas. "We forgot to get a wedding ring," she said. "I've got a wedding ring." Her head snapped around to look at me. I was holding out a ring to her. She took the ring and examined it. "And just where did you get this?" she asked. I made a face at her. "The same time I had your Christmas present reset." She counted on her fingers. "Three months—and you never told me."

She examined the ring. "What are all these initials inside? Did you buy it at a hock shop?" I took the ring. "Here, I'll decipher them for you," I said. "The T stands for to; the M for my; the D for darling; W for wife; M for Maxine; L for love; and B for Billy."

She threw her arms around my neck and gave me a big kiss. The door opened and the bellboy came in, excused himself and started to back out. The justice told him not to leave, that we were about to make it legal.

The bellboy sent us to the best place in town for dinner and after a couple of bottles of champagne, we decided to gamble. We split the money we had and I went to the crap table, while she played roulette. The next morning we had to wire Mom for enough money to get home.

While we were waiting, we drove out and took a tour of Boulder Dam. It was a fabulous piece of engineering, and we went down to its base in an elevator to see the tremendous turbines that turned bigger generators. They had just been put on line a few years before and they sparkled with newness.

When we got back to the hotel we composed a telegram to the serial gang. Maxine knew them as well as I did. It took us an hour. About twenty pieces of paper later we came up with one we thought fit the occasion: "Married today—stop. Had wild episode ending—stop. Take out some time in distant future—stop."

Maxine and I drove home the next day. The serial offices at the studio had a bulletin board on the wall near the door. When I closed the door I glanced at the board and froze. We had sent the telegram from Las Vegas to Bob Beche. The sneaky so and so had pinned it on the bulletin board. It had been meant for the serial gang's eyes only. I tore it off the board and headed for Bob's office.

"What are you upset about? Pinning it on the board made you famous. The whole studio has paraded through here to read it," Bob told me. I could feel my face turn red. "Why didn't you call the *Reporter* and *Variety* and have them reprint it? You might just as well have." Bob got that dirty little grin on his face. "I did, I did." He stood up and held out his hand with a big smile. "Congratulations." "Bob," I stopped and thought, "I'd have done the same heckle job," and laughed, took his hand and said, "Thanks."

Cupid had been asleep all winter, but when he woke up, boy did he ever get busy that April. He fired a multi-headed arrow straight into the serial department. It read like the title credits on the front of each episode. Maxine and I were first, followed by Bob Beche, producer, Lee Lukather, grip, Pete Adreon and Ron Davidson, writers, Joe Kane, director, Bud Springsteen, script supervisor, and Louie Germonprez, assistant director. Maxine's comment was apt: "Cupid sure made a lot of people honest."

Bob told me that Manny Goldstein wanted to see me, and waited for my reaction. When I said "okay" he said, "Try not to blow your stack like you did last time." I frowned. "Bob, why don't you keep up to date on things in the department that you boss? Manny and I are friends." As I walked out, he said, "I'll be damned."

I thought Manny was going to put me on layoff. The contract said he could give me six weeks. It wouldn't matter because I'd had my contract prorated over the entire twenty-six weeks, so I'd have a check coming in every week. If you didn't get any time off they paid you a lump sum at the end of the option for the time you'd worked over the twenty work weeks. I was looking forward to the time off, so Maxine and I could move into the Tarzana house. I had not had a vacation since I'd gone to work for Mascot.

As I sat down in front of Manny's desk I noticed he didn't look mean anymore. He congratulated me on my marriage to Maxine. He knew her from the contract sessions he'd had with her when she worked at the studio. He said, "You're not very busy at the moment, are you?" I answered, "Just cutting sessions and some work with the writers." "Would you do us a favor?" he asked. "It's not in line with your contract work." I said, "Sure, shoot."

"Mister Yates is bringing all the exchange people that sell our pictures to Hollywood for three days. We're showing them all our new pictures and telling them about the products we're producing in the future. We want it to be like a party. I want you to dream up a stunt we can show them on the back lot." I thought about it a moment. "Do I have any money to spend?" He nodded, "How much do you need?" I held out my hands and shrugged. "I'm not sure. Five hundred, maybe. How about a Running W horse fall?" He was enthusiastic. "That should give them something to remember. Set it up and I'll tell you later the time and date."

I stood up to go, but he held up a hand. "One other thing. Do you think Maxine would entertain them at the dinner we're throwing for them on the last night before they go home?" I frowned. "Manny, she hasn't danced or sung for a year. Why don't you hire a professional entertainer?" Manny thought for a moment. Then he said, "They'll feel they know her from the westerns she's made for us, and *SOS Coast Guard*. She was a dancer, wasn't she?" I smiled. "And a damn good one. I'll ask her."

Maxine was all smiles. "How long have I got to practice? I need at least two weeks." I said, "You've got it." Maxine went to see the head of the music department, Sy Feuer, who later had several hit musicals on Broadway. He was delighted to arrange her music. They hired a dance director who she had worked with when she was at MGM, and she picked a beautiful evening gown out of wardrobe. The girls in wardrobe fitted her, or rather poured her into it I later found out, and she was ready.

We worked all morning on the western street preparing the Running W.

Yakima was going to do the stunt. We decided to add a small trick to give it more excitement. An explosion would make it look like it blew the horse to the ground. Roy Wade was the prop man rigging it. We dug the ground up and mixed in some sawdust on the spot the horse was to hit the ground. It was as soft as a feather bed. I told Yak, "You always said you wanted to do your last Running W in an acre of tits. This is as close as you'll ever get to it."

Roy set the mortar and hid it in a pit with only the muzzle showing inches above the ground. We hid it with a piece of cheesecloth painted like dirt. We were ready. The exhibitors walked down to the western street from a sound stage where they had had a catered lunch. We never told them what they were going to see, just some special action for their entertainment. They lined the boardwalk on each side of the street. The announcer said over the speaker system, "Ladies and gentlemen, I'd like to introduce to you the world champion cowboy, the stuntman who has thrilled you in all our great action serials, Mr. Yakima Canutt."

Yak was sitting on his horse at the end of the street. He took his hat off to them. I noticed when he put it back on, he pulled it down over his ears. He was ready. "And now watch closely. He's going to show you some motion picture magic!"

I was standing in a doorway with Roy opposite where the horse was to fall. "Ready Roy?" I asked. He mumbled something that sounded like "Big explosion, big explosion." I said earlier to him, "Load it up, Roy. No little puff now." I signaled Yak. He spurred the horse down the street. No one noticed the hobbles or the trailing wire attached to the horse. When the horse cleared the mortar, Roy set off the explosion. It wasn't a little puff, and the horse went down in the soft earth.

The explosion echoed through the empty buildings on the western street and threw up a great cloud of fuller's earth. I stood silently saying a little prayer. Yak had come off the horse like a ballet dancer and landed on his feet and rolled. Now the horse got up and shook himself. I stopped praying. The cable had broken off the horse and lay harmlessly in the street. The dust from the explosion covered it. Now Yak ran to the horse, remounted, and rode him down the street and out of sight around the corner where a wrangler took him. Then Yak came back on foot, took off his hat to the crowd and the big ham took a bow. The exhibitors applauded and all moved down the street where they surrounded Yak. They all thought the explosion had knocked the horse down, and I'll guarantee you, Yak wasn't about to set them straight.

Roy and I stood alone in the doorway watching. Roy moved to retrieve the still smoking mortar. His muttering sounded like, "I rig the damn thing and Yak gets all the credit."

The dinner party for the last night of the convention was set up at the

Roosevelt Hotel in Hollywood. It was a formal affair, but I had never owned a tux. I borrowed one from Barry Shipman, the writer. I tried the coat on. It fit okay, but the pants were a little loose. With all the booze that would be flowing, I figured no one would notice. When Maxine and I got dressed that night she had on her own evening gown. She would change to the costume at the hotel. When I put on Barry's shirt I found the detachable collar was too small. Maxine solved the problem. She took a pair of scissors and cut it up the back. The tie held it together and the coat hid the cut. It wasn't very comfortable.

The ballroom was packed with exhibitors, directors and producers, actors and executives. Yates sat at the head table. He still ran the studio from New York and only came to California for an event like this one. The entertainment was to be after dinner. There were five acts to set up. Maxine was in the middle. When dinner was finished, Maxine looked at me and said, "Let's go. I've got to get dressed."

I watched as she wriggled into her costume. My eyes bugged out. I knew she had a blouse full of goodies, but in this outfit, they were overflowing. "My God, honey, you can't go out and dance in that." I pointed to the bulges above the neckline of the dress. "What if one of them falls out?" She broke up. When she finished laughing, she said, "That's the idea. All eyes will be watching, and hoping it'll happen, but it won't, so don't worry. That's show biz!"

Her act went off like clockwork. She stepped up to the microphone and sang, then danced. At the end of her routine she did a "walk over forward," which is like a cartwheel combined with a front flip. She did about ten of these in a series, all on the same spot. She did them so fast that she became a blur on the floor. Then she stopped. I held my breath as I checked for a fallout. There was none. She stepped up to the microphone and finished the song. She stopped the show.

For the next three years she was invited to entertain at the yearly convention. The third year when it came time to do her finale, the "walk over forward" routine, she stopped, made a rolling motion with her hands and said, "Remember, this is where I used to do this." Then she went on with her routine. She again stopped the show.

I'll never forget the final act that night. The music department knew Yates was going back to New York the next day, so they wrote a farewell song for the occasion. Gene Autry and Roy Rogers sang it. The song concluded with, "And remember that we Yates to see you go."

The next day the headlines in *Variety* said, "Worst Pun of the Year: We Yates to see you go."

Maxine, Cappy, and I moved into the Tarzana house. Mom moved in with one of her bridge buddies, and Maxine's mother went back to San Francisco to be with her two sisters.

The furnishings in the house included a set of love seats given to us by one of Maxine's closest friends, Joan Gale. Joan was one of the Gale quadruplets who had starred in the George White Scandals. She was now Joan Schreiber, having married Lou Schreiber who was casting director at 20th Century–Fox. We also had a bedroom set that Pickie and Bert had donated, and a bunch of apple boxes I borrowed from the studio. We moved in three big boxes of photographs that Maxine had collected when she was mistress of ceremonies at the Earl Theatre. There was one signed, "Lester Towns Hope." She said every time Bob Hope played the theater, her boss took him aside and warned him, "Keep it clean!" It seems he never did.

Madam Shuman Hienk was an opera star who had one son fighting for Germany and one for the United States during World War I. I knew her; she had retired in Coronado and I went to school with one of her grandkids. The three boxes were full of autographed pictures to her from everyone who was anyone in vaudeville and motion pictures. There was one of William Powell. She'd worked with him on a picture at Warners. I asked her what kind of a man he was to work with. She said, "A doll."

One day some visitors came on the set. One lady came up to him and gushed, "Oh, Mr. Powell, could I have a lock of your hair?" He reached up and pulled his toupee off and said, "Madam, you can have the whole thing." The one she was the most proud of was signed, "To my God daughter, Maxine, All my love, Charlie Murray." Charlie had been on every stage in America. He was most famous for his great silent series, *The Cohens and the Kellys*. He was a great comedian. She had worked with him for a period of time when she was working for the Fanchon-Marco Revues and he had "adopted" her and her mother. He and his wife came out and checked me out like an old mother hen looking after a chick.

My mother came out to see how we were getting along. She had written to my sister Julie in Quantico that I'd gotten married. I'd written to her too, but hadn't had an answer. Mom had. Julie was mad as hell at her and Pickie and Bert for letting me marry a chorus girl. It broke me up. I handed the letter to Maxine, but the smile on her face turned to a big scowl. I asked Mom, "What did you tell Julie in your letter?" Mom loved Maxine. The "chorus girl" in Julie's letter never sank in. "That you'd married an actress who had been a singer and dancer on the stage."

I looked at Maxine. She was still scowling. I laughed. "Maybe Julie has heard the old vaudeville expression about chorus girls. 'First they dance on one leg, and then on the other, and between them both they make their living.'" My mother's eyes narrowed down and she pointed the usual finger at me, "I ought to…" "What, Mom?" I asked. Maxine spoke for her, "Wash your mouth out with soap." I put my arm around Maxine. "Forget it," I told her. "I'll write the redhead and set her straight." She pulled away from me. "Don't bother. When I meet her I'll set her straight." Both Mom and I knew Julie. Now we both knew Maxine. The battle was joined, and the firefight was sure to follow.

A few days after we moved in, Paul and Dorothy Kelly stopped by. Paul was under contract to MGM and they had a beautiful horse ranch in Chatsworth not too far from us. They had become friends with Maxine when she was mistress of ceremonies in Washington. Paul had spent two years in San Quentin for manslaughter, and Dorothy one. The story behind the jail sentence had been headline news in Hollywood in 1927. Dorothy Mackay had married song and dance man Ray Raymond. When Ray accused Paul of trying to steal Dorothy from him, a fight ensued. Ray suffered a bad beating and died two days later. Paul was sent to prison and Dorothy, not present during the fight, was also incarcerated for refusing to testify against Paul and concealing information as to Ray's death.

After they both were free, they were married in 1931 and Paul adopted Dorothy's young daughter that she'd had with her former husband. Paul had since picked up his career and was considered a star. As far as I was concerned, they were both great people. He was still on probation and had to report to the warden at San Quentin once a year. He'd bought an old Rolls Royce that he kept in the barn and only used when he and Dorothy drove up to San Quentin to check in with the warden, who was a good friend of theirs. He would pull up to the main gate and toot the horn on the old Rolls to announce his arrival.

They looked over our property, wading through the weeds. I told Paul my plans for rebuilding the rabbit house into a barn. When they came into the house they sat on apple boxes to have a beer with us. Dorothy asked if we had named the place. It seems every ranch should have a name. When we said we hadn't thought about it, she had a suggestion: Stoney Broke Farm. It fit perfectly, so Stoney Broke it became.

There was a small square window in the front door that you could open to talk to someone on the other side. They had a piece of metal with a Saint Bernard head silhouette cut out in the middle and Stoney Broke in a circle surrounding it made up to fit in back of the glass. It was still there thirty-seven years later when I sold the property.

Dorothy had a wonderful sense of humor. Every time she heard a bell ring, whether telephone, doorbell, or on the radio, she would jump up if she was sitting in a chair or at a table, and walk around it and sit again. It seems that every time the cell doors at San Quentin would open or close a bell rang. She said prison life was okay but it left her ringy.

In early January of 1940 Dorothy was killed in a rainy night auto accident after she had left our house. That was over fifty years ago and as I write these words, I can close my eyes and still see her pretty smiling Irish face. She was always ready for a laugh.

But there were no laughs for anyone early one June morning in 1938 when I was informed by the serial gang that Larry Wickland had passed away the night before. He had had a ruptured appendix and died on the operating table. We all thought the world of Larry and respected his knowledge and friendship. I think it hit me harder than anyone else. Larry was the one who had given me so much advice about life, the picture business and how to treat other people in order to get along in life.

I went to the stable, saddled a horse and took off for the hills. The only other death that I had known was my father when I was four. All I really remember was crying because my mother and sisters cried. It was hard to come face to face with the reality that my best friend was gone. Larry was only thirty-nine years old. My mother told me that if someone dies and there are no tears shed for them, they won't go to heaven. Just my tears alone would assure Larry of a special welcome.

The Director's Guild

S hortly after Larry died, we started the next serial, *Dick Tracy Returns*. It starred my good friend Ralph Byrd. We had a better than average story. It was about a father and his five sons all dedicated to making money the easy way. We killed them off one at a time.

Charles Middleton played the father. Charlie had the meanest face I'd ever seen. He was always cast as the head of the orphanage—the one who loved to beat little kids. In real life he was the nicest, most gentle person imaginable. He was devoted to his wife, who was ill with a weird malady called tick del la rue, the tick of death, where suddenly the face goes into a spasm. It's extremely painful, and at that time there was no cure for it. Charlie was a gentleman who had learned to act on the stage.

Dick Tracy's sidekick was new to me. He was a stuntman named David Sharpe, who had been in pictures since he was twelve years old. Before he was sixteen he doubled Douglas Fairbanks, Sr., doing the fantastic jumps that Fairbanks was famous for. He had been an Olympic tumbler and had his own series when he was in his teens. He was a handsome man and a good actor.

Maxine handled the money. Money to me was only important if you didn't have it. Leaving the house one morning I asked her for a little lettuce, short for the green stuff. She said, "I gave you some yesterday, and the day before. Lunch sure doesn't cost that much, does it?" I didn't answer her. She said, "Well?" I decided I might as well tell her. "Once in a while, usually between pictures, there will be a cowboy at the gate, one of the riders who works all the time for me. The conversation is always the same with all of the riders. They ask if there's any work for them. I ask how bad, they say pretty bad, the larder's low. I pull out my wallet and give them whatever is in it. I never count it, and end up saying it's not a loan, but a gift for the way they ride for me. Maxine, these guys, when I yell for them to come on and knock on it, they turn the horses loose down through the rocks, up the hill, through the trees. They take their lives in their own hands to make me look good. They only make ten dollars a day. A tenner doesn't go very far these days, when you have kids to feed. Some of them pay me back. I've turned down horses they want to give me. One of them offered me an old car."

She nodded and said, "In vaudeville it's called the 'panic list'—someone who is desperate for work. How about carrying no more than ten dollars in your wallet? If it doesn't happen too often we should be able to handle it." For the next twenty years I never carried more than a ten spot, and for the next twenty years the riders still stopped me at the gate once in a while, and for the next twenty years they were all my friends and knocked the horses up and down the hills at breakneck speeds. Some of their kids that I watched grow up rode for me in later years.

John Merton had a good part in the Tracy serial. He usually played heavies, and he could fight and ride and act. Because he had five kids, he was always at the top of the panic list. I watched them all grow up. A couple of them were in the picture business as crew members, and one of them turned out to be as good an actor and fight man as his dad. Lane Bradford was also as quiet and gentlemanly as his old man.

The climax of the Tracy serial was built around a delayed parachute jump. Tracy is held hostage by the heavy in an open cockpit plane. There is a parachute on the seat that he scooches down and wiggles into the harness so that the heavy can't see him. He then rolls the plane on its back and falls out, leaving the heavy, who can't fly, in one hell of a spot. Bud Thackery was the cameraman. He set the camera up in the Goodyear blimp. The stuntman was to jump from beside the camera and not pull the rip cord on the chute until he got near the ground. With the weight of the camera, Bud, the stuntman, and the big batteries that ran the camera, the poor little blimp was loaded. We watched it take off and set up in a grove of trees to shoot the parachute landing. The trees hid us from Bud's camera. It was a hot day. The blimp circled and circled. It could only get up to about a thousand feet. The stuntman knew where we were and was going to guide the parachute as close to us as he could. When the blimp could not get any more altitude, Bud decided to make the shot anyway. We were ready and on the next circle the stuntman jumped. He had more guts than I have. He fell—and fell, and fell. I started to yell, "Pop it, pop it!"

He was too close to the ground to suit me when he pulled the rip cord. The chute popped open. We could hear the sound, like an explosion. A second later the safety chute popped open. Now he was coming down with two open parachutes. There was no way he could guide them in our direction. He was drifting toward a big hog feeding lot. The man who owned it ran out of a shed and started yelling at him, "You can't land here! Go away!" He was waving him off. The stuntman landed in the middle of the pigpen loaded with hogs. The chute settled over them. We had never rolled our camera. Now the pigs started to run out from under the chute. Mack Sennett would have loved it.

We rescued the stuntman and the chutes and paid off the owner. I'd say it was the "stinkingest" shot anybody in the picture business ever made, and that's literally. The stuntman told me that the force of the sudden stop when the first chute opened ripped the safety chute open. The force of the stop left him with some deep black and blue marks where the harness came over his shoulders. If the audience was observant, they could see the hogs running out from under the white blanket from Bud's high angle in the blimp.

About that same time, I walked into the house one night after work and Maxine was sitting in a chair reading. She looked up and said, "Want a drink?" She knew my answer, and stood up. As she did, a mouse got out of the chair with her and zig-zagged across the floor and disappeared into the kitchen. She screamed and jumped up on a chair. I laughed, but she didn't. "I'm not going to go in the kitchen. Make your own drink. Make me one, too. And while you're at it, set about a thousand traps. Make that two."

The house hadn't been lived in for several years and the field mice had taken it over as their own. I brought her drink back with me. She was beating on the chair with the fireplace brush. Then she went to the door and called Cappy. He was still a gangly puppy. "He's sure no mouser. They ran over the top of him. He doesn't pay any attention to them!" she exclaimed. I had a solution. "Why don't I go and see if I can find that old snake friend of yours?" I said. She sat on the very edge of the chair. "Go find him. I can't take these damn dirty little things scaring me half to death anymore." She was deadly serious. We ate out that night.

The next day I worked I told Bill Nobles about my problems. He had a chicken ranch and knew about mice. He had the same problem. He laughed, "I've been through the same thing with my wife. Follow me home tonight and I'll give you a cat. I've got one that's a hell of a mouser, but lately he's been killing some baby chicks. I'll give him to you." We caught the cat, a big black one, put him in a gunny sack, tied the top and I took off for home. The cat growled at me all the way.

"What's in the bag?" Maxine asked when she met me at the door. I told her it was the greatest mouse trap that had ever been invented. The growl from the sack told her it was a cat. Cappy sniffed at the sack and growled back at it. We shoved him outside, opened all the cupboards and I dumped the sack upside down. The cat hit the floor on four feet. Just at that moment a mouse made a noise under the cupboards. The cat dove after him. The sound effects of pots and pans being thrown out of the way continued for a couple of seconds. Then it got deathly still. We were frozen in time as we waited to see what had happened. The cat came out the door holding a mouse by the head. He looked at Maxine and closed his jaws. The breaking bones sounded like a clap of thunder. I turned and looked at Maxine. She threw up. We ate out again that night.

The next morning the cat's belly looked like it was about to blow up it was so big. The old tomcat taught Cappy about cats. Lesson number one: stay at a safe distance. Lesson number two: don't chase. Cats can stop, turn on a dime and bloody your nose.

When Maxine and I were married she didn't know how to boil water. She was working when most girls her age were learning to cook. Her mother was the cook, but she was willing to learn. I got some of the craziest meals that were ever thrown together. Now mashed potatoes and gravy doesn't sound too bad— or does it? My mother taught her how to make gravy. You've heard people brag, "Gravy like my mother used to make." Well, my mother made the worst gravy in the world, bar none. To this day I don't eat gravy. When I refused to eat it, she got mad and said, "If you don't eat it, I'll feed it to Cappy." When I laughed at her, she went to the door and let Cappy in. She grabbed my plate, set it in front of him, and looked at me, saying, "You can go hungry." Cappy sniffed at it, turned, and went into the living room to lay down. I didn't dare laugh. I'm sure she would have decorated the top of my head with the plate. She sat down and took a big forkful of potatoes and tasted it. She grinned at me, "Let's go out for dinner. I'm hungry."

Ralph and Virginia Byrd had a sister who moved to Reseda not far from us. Fran and Emmy Peet were delightful people. Fran was Virginia's sister. Emmerson W. Peet looked just like the band leader Paul Whiteman. He was fat, but solid as a rock—a big rock—and played a great game of badminton. He was from the wealthy Peet Railroad family. Knowing his son, when Emmy's father died all the money he left to Emmy was tied up tighter than a drum. Emmy got a monthly check, which he could never live on. He spent the rest of his life trying to loosen up the drum it was tied up in.

Ralph and Virginia bought a house in Reseda in a two-acre walnut grove. It had a huge barn in back of the house. Maxine and I were delighted. They were only going to be five minutes from us. We finished the serial and we all helped them move in. The housewarming party was held in the big barn. It was the first of many parties over the next ten years.

Emmy came to me one day and said, "Will you kite a check with me?" I'd never heard the expression. It was four days before the first of the month when he would get his check. He was broke. He explained how it worked. I write a check to him for X amount of dollars. He writes a check to me for X amount of dollars. We cash them at our respective banks. His was in Hollywood. Mine was in Reseda. It would take at least four days for the checks to clear the banks. First they went down to the central clearing house in downtown Los Angeles. Then they were sorted and sent to the bank they were drawn on. On the first of the month when his check came in he could cover his, and on the first of the month my paycheck would cover mine. We had the use of the cash for four days. It made sense. I wondered why I'd never thought about it. Emmy had put a lot of thought into it. It worked—for the next three months. Then one month the clearing house checks got to the bank on the thirty-first. Both checks bounced. Maxine said they were sending them by carrier pigeon. From then on the word "kite" was something on a string up in the air.

On a lazy Sunday morning we'd been out to look at some horses that were for sale. Cappy had outgrown the coupe and was sprawled out in the back of the new station wagon. When we stopped he stood up to see where we were, then started to wag his tail. It was his old stomping grounds. The La Fonda was a bar and restaurant near the studio where we often had lunch. It was run by a big friendly gal named Rae.

When I opened the door, Cappy pushed through us and ran inside, circled behind the bar and buried his head in the overflow bucket under the beer kegs. Rae came in from the restaurant. The whole place was deserted this time of the morning. She greeted us, "The same as Cappy?" She drew us two beers. "I wish I had more customers like him. I'd make my first million." She ruffed up his ears and laughed, "He does love his beer." Maxine took a sip and said, "Breezy Eason lives near here, doesn't he?" I nodded. "I've never met him. From the stories you tell, he must have a great sense of humor."

We pulled into Breezy's driveway. He had a couple of acres and a small frame house with a big garden. In the back were two of almost every domestic animal, all living peacefully together in a green pasture. Breezy was in the yard, and his wife Jimmsy was pulling weeds. They greeted me with open arms. "Breezy, Jimmsy, I want you to meet Maxine. We were married a couple of months ago." Jimmsy gave Maxine a big hug. "Welcome to the family." Breezy stood back appraising her, then turned to me. "So you didn't marry that stripper you've been chasing after?" Maxine laughed and answered, "Nope." Then she asked, "You Irish, Breezy?" Jimmsy answered, "As Patty's pig." Maxine continued, "Lace curtain or shanty?" Breezy laughed, "Maxine, if I said lace curtain, I'd be lying. And you?" Maxine grinned, "Guess." From that day on Breezy called Maxine "Shanty."

We sat on the porch. Breezy made a big show of asking what we wanted to drink. Maxine wanted a beer. He repeated, "One beer" and held up one finger. "One beer." I wanted a bourbon and soda. Again he repeated, "One bourbon and soda." Jimmsy said "the usual." I'd been on this route before. All the drinks came out gin and ginger ale.

Drinks in hand we toured the barnyard. The twin baby goats fascinated Maxine. One of them tried to butt her. She sidestepped it and said, "Olé" When the old gander tried to bluff her by running head down at her, squawking, she stood her ground, stamped her feet and ended up chasing him away. This was the routine all newcomers to the barnyard got as a greeting. Breezy turned to me. "It behooves you to note, my friend, she's got guts."

We came to the flower garden. There was a statue of a little boy in the middle of the birdbath. I don't know how many people remember the sales logo for a brand of Mexican beer. It had a little boy piddling in the middle of a small quiet pond with all the ripple effects. With the printed logo, "No beban agua," (don't drink the water). Breezy's little boy looked just like him, but no water was coming out at the moment. He walked Maxine over in front of the birdbath. Jimmsy said, "Breezy!" I held up my hand to stop her. She was about to say, "Don't." Breezy stepped on the "piddle button" and the little innocent-looking kid piddled on Maxine. She looked down at her wet blouse, then at the little boy and started to laugh. Breezy grabbed her, gave her a big hug, and said, "Welcome to the family." She had passed the test.

They gave us a big cookbook which I still have, and Cappy had company in the back of the station wagon on the way home. He gave Maxine the little baby goat that she was already acquainted with. I wanted to name it Olé. Maxine said it was too masculine sounding for a nanny. It turned out to be Susie Belle.

Breezy asked me if I'd gotten a call about a meeting to be held by all the directors to further plans for the screen director's guild. It had been organized in 1936 but had been lying in limbo. When I told him no, he said, "I think you should come. I feel we need a strong one." He wrote the time and place on a piece of paper and asked me if I'd pass the word on to the rest of Republic's directors.

The director's guild meeting was held on the second floor of the Hollywood Athletic Club on Sunset Boulevard, just east of Vine. There were about forty directors in the room, including Jack English, Breezy, Joe Kane and myself. The rest I didn't know. As a matter of fact, I'd never seen any of them before. Frank Capra was running the meeting. There had been some meetings before this, but apparently nothing had been accomplished. They wanted input from everybody to see what was going to be needed in the bylaws. A man with a thick accent stood up to speak. I think it was Joseph Von Sternberg, but I'm not sure. The meeting was over fifty years ago, so you'll have to forgive me if I'm wrong.

"Frankie, there should be something in the bylaws so what's happening to me shouldn't. I'm making a picture at MGM. I'm going to the studio one morning and the gate man is not letting me in. I go across the street to get a cup of coffee and read in the *Variety* that I've been replaced. Now there should be something in the bylaws that says they have to tell me before they tell the *Variety*."

Capra held up his hand to stop the laughter. "And I know why you were replaced. You shot sixty thousand feet of film of pigeons flying around a loft." Now all eyes turned to the proposer of the new bylaw. "Ah, yes. Sixty thousand feet. I say shoot that one, now shoot that one. They were so graceful. So much poetry in flight. It's true: sixty thousand."

The talk turned to minimum wages. A gray haired gentleman stood up. I believe it was George Cukor, but again I'm not sure. In an actor's voice with every syllable in place, he said, "I see no reason to waste time on discussing this. Is there anyone here who doesn't make at least seventy thousand dollars a year?" Even Frank Capra couldn't stop the laughter for five minutes. At the end of the meeting it was decided that we wouldn't ask anything for the directors but fight to help the assistant directors who we all felt were overworked and underpaid.

The Screen Director's Guild had a constant fight with the producers. King Vidor was its first president, Frank Capra the second. It was under Capra that the producers finally gave the Guild recognition. With it, we won minimum wages and working conditions for the assistants. The first agreement with the Hollywood producers was signed in 1939, and I believe there were only around two hundred and fifty members, including the assistant directors.

The board of directors hired J. P. McGowan as executive director of the Guild. Mack had been a serial and feature director during the silent days and the early sound era. When the Depression hit the country in the late twenties Mack became an actor to keep body and soul together. We had worked together a few times; he was a wonderful, smart gentleman. I still think that without Mack's and Frank Capra's dedication to the Guild during the first stormy years the Guild might not have survived.

There were more meetings. No one missed them. They were lively to say the least. I can't remember who was holding down the president's spot at the time, but there was one hell of an argument from the floor. The president held up his hands in frustration. "It's impossible to get any two directors to agree on anything, but I have a proposition that I'll guarantee everyone will agree on." It broke the place up. When he finally got the floor back, he said in a loud sure voice, "Ida Lupino is the prettiest director in the Guild." (She was, I believe, the second lady to join.)

Around this time I started work on the next serial: *Hawk of the Wilderness*. We bought a book written by William L. Chester. It was a Tarzan-like story. Jack and I scouted locations and both of us fell in love with Mammoth Lakes,

California. There are seven lakes nestled in the southern High Sierras around the seventy-five hundred foot level, with big pine trees and blue skies. We picked Olympic champion Herman Brix to be the lead, and added Ray Mala to play his sidekick. We cast Monte Blue as an Indian. He had been a silent screen star, but this was the first time we had worked with him. He made a great Indian. Jack and I decided to put him on the rating list we kept on actors. Also in the cast was an Englishman with a great face, William Royle, who also went on our list—right at the top.

There was a dog that had a lot to do. A Saint Bernard like Buck didn't fit, so we interviewed several trained dogs. One of them was an Australian sheepdog named Tuffie. He was trained by a man from Texas. When they came into the office, Tuffie sat at the trainer's feet while we talked about what the dog had to do. In the same tone of voice that he used with us in conversation, he suddenly said, "Tuffie, it's dark in here. Turn on the light." We watched as the dog jumped up, searched the room, and spotted the light switch. He came to my chair, which was closest to the switch, and tried to pull it toward the switch. I stood up. He pulled the chair to the wall, jumped up on it, put his feet up on the wall and with one paw turned the light on. Everybody in the room "saw the light." Tuffie got the job. He was as smart as old Cappy.

You've probably heard the expression "two dollar dog." It came out of the picture business. There was a quickie producer on poverty row who had a dog in his picture. He had his choice of two dogs. One made two dollars a day, the other five. He figured out on his fingers how much he'd save on the cheap one, and hired him. The dog was about as half-ass trained as the half-ass producer that hired him. Once the dog was established in the picture, it was too late to replace him. He again was counting his fingers, only this time it was the takes it took to get the scene finished. He didn't have enough fingers or toes to figure out what the two-dollar dog had cost him in wasted film and time.

We had been working in the High Sierras for two days when a disgruntled call came from the studio. "Too much headroom. You're cutting the actors at the chin." The head cameraman lights the set and is responsible overall for everything concerning the camera. The operator is the cameraman who looks through the finder. He's the one who balances the picture; like an artist, he tries to make a pretty picture of every frame, framing a tree limb or a reflection in the water. Headroom is the name given to the empty space between the top frame line and the top of an actor's head.

Bob Beche was the producer. He was grinning when he told the camera operator about the phone call. He was an artist at his trade. We all looked up at the sky. Big cumulus clouds floated lazily across the tops of the big pines. Eddie Lyons, the cameraman, shook his head. "I'm guilty, Bob, but you'll have to admit they're prettier than the actors." We all agreed.

The studio said that the bottom frame was cutting across the actors' chins. They also said the clouds were beautiful, but something had to be done. I had a solution. "Let's shoot all the close shots with a one-inch lens. That way we can still get the clouds in the frame without all the headroom." To get a close shot with a one-inch lens, the lens has to be practically down the actor's throat. Now the soundman protested, "I can't keep the camera noise out." A one-inch lens also takes in the whole world. His mike would be farther away than usual to keep it out of the picture. We compromised. We'd only use the one-inch on silent shots. The picture was beautifully photographed. Bill Nobles was a master with the use of filters. On the screen it seemed like the goobers stood out in three-D. Did I say goobers? That's picture parlance for beautiful clouds.

We finished the picture in October under threatening black clouds. We were glad to get out of the beautiful high country before the snow started. On the way home Jack and I discussed how pleasant the picture had been to make. The actors had all been great to work with, and we knew we had a number one crew. We decided from here on out to have more to say about the casting. I guess we'd been lazy. The producer and casting director had been making the decisions, often without even asking our okay. We'd lucked out on this picture, and we weren't going to leave it to luck anymore.

Maxine and Cappy greeted me at the door with a kiss and a tail wag. I picked up the suitcase and stepped into the living room and stopped. "What the hell is that?" There was a very large bouquet of flowers set in a monstrous wooden bowl that practically covered the dining room table. Maxine smiled, "Read the card." The card said: "I just found out about your marriage. Best of luck and happiness to the both of you." It was signed "Arthur Godfrey."

I could feel the hair standing up on the back of my neck. "The son of a bitch!" Maxine took the card out of my hand. "Come on, honey. Grow up. He was just a friend." I picked up the flowers and headed for the door. She watched me. I took them outside and set them on a bunch of rocks around the fish pond. Cappy sniffed them, then lifted his leg. He thought they looked a little dry. I was tempted to do the same thing. I came back in and went into the kitchen to fix a drink. She stood in the doorway. "Better fix me one too." There was nothing more said about the flowers until that Christmas when another huge bunch of flowers arrived in a big wooden bowl. The card read Merry Christmas, and it was signed Arthur Godfrey. This time we both laughed, and took it outside. Cappy was waiting. I don't think Arthur missed a Christmas for the next three or four years. Maxine would say, "Cappy got his Christmas present from Arthur today."

Let's fast forward about eight years. As the old song says, "and baby makes three." Maxine and I had been blessed with the birth of a baby boy.

I was working on one of the sound stages when the assistant tapped me on the shoulder and said, "Mister Yates wants to talk to you." He pointed in back of me and I turned to see Yates standing with another man. They had just come through the door. As I approached them the other man looked familiar and Yates said, "Kid, I want you to meet Arthur Godfrey." As we shook hands I sized him up and vice versa. He was neat, trim, a little older than me. Nice looking. As he spoke I recognized his voice from listening to his radio show. He was famous for kidding the product he was doing the commercials for.

After a polite bit of the usual chitchat he said, "I hear you and Maxine have a new baby. I'd like your permission to say hello to her and see the baby." There was an awkward silence for a long moment before I spoke. "It's okay as far as I'm concerned, but you'd better call Maxine and talk to her first. I'll give you the phone number. Are you going in a studio car?" When he said yes, I told him the driver would know where I lived.

Someone on the set yelled, "We're ready." Before I turned to go back I said, "There's one condition." He looked surprised. I continued, "Please, no more Christmas baskets. We're running out of space to store them." He laughed and held out his hand. "You've got a deal." A quick handshake and he and Yates headed for the door. I watched him walk away in his two-hundred-dollar silk summer suit and with a frown on my face I went back to work.

Maxine was waiting for me at the door. The baby was in one arm, and a drink for me was in the other hand. She held out the baby. "Take him. You sure as hell can't deny him. Let me tell you what happened today. When Arthur got here the baby was asleep in his crib out on the patio. He said not to wake him up, so we sat and talked about his horses and a lot of people that we both knew in Washington. The baby started to make noises about a half hour later, so we both went outside. I picked him up. Arthur said, 'Let me carry him in the house for you.' I told him it wouldn't be safe until I changed him. He insisted. The minute I handed him to Arthur he pulled a Cappy and wet all over his beautiful suit." I held the baby out at arm's length and said, "That's my boy!"

The Lone Ranger had been one of Republic's most successful pictures. It was rolling up the profits in just the first few months of release, so the studio made a deal for another one, *The Lone Ranger Rides Again*. They were willing to spend more money on it than any of the other pictures to date. Jack and I made it clear we intended to be in the middle of the casting process.

The script wasn't as good as the first one. This one was the old story of the homesteaders against the cattle baron. The studio had Bob Livingston under contract and wanted to use him. His head had healed up and his back was okay.

We cast Duncan Renaldo as his sidekick. Chief Thunder Cloud was Tonto again, the same as in the first picture. Little fat Billy Bletcher was again to do the voice.

Actors are strange people sometimes. You ask them if they can swim. The answer is always, "a little"; if they can ski, "a little"; but when you say can you ride a horse, they were all born on a ranch. Of course they could ride.

We cast a girl names Jinx Falkenburg, a tall, pretty brunette who later became famous as a television personality. The heavy's name was Ralph Dunn. We asked them both if they could ride, and they were both "born on a ranch." The first scene of the picture on the first day they were to ride in from different directions, meet, and pull to a stop. They rode in fine. The stop was something else. They both fell off.

The studio was growing. They enlarged the western street and built a beautiful big new sound stage. We all thought it was a great idea when Mister Yates dedicated it to Mabel Normand, the great comedienne whose pictures had helped Sennett build the studio.

We were slowly becoming a major studio. They brought in a production manager to oversee all the pictures produced on the Republic lot. His name was Al Wilson. He was knowledgeable, had a great sense of humor, and I liked him. We always worked until eleven fifty-nine and a half on Saturday nights. The Actors Guild had been reactivated and their contract said the actors had to have twelve hours between calls or they received an extra day's pay. Sunday gave them the twelve hours.

It was around 11:00 at night and Al came on the set, pulled a chair up next to mine and stared at me. "You looked tired." I stared back at him. "Pooped is the word," I replied. "We've been on this friggin' set since 7:30 this morning. That's fifteen and a half hours, Al, and you come in here and say I look tired." He didn't say anything. "Al, did you ever hear the story that went around Mascot in the old days?" I asked. He shook his head. I continued, "There was this grip who asked Levine if he could have a few hours off. His wife was going to have a baby. Levine said, 'I didn't even know she was pregnant.' The grip answered the question. 'If you'll give me a few hours off, she will.'" Al was still looking at me. He nodded his head. "I understand. Was it a boy or a girl?"

When *The Lone Ranger Rides Again* was finished I asked Manny Goldstein if I could have a couple of weeks off. He told me to go ahead and take them, but he didn't want to put me on layoff. He said the studio was so busy he'd

Because Bob Livingston was a fine horseman it made him a pleasure to work with in *The Lone Ranger Rides Again.*

rather have the option of bringing me back if something should happen and he needed me.

One of the cowboys who worked with us on every picture told me he had a little horse he'd like to give me for Maxine. It was old and reliable. His kids had outgrown it and he'd like to find a home for her. He brought the little horse to the house and Maxine fell in love with Blackie. We had carpenter line the rabbit house with heavy timber and it made four big stalls with separate corrals attached to each stall. I found a big horse that I thought might make a good jumper. We were back in the horse business. Maxine and I took off for the hills.

We stayed out too long the first day and the second day there were a couple of sore bottoms.

The city of Tarzana was on the corner where Reseda Boulevard dead-ended into Ventura Boulevard. There was a gas station on one corner, and on the other corner was a drugstore. Across the street on Ventura was a long old wooden building with wooden floors. It was a grocery store owned by Isador Cutler and family. Izzy had owned a liquor store in Canoga Park, which was strictly farm country with ninety-nine percent Mexican population. He learned to speak Spanish. I loved to hear him speak it with a Jewish accent. His store was the only place to shop for miles around and everybody loved him.

I ran into Earl Bunn, the one-legged stuntman who was responsible for us moving to Tarzana, outside in the parking area. I looked at his peg leg. Usually he had a normal leg with a shoe on it. He told me the stump was sore and the wooden peg leg gave him some relief from the pain. We walked into the store together. Izzy's eyes were wide open when he saw the peg leg. He'd never seen Bunny without the normal leg. He pointed to the wooden leg. "Mister Bunn, oh my goodness, what happened?" Bunny never batted an eye. "I had a bad hangnail, Izzy, and they cut it off yesterday. Got any good steaks?"

Maxine came home from Izzy's one afternoon and said she'd run into an old vaudeville team she had worked with many times. They asked her if I could get them into the picture business. They wanted to be stuntmen. "Maxine, everybody wants to be a stuntman," I told her. This was about half true. She said they had a great act. It started out with the two men and the girl doing a ballroom waltz. They twirl the girl around from one to the other really gracefully, when something goes wrong and she lands in a chair and goes over backward. The two run to her, pick her up, dust her off, and then they go into the same routine again, but when it comes to the twirl she spins one of the guys off the stage into the pit. He crawls back on the stage and the free-for-all is on with the gal coming out the winner. She said they were honest to God great athletes. I told her to call them and tell them to come to the studio as soon as I got back to work. She wrote their names on a piece of paper for me: Jimmy Fawcett, Ken Terrell, and Helen Thurston. Helen was Jimmy's wife.

Maxine was right. They turned out to be as good as their billing. They became a part of our serial stunt team. Ken Terrell had been Mr. America three or four times. He was the one with the muscles, but he could also tumble, which is unusual for a bodybuilder with bulging muscles. Jimmy Fawcett was a great high fall man and all-around athlete. Helen Thurston became the number one stunt girl in the entire picture business.

We were doing a fight in a western saloon. There was a fall off the balcony. Usually there was a net under them and you never saw them hit the floor. Jimmy came to me and said, "I can come off the balcony onto a table." I told him we'd never planned it that way. We didn't have a breakaway balsa wood table. They cost too much to make. He told me, "I don't want a breakaway. Can you afford to ruin one of these old tables?" I looked at the table and told him we sure could. He got a saw from a grip and carefully sawed each leg at an angle.

As I watched him work, I realized he'd probably tried this in his backyard. We made the shot. Jimmy came over the balcony rail and did a flat layout. He landed on the flat table on his back. The table legs collapsed, which broke the force of his fall, and he rolled onto the floor. It was one of the wildest stunts of that kind I'd ever seen. He said, "How was it?" He was ready to do that all day. It started a new trend in barroom fights.

He came to me another time and said, "Ken and I can give you something different to put into the usual fights. Ken can throw me high up onto a wall so I'll hit the wall with my back and my feet will be near the ceiling. I'll be head down." I laughed, "Look, Jimmy, I like you. Now if you're upside down on the wall with your head six feet off the ground, you're not going to stick to the wall like a fly. You're going to come down on your head. I need you. I sure as hell don't want to get you hurt." Jimmy shook his head. "Let me show you." He was adamant. "Okay," I said, "but we'll have to have a ceiling piece put in the set." We braced the hell out of the spot Jimmy was going to hit, put the ceiling piece in and made the shot. It came out exactly as planned. When he hit the wall on his back, he kicked off the wall with his feet and instead of falling straight down on his head, he landed rolling back into the set. Great athletic ability makes stunt work look so easy that the audience thinks anybody can do it.

Daredevils of the Red Circle

Near the end of my two week vacation, Bob Beche called me and asked if I could come in and talk to the writers about the next serial. He had already called Jack English. The title was *Daredevils of the Red Circle.*

Barry Shipman, Pete Adreon, Ron Davidson, Sol Shor, and Rex Taylor were all in Bob's office when Jack and I joined them. I thought to myself as I appraised the serial writing team, "This is probably the greatest collection of characters ever assembled in one room."

Barry Shipman, being the senior writer, was the spokesman. He gave us a thumbnail sketch of the story. "There are these three great athletes who have a circus act. The high diver dives off a hundred foot ladder into a cup of water. As he hits the water another one slides down a wire held at the bottom of the ladder by the strong man who holds the end of the wire in his teeth while hanging onto a stanchion to keep the wire tight."

Jack interrupted Barry's dramatic delivery. "We've got to cast a young man in the part—one with dentures won't be believable." Barry nodded. "Right. Now the heavy is out for revenge on a very wealthy guy, who he kidnaps and holds in a cell. He's mad as hell at the wealthy guy for sending him to jail. He takes the wealthy guy's place by using a lifelike mask of him. He sets out to destroy all the wealthy guy's projects and leave him broke."

Barry had been walking around the room using his hands to sell a point. He stopped and looked at Jack and me. Jack looked at me, then said, "Barry, run that lifelike mask bit past me again." I had a different idea. "Why not run it to the nearest garbage can?" I asked. "I think you guys should stop drinking and give yourselves a chance to get over the DTs." Bob Beche had been sitting silently. As the producer he'd okayed the story. "If you think this came out of a drunken dream, you ain't heard nothin' yet. Tell them why we invited these two gentlemen in, Barry."

"Gladly, Bob, gladly," Barry continued. "Now we come to the episode ending in the first chapter. So far it's in the talking stage. We want to know if you think it can be done before we put it down in our beautiful words. One of the wealthy guy's projects was to build a tunnel from Catalina Island to Los Angeles, twenty-one miles right under the Pacific Ocean. When we pick up the story, the tunnel has been finished and the grand opening is about to take place. We see a long cavalcade of cars waiting for the speeches to end and the ribbon to be cut. Now the heavy naturally has other plans. He is going to flood the tunnel."

Jack looked at me. "No shit." Barry said, "No shit. Now here is the part of the sequence where we need your expertise: the hero has been informed of the plot and goes into the tunnel on a motorcycle to make sure the tunnel hasn't sprung a leak." I held up my hand with one finger sticking in the air. Barry looked at me and stopped talking. "You just reminded me I've got to go potty." Bob shook his head. "You'd better stick around and hear the rest. You'll probably be holding up two fingers."

Barry had caught his breath. "Now there is an offshore oil well near the tunnel that the villains have taken over and made the drillers change the course of their drill bit to hit the top of the tunnel. They have synchronized their watches to start drilling again as soon as the cavalcade is in the tunnel. The hero on the motorcycle sees the bit come through the tunnel and the water starts to gush in. He turns around and heads back to warn the cavalcade. The tunnel collapses and a wall of water starts down the tunnel, chasing the hero. In the episode ending we see it overtake him. As the water covers the camera we fade out." Barry took a deep breath. "That ought to bring the little bastards back the next week."

Silence. Jack spoke first. "The little bastards' mothers will probably be with them to see why they won't go in the bathtub to take a bath, so we have a stinking audience." We all agreed that it was a possibility. "Barry, you'd better tell us about the take out. It might involve something more complicated. I can guess. They don't build a tunnel without waterproof doors that can be closed." Barry replied, "Exactly." I said, "That we can handle. The rest I believe we'd better go into animation."

Jack asked Bob, "Have you tried this out on the miniature department?" Bob smiled. "Of course. I went right to the boss, Babe Lydecker himself." Jack smiled back. "And?" "The mighty Babe felt like you do. He thought we were nuts." Barry turned to the writers and said, "Genius still goes unrecognized." I stood up. "Let's go down and talk to Babe." "Put your genius on hold, Shippee. We'll be back to you in a little while." Bob always wanted the last word. "Barry and the rest of my slaves will be waiting with bated breath." Jack turned at the door. "You mean alcoholic, Bob, not bated."

Barry Shipman was a good looking kid with dark eyes and lashes that any girl could envy. He had been raised in the picture business. His mother had been a star in the not too distant past silent picture days. Nell Shipman was probably the first woman director in the business. She not only wrote and directed, she also raised her own money and produced. She loved animals and the big outdoors. When she passed away she left Barry an autobiography that describes the trials and problems of a lone woman making a picture in the vast wilderness. When I read it I thought, "And we think we've got problems."

The miniature department was in the back part of the carpenter's mill where the sets were made before they were put on the stages. Our walk down had been silent, with both of us deep in our own thoughts. Jack stopped before we went into the building. "I like it." I agreed, "It's at least different."

Babe liked the idea too. Babe was a tall, slender, preternaturally balding man, who was also a nice person. He and his brother ran the miniature department. Babe was the brains. Larry Wickland had hired him about the same time Barry and I had joined the Mascot Picture gang. We had all had our basic training under Larry and Jack Coyle.

We talked for two hours and set down on paper what we would shoot and what Babe would shoot. We had to find a tunnel with a curve in it so you couldn't see out the other end. Babe would match the tunnel in miniature for the tunnel collapsing and the water flooding it. He would shoot a moving process plate of the water chasing the camera down the tunnel so we could put our lead on the motorcycle in front of the process screen. We would also shoot the run-throughs of the motorcycle in the real tunnel. Babe would shoot the watertight doors closing to stop the water so we could put our set in front of it, with the lead spinning a big wheel to close the doors. Now all we had to do was find a tunnel with enough curve in it so we couldn't see out the other end.

Mack D'Agostino, our unit manager, went down to the Los Angeles street department and got a list of the tunnels with curves. We looked at them all and picked one in downtown Los Angeles near the city hall. It was an old tunnel that was tiled with small white tile. Mack thought that we'd have to tarp off one end to black out the reflected light. We'd need a generator and lights. The white tile would be to our advantage—no big deal. In those bygone days Los Angeles didn't have any traffic problems, and we got an okay by the police department to block traffic for one day. We told Barry to go ahead and put down his beautiful words on paper.

The usual weekly get-together of our gang was at Ralph and Virginia Byrd's house. Although it was March, we'd had an early spring and a badminton game was in full swing. A car pulled into the driveway and a couple got out and walked across the lawn toward us. Ralph greeted the man. He worked for Mitch Gertz, Ralph's agent. He introduced us to the girl, Carole Landis. She was wearing a simple silk dress that clung to one of the most beautiful bodies

I'd ever seen. When I got around to seeing if the body had a head, which it did, it was as spectacular as the body. Maxine said in a low voice, "Go inside and get a big towel for me to wrap myself up in." My answer, "The poor thing hasn't seen her feet since she was four."

Carole was an actress trying to break into pictures. She also played a damn good game of badminton and mixed easily with our crowd, proving that she had to have a sense of humor to go along with her beauty. Jack and I knew we'd be looking for a leading lady for the next serial and told the agent to bring her in to see us on Monday. She got the job. When she left, Bob Beche said, "She sure as hell wasn't in the back of the line when they were handing out knockers." We all agreed. Bob continued after a moment's thought, "We never asked her if she could act." Jack and I sounded like a chorus. "Who cares?"

We again picked Herman Brix as the strong man of the three leads. David Sharpe, whom we had first used in a small part in the *Dick Tracy Returns* and *The Lone Ranger Rides Again*, was cast as the tumbler and escape artist, and a new man, Charles Quigley, as the high diver. Charlie Middleton of the great disposition and mean face played the heavy. We also used Helen Thurston to double Carole Landis and Jimmy Fawcett to do all the stunts. David Sharpe could do them, but once an actor is established in a part you can't take a chance on him being hurt. Dave wasn't too happy about this because Jimmy would wind up making more money than he would as an actor, but he understood. Ken Terrell also got a part as a heavy and doubled other people throughout the production. There was a dog that belonged to the three daredevils. He had a big part. We again used Tuffie. We knew he could do it all.

We needed a circus performer who could dive from a high ladder into a tank. Mack D'Agostino found one working in a small carnival in east Los Angeles. Bob, Jack and Mack decided we'd give our wives a night out one evening. We all headed to east L.A. to catch his act. We decided it would be better not to approach him about working for us until after we'd seen him dive.

It was early evening and there was no one around the tall ladder sticking up in the air with a large tank of water sitting at its base. We couldn't get very close. There was a small picket fence surrounding it and the base of the guy wires that held it up. The ladder was in seven sections with about sixteen rungs to each section. The rungs looked about eighteen or twenty inches apart. The tank was about eight feet deep and ten feet in diameter. It's hard to judge distances in the dark. We had time to kill, so we took in the freak show and had hot dogs and beer for dinner.

The loudspeaker music stopped and an announcer's voice replaced it. "Ladies and gentlemen, if you'll step over to the tall ladder, our show is about to begin!" He said the dive was a hundred death-defying feet into five feet of water. A spot came on and picked up a man in white tights standing on the bottom rung of the ladder. He held onto a rung with one hand, leaned far out and acknowledged the crowd. Everyone, including our gang, applauded.

The announcer kept up a running string of statistics, like how fast he'd be going when he hit the water, and so forth. As he slowly climbed the ladder—I'll swear it took him ten minutes—he spent another five balancing at the top. Then with the roll of a drum through the loudspeaker, he took off in what looked like a straight out jump that turned into a pretty good swan dive. When he hit the water, there was a big splash and in less than three seconds, using the side of the tank, he vaulted out of the water and stood taking a bow.

We decided it was a damn good act as we applauded and followed him to his trailer. We gave him ten minutes to change his wet clothes. A deep gruff voice said, "Yeah" in answer to our knock. Through the door Bob explained what we wanted. When the door opened we all got a shock. Instead of someone who looked like David Sharpe, a beat-up, unshaven man in a greasy shirt and pants stood in the doorway. Over his shoulder we could see the inside of the trailer. A high diver he might be. A housekeeper he wasn't.

We walked back over to the high ladder and tank. He found us some chairs and boxes and we sat down to talk business. He smelled like he'd just had a drink. We asked him how high up the ladder extended. He said about a hundred feet. I said, "I counted the rungs on the ladder." He held up his hands. I stopped talking. He laughed. "Tell you a secret. The rungs on the bottom section are wide apart. From there on up, they get progressively closer to each other. When you look up at them they all look like the bottom section. I'm actually dropping around seventy-five or eighty feet."

I looked at his hands. They were calloused and deformed. I said, "You put up your own ladder and assemble the tank?" He nodded. "Can't afford any help." He looked at his greasy, beat-up hands. "The grease is from the nuts and bolts that hold the ladder together. The calluses are from the sledge I use to drive in the metal stakes that dead-man the guy wires. The knotted fingers are from hitting the water." We were all quiet as we looked at the broken hands. We were getting a lesson in the glamorous profession of being a high diver. "You know, water cannot be compressed, so it has to be parted. As I enter the water I hit it with my fists, then double up in a ball and spin so I won't hit bottom. The broken fingers come when you don't make a fist fast enough and your fingers take the place of your fists."

Mack made a deal with him and we all wound up in his little messy trailer having a drink on the deal. On the way home Maxine said, "Did you see the drink he poured for himself?" I nodded. "Didn't he have another dive to make tonight?" "I'll tell you something, Maxine, if I'd had to make that dive I'd have taken the drink right out of the bottle."

The opening action sequence in the first episode took place in an amusement park. It involved three daredevils, of the "Red Circle" presenting their act to an audience. The high diver climbs to the top of the hundred foot ladder, stands on the platform, and the announcer informs the audience that the flare he is about to light only burns two minutes. This is to see if the straitjacketed escape artist, who is strung up by his feet, can get free by the time he is pulled to the top by the strong man. The high diver lights the flare. The strong man pulls the struggling escape artist slowly to the top of the ladder. He gets out of the straight jacket just as he reaches the top. The high diver throws the flare down into the tank of water below him to show the height, and then takes off after the flare in a swan dive. As he hits the water the escape artist slides down a wire that the strong man is holding in his teeth.

We then meet the three daredevils face to face, as well as a young boy who is the brother of the high diver. We also meet the heavies who apparently don't like the act because for the night performance they drain the water out of the tank and fill it with gasoline. The act goes on and is thrilling the audience. When the high diver throws the flare down into the tank just before his dive, the tank explodes. This puts the high diver and the escape artist in an embarrassing position. They both have to slide down the wire holding on to each other while praying the strong man's teeth can take the extra weight. (If the Stick Tight Denture Creme Company had been in business when we made this serial, they could have claimed that the strong man was using their product. What a commercial that would have been!)

The three daredevils save the girl who is trying to help the little brother escape the flames. The little brother dies from injuries suffered in the fire. The daredevils swear revenge on the man who filled the tank with gasoline. The rest of the serial details how they bring the heavy to justice.

I asked the producer how come somebody didn't smell a big open tank of gasoline. He had a simple answer. Somebody invented the motion picture camera. Somebody else invented sound. Nobody has yet invented smell to go with them. I nodded and observed, "We just did."

The minute I read "fire" in a script I knew I'd be shooting the sequence. In one of our earlier films together, a fire sequence had fallen on Jack English's day with the camera. It was a sequence of a fire burning in a store on the western street. Early the next morning before I went to work, I read a small squib in the daily morning paper about a fire on the back lot of Republic Studio. It drew every fire company within twenty miles to the scene, but had been put out with only minor damage.

When you say studio fire, it brings back memories to all of Hollywood about some major disasters that had happened in the past. The studio back lots are full of standing sets—western streets, New York streets, apartment houses. They are fronts only. The fronts are held up by wood shoring in the back. Some of these sets are thirty years old. They are a five alarm fire waiting to happen. When the fire department gets a call to come to a studio, they break out all nearby stations, even if it's just a smoldering cigarette.

When I got to the studio I immediately went to the western street. It was my day to play fun and games with the camera. I was to pick up the sequence after the fire. We had planned to use black paint to show the smoke damage to the next door buildings. We didn't need black paint. They were charred.

The studio fire chief and his assistant were there with the studio fire truck. They'd been there all night in case of a flare up. I asked what had gone wrong. The chief said, "Jack." I looked at the charred building. "What the hell did Jack have to do with it?" The chief shook his head, "He wouldn't yell 'cut.'"

The crew gathered around us. It seemed like the prop men had set a pretty hot fire inside. That's what Jack wanted. He yelled "action." Some stuntmen ran out, one dragging a burning sack. He dropped it in front of the camera. Jack leaned forward and stared at it as the blaze built inside the building. The fire chief was standing by, hose in hand. The assistant was inside with a fire hose. Jack never yelled or signalled cut, and the big butane burners caught some of the set on fire. Jack still leaned forward like he was in a trance. A big cloud of smoke billowed into the air. Someone across the street watering their lawn saw the smoke and called the fire department.

Bill Nobles, the cameraman, looked at Jack, still sitting and staring at the fire, and yelled, "Cut. Put it out." The entire crew grabbed wet sacks and started to beat at the flames. The big fire hoses hit the fire from inside and out. The fire trucks started to roll into the studio. The studio offices emptied out onto the lawn. A big bellow of steam rose into the air, and the fire was out. Fire engines rolled onto the back lot for the next ten minutes.

Jack came on the set after looking at the dailies. I guess the scene on screen was particularly spectacular. He pulled up a chair beside me. I asked him how the dailies came out. He was shaky. "Did they tell you what happened?" I nodded. "I damn near burned the studio down." He was thoughtful. "Thinking back, I made a hell of a mistake. I should have turned the camera around and shot all the fire trucks pouring onto the street, sirens screaming. It was more exciting than anything we've ever had in any of our serials."

After that I could look at the big production board and find the fire sequence, and count backwards every other day to the start of the serial to tell whether I had the first or second day of shooting. I accused Jack of doing it on purpose so he wouldn't have to go through those miserable fire days. He denied the accusation, but did add, "If I'd thought about it, I might have."

So that brings me to the fire sequence in *Daredevils*. The amusement park was built inside one of our very small stages. We had shot the long shot with doubles. The girl sees the little boy fall and runs to him and then the three

Carole Landis and Robert Winkler. The fire in *Daredevils of the Red Circle* would get a lot hotter than this.

daredevils run in, grab the girl, pick up the little boy and run out as flaming debris just misses them. It had been a pretty hot fire, and by the time the firemen and prop men put it out, the floor of the stage was swimming in water.

The big doors were never opened until every bit of flame was out. When open they could cause a draft that might fire up a spark that had floated up to the insulation that soundproofed the ceiling. After an inspection, they were opened to air the stage and the big fans were turned on to get the smoke out. Then they were closed again and the burlap sacks nailed to the wall again and soaked with kerosene to get ready for the next scene. The last step, just before the camera rolled, was when a prop man fired up a kerosene torch. When the cameraman said "ready," the director yelled "light 'em up" and the prop man ran through the set, touching off the burlap sacks on the walls. Then he fired up the pieces of kerosene soaked cotton in the butane burners. These acted like wicks that touched off the butane when the big tanks were turned on. The fire was held back until the last moment. You could only let it burn for a minute or two at the most.

We were lining up for the close shots that involved the principal people. Carole Landis was to run in to the little boy who had been knocked down by falling debris and try to drag him out. We had cut the fire down to the walls in the far background and only the butane fire trough we were using was under the camera, between the principals and the camera. The doors had been closed for probably ten minutes and while the prop man splashed kerosene on the rags hanging from the walls I stood talking to Carole and the little boy. We'd re-hearsed the scene—where she runs in to him where he is lying on the ground—several times. The kid's father was standing in back of him. He wanted to be sure I wasn't putting the kid in danger.

I saw the prop man light up the torch and a second later there was a "whoosh," like a small explosion, and a bright blue flame swept through the stage at waist level. Searing heat engulfed our legs and swept over the small boy's head. I reached for him, but the father beat me to it and held him high in the air. Then the flame was gone. I ran my hand over the kid's head to be sure his hair wasn't on fire. His hair was singed, and I could smell it. I yelled to open the big doors, and told the father to get the kid out and over to the studio first aid station.

I turned to Carole. She had her dress pulled up and was beating at her panties. Her dress wasn't smoking. I said, "Carole, it's all over." She stopped beating and looked at me. Her breath was coming in gasps. "What the hell was that?" I guessed, "Butane is a heavy gas. There must have been a leak in one of the lines, and the gas went down to the cold wet floor and stayed there. When the prop man lit the torch, the flame touched off the butane." (Later my guess proved correct.) Carole nodded, "It went right up my dress." She was still hold-ing her dress under her chin. She looked down at her panties, then very lady-like, dropped her skirt. "It could have ruined my little money maker."

We'd been into the serial for a couple of weeks and everything had settled down to the usual grind. The sequence with the flood in the tunnel turned out better than we'd expected. One morning the wardrobe girl came to me. "Billy, I can't get Carole to wear a brassiere." "She says it's too hot." I laughed, "Great. She needs one like a hole in the head." The wardrobe girl didn't laugh. "But the motion picture code!" she said. I closed my eyes and visualized her without the brassiere. "To hell with the code," I replied. She turned and stomped off the set. In two minutes the head of the department came on the stage followed by the wardrobe girl. She stormed up to me. "Do you want us all to lose our jobs?" I laughed, "Relax. I was just kidding."

I knew the code of decency would probably make us cut out any scenes of Carole without a brassiere. "Bring her here and let me talk to her," I told them. When she walked on the set I took a good look at her. In later years after she had become a star, Earl Wilson, the New York columnist, described her as "looking like an ornate French bureau with the top drawer pulled out." I sighed. "Carole, go put on a brassiere." She protested, "It's too hot." I asked her, "Have you ever heard of the code of decency that governs what you can and can't do in order to release a picture?" She shook her head no. "Well, you will. Carole, close your eyes a moment and visualize me walking down the road, holes in my shoes and a bundle on a stick over my shoulder, all because of a brassiere." She laughed and said, "You win." She turned and walked out of the stage. The wardrobe people followed her, just to make sure. I turned to the crew who had been listening. "Look, I'm crying too. Now get the hell back to work," I told them.

Carole had stardust sprinkled all over her. She was talented, pretty, and had a hell of a figure. She went on to star in many pictures, but was probably best remembered for *Four Jills and a Jeep*. I was shocked to pick up the paper one morning a few years later to read that she had committed suicide.

Remembering the code set forth by the Motion Picture Producers and Distributors of America, Inc., in those bygone days of the 1940s and 50s, and what we see on the screen today, is the difference between going to church in the old days and the burlesque theatre today—or putting it bluntly, the difference between a flower garden and a garbage dump. There is more blood shown spouting from people's bodies in one picture today than all of the pictures produced under the code.

We couldn't even show a person being hit on the head. There had to be two cuts. A person striking something off screen, then the recipient falling to the ground. Profanity of any kind was forbidden. I am not sure just why, but over a period of time they threw the code out the window and exchanged it for the dirty language and pornographic stories and nudity of today's cinema. The old pictures made under the code will last forever: *Gone with the Wind*, *Snow White*, *Casablanca*, *Stagecoach*. Will the new ones survive?

The year 1973 was the first time I'd ever shot a nude scene. The girl had to be interviewed to make sure she didn't have any imperfections like birth marks, or scars from operations, or implants. I insisted that we have the wardrobe woman and make up girl in the room with me. I also excluded even the producer. It was one of the most embarrassing moments of my life—and I might add that it was the first and the last time for me.

But back to *Daredevils of the Red Circle*. Dave Sharpe turned in a great athletic performance as the escape artist. It was a director's dream to have a leading man capable of doing his own fight sequences. It meant you could keep the camera close to him and it gave us a chance to show him off.

Dave smoked cigars. Optimos to be exact. He would keep one in his mouth during the rehearsals. Then, when the scene was ready to shoot he'd take it out of his mouth and carefully lay it on a rock, camera case, or chair edge, and do the stunt. When the director said cut, he'd walk over, pick it up and stick it back in his mouth, and come over to the director saying, "How was it?" I think it was a good luck omen, like keeping your fingers crossed.

I once asked one of his many wives if he used the same routine with the cigar when he jumped into bed at night. She looked at me with a big grin on her face. "You've been peeking!"

Dave was a heckler at heart. He was always ready for a laugh, and could laugh at himself. We were working on the back lot at night. It was a fire sequence and Dave was to dive out of a third story window with flame shooting out of it, fall through the flames shooting out of the second and first floor, and into a net held by firemen waiting below. We had the real fire department from North Hollywood down below to catch him. Dave and I were sitting next to each other watching the prop men adjust the butane burners that shot the flames out of the windows.

The fire chief in charge of the men holding the net walked up to us. He had on his helmet and big fireproof coat. He pointed to Dave and asked me if this was the young man who was jumping out of the window. I introduced him to Dave, who stood up and shook his hand. He asked Dave if he was worried about the fall. Dave looked up at the flames coming out of the window and said in a very meek voice, "My, it is a long way up." I turned and looked at him and started to say something when the fire chief said, "Watch me and do exactly like I do and you'll be okay." He took off toward the door of the building and disappeared inside. Dave looked at me and pointed to the window he was going to jump from. "Well, it is a long way up." I shook my head, "Davy, if there were two more stories, it wouldn't be a long way up to you." I yelled to the prop men to turn off the burners.

The fire chief appeared in the window, looked down at us and yelled, "Remember, do just as I do. You ready below?" The firemen holding the net yelled back, "Ready, Chief. Turn 'er loose!" I yelled, "Hold it, Chief." He yelled, "Be right down," and jumped. The net men caught him like the bunch of pros they were. When they lowered the net to the ground the chief never stood up, and the firemen gathered around. Dave and I ran over to the group. One of the chief's legs had hit the iron ring that acted as a handle for the net holders.

When they were putting him in the ambulance I spoke to him and told him we were sorry about the accident. He said, "Just part of the game." Dave looked down at him and asked, "Chief, I don't have to do it *exactly* like you, do I?"

We finished the picture on schedule and at the party we always had to celebrate "another one in the bag." Fred Toones came up to thank me for the job. He billed himself as "Snowflake." Fred was black. He also ran the shoe shine stand at the studio and everyone loved him. Blacks were typecast in those days, and there wasn't much work for them. We tried to write Snowflake into as many serials as we could. The word discrimination in those days was a word that you seldom heard, and as far as I'm concerned, it's still a word that should be seldom heard.

Lower left is Charles Quigley, lower right Herman Brix and top David Sharpe. I felt these three actors fit their parts and were totally believable. They were all great to work with.

The cast, crew, and stuntmen all gathered around the central meeting place. The bar had been set up in the middle of the set that we had just finished using. The talk turned to the war clouds gathering in Europe. Jimmy Fawcett, Ken Terrell and Jimmy's wife Helen Thurston held center stage. Just before they came into the picture business, they had toured Europe with their knockdown drag-out vaudeville act. They told us that in Germany there were blocks of buildings that had toy factory names on the outside of the buildings. They asked one of the theater managers how they could sell that many toys. He told them to get up early in the morning and watch the toys being shipped out. They did and the next morning, just before dawn, twelve big tanks rumbled out of the back gates and disappeared down the street into the darkness. They told us that when they went to the U.S. Embassy to have their passports stamped to reenter the United States, there were block lines of Jews trying to get visas. They talked about Hitler's secret police. It was the first time any of us had any idea how serious the situation in Germany had become.

One of the grips remarked, "Hell, I don't see what Hitler has to do with us." It wasn't a year later that I saw him in uniform. It certainly answered the question he asked better than any spoken word.

Jack and I went into the projection room to check the composite print of the first episode of *Daredevils* before it was shipped to the exchanges. Everyone in the projection room seemed to think this was the best serial we had made to date. We were all learning by trial and error and the serials were playing in better theaters and were making more money for the studios than they ever had before.

Time, when you're not working, seems to fly by, and Jack and I started to cast for the next serial. It was another Tracy with our good friend Ralph Byrd. This one was called *Dick Tracy's G-Men*. It was about a master spy. We interviewed a bunch of actors for the spy roll, and finally chose Irving Pichel. Irving

Ralph Byrd and Phylis Isley made a good looking team.

came from New York and had directed several pictures. We had picked the leading lady and Tracy's sidekick from a list of good actors when we were told by Bob Beche, the producer, to forget them. The front office had already picked them for us.

Jack looked at me. "Here we go again!" I asked, "Whose relatives are they, Bob? Remember the last time we got stuck with a leading lady that was sleeping with someone in the front office?" Bob nodded, "A disaster."

We met the girl a few days before we were to start production when we went to ladies wardrobe to check out the clothes she was to wear. Phylis Isley was tall, dark and slender. She wasn't a beauty, but pretty in a clean, girl-next-door sort of way. She introduced us to her husband Robert Walker. They were just married and seemed like a couple of happy kids. Isley was her maiden name, and her father owned theaters in Oklahoma. They had both been to acting school and came to Hollywood to get into the movies. Mister Yates had put her under contract—I imagine out of deference to her dad, who might be talked into playing Republic's pictures.

The other actor who was wished off on us was named Ted Pearson. When he came to Hollywood he forgot to bring his talent with him.

Jack and I rarely ever went in to see our own dailies. We were too busy preparing for the next day's shooting. The producer checked them out and if there was anything wrong, he'd set up projection time late in the day and he and the director would look at it together. The first day I worked with Ted, I knew we had a disaster on our hands. I told Bob Beche to let me know what time they were running my dailies. I wanted to be there to defend myself.

When I came into the projection room, the lights had been turned off. The projectionist usually let you sit in darkness for a couple of minutes before he rolled the projection machine. This was to let your eyes adjust from the daylight outside to the dim light on the screen. The top row of seats were big leather chairs set in back of a long desk that ran the length of the back row. Each seat had a small adjustable lamp so you could take notes. It also had a button in front of each seat so you could press it and a buzzer sounded in the projection booth. The projectionist would then stop the picture. Press it again and he'd start it running again.

My eyes were blinded by the darkness, but a hand come out and Bob Beche's voice said, "There's a vacant seat next to me." The hand guided me into a seat next to him. The picture came on the screen. The slate with the sync marker on top was slapped together and I heard myself saying "action" and Ted came on the screen.

There is an old saying in the picture business: "The scene was great until they pulled the slate out." In this instance, the saying was a thousand percent right. I listened for a moment to Ted, then cringed for fifteen minutes more.

The slates went by and Ted didn't get any better. I was completely cringed out when the buzzer sounded. The picture stopped and the lights came on. To my surprise, I was sitting between Bob and my old nemesis, Moe Siegel. Moe turned to me. "I've seen thousands of feet of film run through this projection machine, but that's the worst acting I've ever seen." I could feel the hair on the back of my neck stand up. "I agree with you. We didn't hire him. He was forced on us by someone in the front office." Moe didn't say anything, but glared at me. I broke the silence. "This dumb son of a bitch can't even drive a car." Moe said, in a very low voice, "I can't drive a car either." Before I could answer, he pressed the buzzer and the picture came on the screen.

Bob and I walked back to the office when the dailies were finished. Moe had left the room without another word. Bob broke the silence. He had a grin on his face. "May I ask what you were going to say when Moe pressed the buzzer and cut you off?" I grinned back at him. "Guess." Bob's grin widened. "I've known you for a long time. The odds are in my favor. But if Moe hadn't pressed the button when he did, we both might be walking out the gate instead of back to our offices. I was looking at you. Your lips had already formed the word 'no.' If you hadn't said it, I probably would have. The other word was 'shit.'"

I opened his office door for him. "Enter, oh great reader of minds," I told him. Bob stopped. "Let me delve into that vast expanse of nothing you've got between your ears once more. You're thinking, 'Ted was given to us by Moe.'"

The picture wrapped up and Jack and I were going over our list of actors to put on our "good" list. Ted's name never even came up. Phylis got one vote from me. Jack said, "She's clumsy. She can't walk across the room without tripping over her own feet." My rebuttal was, "With those big dark expressive eyes, put her in *Orphans of the Storm* and you've got a winner."

I wanted to use her on the next serial, but casting told me she was no longer under contract. I asked Manny Goldstein what happened to her. He said Yates let her out of her contract because she wanted to go home. He thought she might be pregnant and her husband wanted to go back to acting school. This was near the end of 1939. She returned to Hollywood in 1943 and won an Academy Award for best actress in Song of Bernadette under a new name: Jennifer Jones. Her husband, Robert Walker, also became a big star a short time later.

Shortly after finishing *Dick Tracy's G-Men*, Maxine and I had just come home from a long ride up in the hills and were turning the horses out into the corral when the sound of a horse galloping on pavement turned our attention to the street. A riderless horse that belonged to the girl who lived down the street from us ran up to our corral fence and sniffed noses with our horses. Maxine said, "Something's happened to Bea." We had met her on the trail a half hour before and stopped and talked for a few minutes. She owned a health food store and was a nut on the subject. She had told Maxine she loved to ride into the hills and get a tan. She sometimes took off her shirt.

We both liked Bea. She was a good neighbor. She was also young, pretty, and busty. I opened the big gate and caught the little horse. Bea's shirt was hanging on the saddle horn. Maxine was concerned. "Maybe she fell off. She could be hurt." She lifted the shirt off the saddle horn. "She must have taken off her shirt to get a tan." There was something else hanging with the shirt. Maxine separated them and held up a brassiere—not just an ordinary brassiere, but a very large one.

I tied the horse to the fence and headed for the garage to get the car. As I started the engine, Maxine opened the door on the passenger side, shirt and bra in hand. "If you think for one moment you're going looking for her by your-self, you're dead wrong, buster! Let's go."

We found Bea hiding behind a tree. It seems she got off the horse and turned him loose to graze for a few minutes and he took off for home without her. Maxine hollered, "Stay put. I'll bring your shirt." She turned to me. "Now aren't you glad I came along? Think of how embarrassed you would have been walking up to her and handing her this." She held up the bra. As she walked away she turned back to me and stuck her tongue out.

Things at home couldn't have been better. One day Maxine was sitting in a chair and Cappy had backed up to her and was sitting on her lap with his front feet on the floor. It was his favorite way to relax. I came from the kitchen with a couple of beers. I set hers down and she just beat Cappy to it. "You'll get yours later." She pushed him off her lap and he sprawled on the floor. "Let's get him a playmate," she said. "He's lonesome. Remember how cute he was when we first got him? We could have a whole yard full of them, sell them and make a fortune." I groaned, "Hell fire, by the time they were big enough to sell, we'd be so broke we'd have to feed the horses to them."

Dick and Elaine Walt, the kids who sold us Cappy, had talked us into going to some dog shows. We met a different group of people than our motion picture business friends, and we enjoyed them. We knew Dick had bred an-other litter of puppies with different blood lines than Cappy's, and so another mouth to feed joined our family. We named her Trudy. She was just as lovable and a hell of a lot smarter than Cappy. Maxine made the observation: "The female of any species is always smarter than the male." I thought about the remark for a moment and decided I wouldn't touch it with a forty-foot pole.

A bit later we were visiting my mother. I had never seen my mother happier than when she finished reading a letter from my sister Julie. It seems Julie was pregnant for the first time. I knew my other sister, Pickie, was in the same condition. Their letters had crossed, telling each other of the good news. Mom said it was about time. They had both been married a long time. She turned to Maxine. "Why don't you make it a threesome?" she asked. Maxine patted her hand. "We're trying, Mom. I hope we don't have to wait as long as they did."

The news the daily paper brought every morning was full of the problems that the rest of the world was having with Germany and Hitler. Julie's letter talked of the marine corps buildup, and the intense training Cle was putting his fighter and bomber squadrons through. The marine corps had invented dive bombing in the Nicaraguan campaign. They would wire a bomb to the wing and dive at the target, reach out and cut the wire with a pair of pliers. Then as the bomb took off, the bombers would pull out of the dive. They had found even this crude method pretty successful and were working to find a more sophisticated system.

Zorro's Fighting Legion

S hakespeare said, "The old order changeth, giving place to new." How true. Barry Shipman, the lead writer, left for a better job. Bob Beche, the producer, did the same. Jack and I had lost two good friends. Billy Nobles, the cameraman, had to be replaced because of illness, and a new man, Reggie Lanning, took his place. Bob was replaced as producer by a tall, good-looking young man named Hiram Staunten Brown, Jr.

When Jack and I first met him I asked, "Do I call you Hi, Hiram, Stan, Staunten, Brownie or Junior?" He laughed. Jack observed, "Your parents must have been very brave." He nodded, then asked, "Why do you say that?" Jack said, "Because it would take a lot of bravery to name a small wrinkled up baby Hiram Staunten Brown Junior." He smiled and answered, "That's why, after they thought it over, they called me Bunny."

Bunny's dad had once run RKO Studio. Bunny was a graduate of Princeton and he had a beautiful wife and two pretty little girls. We also found out he'd stop by the bar with us for a drink, and he was smart, with a great sense of humor. We hated to see Bob go, but the old serial gang decided that the studio couldn't have found a better replacement.

Jack and I were having a drink with Bunny at our usual watering hole. He was sitting between us. Jack started a conversation that the two of us had decided was the best way to get a point across to the new producer. "Bill and I are tired of shooting the same old fights day after day." It was my turn. "Bunny, both of us are punch drunk." Jack's turn: "We've seen so many punches thrown we're mentally black and blue."

Bunny's head had turned first to Jack, then to me, then to Jack. He held up his hands. "Wait a minute. Change seats with me, Jack. My neck's getting sore." He and Jack changed seats. "I'm new here, but I just learned something. Don't get in the middle of two old friends. Now go ahead. At least my back's protected." Jack took over. "This next serial is called *Zorro's Fighting Legion*. We've already told you that if they cast John Carroll in the part you can include

160

I'm on the left with Hiram Staunton Brown and Jack English.

us out. We want to replace the phony fist fights with sword fights." We let that sink in a moment and picked up, "If we cast the part of Zorro now, instead of at the last minute, we can send him to school to learn how to handle a fencing foil."

We cast a tall slender actor, Reed Hadley, to play Zorro, and hired Ralph Faulkner to teach him how to handle a fencing foil. Ralph Faulkner was a small wiry gentleman. He had an accent that I believe was Austrian. He was in his forties and could still jump up on a table from a standing position. He had been an Olympic saber champion. He combined the saber technique with the art of fencing and had trained every picture star who had ever held a sword in his hands during a picture. Fencing is an art, and I might say it's dull to watch, but combined with the slashes and feints of saber fighting, it becomes an exciting moment on the big screen.

Ralph had a young son who was as good as his old man. They worked beautifully together. There was a name for every move. It was mostly in French, and they would talk to each other under their breath during their fight, like sixth, third, and ninth, that told the opponent which parry he must use to keep from getting run through. The ballet uses the same technique. Every move has a name.

There was a lot of horse work in the serial, and we talked about all the action and having a scabbard and sword hanging around your waist for the

Ralph Faulkner is on the right. The other actor is Guy D'Emmery. In this picture Ralph was at least sixty years old and still the master fencer and saber champion of all times.

stunts. Someone came up with a brilliant idea. The scabbard was wrapped around Zorro's waist with the sword handle used as a buckle. The Lydeckers designed it for us and it worked perfectly. Of course, once Zorro pulled the sword from the scabbard, we had to cut and give him a real one. To be supple enough to wrap around the waist, it sort of "flopped in the breeze" once it was drawn from the scabbard, but this gimmick let us do away with the usual black cape. We also gave him a bull whip to use with the sword. We figured the sharp explosive noise of the popping whip would at least keep the kids awake. We also used a song over the main title.

The story was sort of like *The Desert Song*. Zorro recruits from his friends a bunch of young people to help fight the heavies, so when they ride with Zorro we decided to let them sing to keep awake. They also wore a Zorro type costume, only instead of black it was gray, and they all wore masks.

There were two incidents that happened during production that still stick in my mind even after fifty years. We had a low setup on the back of the camera car shooting straight back at a four-up team pulling a stage coach. The camera platform was no more than eight inches off the ground. A four-up team has two leaders and the team behind them are the wheelers. The leaders are always the fastest and the best trained. It was the first scene in the morning on the running insert road at the upper Iverson Ranch in Chatsworth.

The first run of any team is always the fastest and wildest. The horses are fresh and ready to run. After the first run they settle down. We started the camera car back up the road so that we had what should have been "horse speed" as we roared by the team. The two pickup men were holding the leaders. They turned them loose and spurred their horses to one side to get out of our picture. The driver pulled the team directly in back of the camera car on a dead run.

I was sitting on the low platform with Joe Novak, the operator cameraman who was on his knees behind the camera. The camera assistant was standing in back of Joe. The minute the team pulled in back of us, I knew we were in trouble. The leaders were pulling closer to the camera car. The stage driver couldn't hold them back. I yelled to the camera car driver to keep going. The leaders overran the camera car platform and I found myself with a horse's leg on each side of me, with his chest pressing against my face. I couldn't move back. I was leaning against the camera car bulk head.

It was only momentary. The camera car surged ahead and pulled the horses off of me. I looked over at Joe. The camera was cocked to one side and Joe was laying up against the bulk head. I could see the assistant cameraman on the next platform. He had pulled his legs up out of the way. Somehow the leaders were still on their feet running. Why they hadn't gone down and piled up the rest of the team with the stage on top of them only God knows. He was surely looking down on us that early morning.

We sent Joe to get an X-ray on his shoulder, and the first aid man put a tape over my broken nose. I thanked God that no one was hurt, but the day had just started. It would get even wilder before sunset.

Those of you who have seen John Ford's *Stagecoach* will surely remember John Wayne falling between the horses of the running six-up team pulling the stagecoach on a dead run, hanging onto the tongue, then letting go and as the stagecoach runs over him, catching the axle and pulling himself back up onto the coach. The man doing the stunt was Yakima Canutt. We had shot the same stunt with Yak several times before Ford did it on *Stagecoach*.

We were set up on the camera car running with the team when Yak, doubling Zorro, spurred his horse next to the running stage and jumped from his horse to the running leaders of the team. We were using a four-up (four horse team) instead of the six-up (six horse team) that John Ford would use in *Stagecoach*.

While the team was getting a breather after the run, Yak put on the "spreaders" for the next part of the stunt. The spreaders were made out of oak and were about three feet long. They were attached between horses to the collars of the team to keep the team from crowding into the tongue and into each other. When we made the run this time, there was a hidden driver inside the

Yak transfers to the four-up team. Note that instead of a regular western stirrup hanging down on the left side of saddle there is one of Yak's inventions "The Step."

boot of the stagecoach driving the team with small cables replacing the leather reins. The leather reins were still in place, but not attached to the horses.

The sequence of events was covered by three separate scenes. Yak transfers to the coach, which we had already shot. Now we were ready to make our second run. The run started with Yak standing on the tongue of the leaders. The driver shoots at him. Yak fires back, hitting the driver, who then falls off the coach. The hidden driver now has control of the horses. A man leans out of the stage window and fires at Yak, who ducks and falls between the leaders, grabs hold of a bar he had engineered under the tongue which ran the length of the tongue. He is now dragging on the ground between the running team.

The next step is the most dangerous. If it's not done exactly right, Yak could end up under the wheels of the stagecoach. He drags for a few seconds until he's sure the horses are lined out straight, that the wheelers are spread apart enough for him to squeeze through, and he cuts loose, being careful that he doesn't roll. He passes through the wheelers and the coach rolls over the top of him, leaving him laying on his back in the middle of the road. That is the way it's supposed to happen.

The camera car was running alongside the stagecoach. The camera was on a low setup. Yak fell between the two horses and grabbed the bar to start his drag. There was a loud "pop." I glanced away from Yak and realized that the spreader on the lead team had snapped. The team came together against the tongue. Yak was ducking the horses' hooves like a fighter. He had to cut loose. One of his knees hit the wagon tongue and he was turned end over end and the coach rolled over him. I yelled at the camera car driver and he swerved off the road. The team ran past us with the pickup men in pursuit.

By the time I jumped off the car and ran back to Yak, he was on his feet. Not one of the big iron wheels had touched him. We used the scene as one of the episode endings in the serial. It is probably the most honest ending that an audience has ever seen, and I'm sure they thought we had used a dummy.

The final cut in the sequence where Yak grabs hold of the axle and climbs back up on the coach wasn't as dangerous as it looked. An outrigger pole is attached to the side of the camera car and the coach's tongue is attached to the end of it. The camera car is now pulling the coach and is running alongside of the camera car. Yak now lays on his back in the middle of the road and the camera car pulls the coach over the top of him at a slow enough speed so he can grab the special bar welded to the axle and hang on to be dragged.

The camera speed dropped to probably fourteen frames per second instead of the usual twenty-four. As he grabs hold of the special bar, the camera car picks up speed so that by the time Yak climbs into the coach, it is moving at race horse speed. The cameraman slowly brings up the camera speed from fourteen to normal.

Otherwise the serial went smoothly. When it was finished, Jack and I added a name to our list of actors. Reed Hadley's name had an "excellent" written next to it.

Just before we started the serial, World War II became a reality when Hitler's troops invaded Poland. Rumors started that there would be a draft. About the same time, each of my sisters had their first child. Pickie and Bert Clark had a little girl named Victoria and Julie and Cle Green had a boy named Cleland Junior.

Trudy, our Saint Bernard female, and Cappy had a litter of pups. One of them looked like Cappy with an off-white ear. We sold or gave away all but the one with the white ear. We named him Barry, hoping he would grow up to be as great a dog as his name sake.

"Bunny, you're out of your mind!" That was Jack's response when Bunny presented us the script to our next serial. Bunny looked at me and carefully took one of the expensive cigarettes he always smoked out of its expensive looking box and lit it with a silver Dunhill lighter. "Jack, I just heard the same statement from Billy, only he used the word nuts. I suppose you've come to the same conclusion about the story that he had," Bunny replied. "The story is good," Jack said. "It's great. It's exciting, but..." Bunny held up his hand. "We can't make it for the money the studio wants to spend." Jack nodded. "You'll end up smoking Camels instead of Benson and Hedges, and I'll end up a nonsmoker and Billy'll have to feed his horses to those big dogs of his." We all looked at the script lying on Bunny's desk. The big title letters looked back challengingly: *Drums of Fu Manchu.*

We started to look for the lead. If Fu Manchu wasn't believable, we didn't have a serial, no matter how much money we spent on production. We interviewed every actor in Hollywood. Nobody came close. We were getting desperate. We were facing a start date. Then fate stepped in. The casting director brought in a tall, dark young man. We had been looking at the older character actors. How could this handsome young man play Doctor Fu Manchu, who was supposed to be a hundred years old and able to operate on anyone's brain and make them his slave forever?

The casting director had given him a page of script that we had been using with all the actors. He was to read it with a Chinese accent. He had the page in his hand. We all wanted to say, "Forget the reading," but with an actor sitting in front of you, well, I know I couldn't be mean enough to say to anyone who wanted a job, "Forget it, you're too young." So to be nice, we talked to him, asking the usual questions. What have you done? The answer was New York plays. How old are you, and so on. We had already made up our minds that he wasn't right for the job.

Finally Bunny looked at his watch. The interview was over. Bunny said, "Would you please read for us? This man *must* have a Chinese accent." Henry Brandon stood up, all six feet two, tossed the page that the other actors had read on the casting director's desk, and from memory recited the page. I closed my eyes and listened, visualizing a Chinese mustache, skin head and heavy eye makeup. I looked at Jack and Bunny. This wasn't Henry Brandon. This was the sinister Doctor Fu Manchu. Henry turned out to be one hell of a good actor, and as nice a person to work with as Jack and I ever wrestled, overworked and prodded through one of the longest schedules of any serial we had ever made.

Fu Manchu's henchmen, the Dacoits, had all had brain operations to make them slaves, so a big scar across their forehead was a must. Bob Mark, the head of makeup, shook his head. "Bunny, just the Chinese makeup is going to make us way over the usual budget." He thought a moment. "What if we made up a bunch of rubber caps that fit over all the Dacoits' heads with the scars already on them?" he asked. "It would give them a shaved head look. We could do the same for Fu Manchu." Bunny looked at Jack and me. Jack said, "Bob, that's a hell of an idea. We owe you a drink."

Jack, Bunny and I stood watching Louis Germonprez, the assistant, moving strips on the big production board. He was a genius at holding the actors down to a minimum number of days worked and loading the daily schedule with work that was possible for Jack and me to finish on a daily basis. We all liked Lou. He was a slim, trim Frenchman who had learned his trade under his brother-in-law, Erich Von Stroheim, the famous German actor director.

Lou was full of stories about Von Stroheim. His favorite story went like this. The scene was the exterior of a small German cottage. The time was World War I. A woman comes out of the cottage door, walks slowly down the path to the mailbox set in the white picket fence, opens the box and takes out a letter. The letter had a black border around it. She looks at the letter, and the black border tells her that her husband has been killed in the war. She doesn't open the letter, but clutches it to her breast, turns and walks slowly back into the house, tears streaming down her face. Cut.

Von Stroheim is sitting in his director's chair, with his head down and nursing a hell of a sick hangover from the night before. When the woman pulls the letter out of the box and looks at it, Von Stroheim says in a weak voice, "cut." Then to the woman, he says, "Bring me the letter." She hands him the envelope, which he tears open and pulls out a blank piece of paper. He yells for the prop man. "How can you expect a woman to cry over a blank piece of paper?" The prop man replies, "But Mr. Von Stroheim, in the script she never opens the letter." Von Stroheim replies, "You expect her to fake the tears like you've faked the death letter. Get the real death notice and put it in the envelope."

The prop man turns to Louis. "Lou, get me a car. I've got to go into town and have the letter printed up at the print shop. I'll see you in a couple of hours." Lou turns to the crew. "Shut the set down until after lunch." He turns to Von Stroheim, who is seen walking slowly, holding his head, back toward the dressing room. Lou follows him. By the time he gets to the dressing room Von Stroheim is lying on the couch sleeping off the night before. Lou shrugs, knowing that after lunch Von Stroheim will feel well enough to go back to work.

Soon we were on location for *Drums of Fu Manchu*. It had rained off and on all day, but we had still managed to get in a day's work. On location, there is a production meeting about the next day's work every night when the crew gets back to the hotel. The next day's location was in a canyon at the end of a dirt road. Lou's instructions to the drivers were, "The road will probably be muddy, so if anyone gets stuck in the mud, pull over to the side of the road so the other trucks can get through."

The four of us worked on the production board for two days. We were to start three days before Christmas, so we had to absorb the Christmas and New Year's holidays. We went over every shooting day and cut out anything we didn't think hurt the picture. We came across an item on the board—"pigeons." Fu Manchu was contacting the hill tribe and telling them when to start the big rebellion against the British by carrier pigeon. No, we couldn't cut them out. It would mean a complete rewrite. I was only kidding when I said, "The great Fu Manchu, I can hear him say now in Chinese: 'Pigeon bring message,' like Tonto said to the Lone Ranger." Bunny looked at me. "All right, smart ass. How about a note on a horse?" Jack tried his Chinese dialect, "Horse bring message." Louie said the great Fu Manchu would use an eagle. We all agreed that an audience had never heard "Eagle bring message" before.

Lou got on the phone and called Curly Twiford, the little guy who supplied all the smaller animals like chickens, rabbits and pigeons, to all the studios. Yes, he had a trained eagle. It was the same price as the pigeons. We hadn't saved any money, but we felt we'd improved the script. Everyone was happy but me. The sequence fell on one of my days. I wished Louis had kept his big mouth shut.

We were set up on the top of a big rock at Iverson Ranch. There was a canyon below us that opened up into the Chatsworth area of the San Fernando Valley. In those days there were orange groves and chicken ranches. Now it's wall to wall houses. We had one of the stuntmen dressed in an Arab costume with an eagle, a big eagle, on his arm. The bird had a hood over his head. Another stuntman was attaching a message holder to one of his legs. We were ready to shoot; the stuntman was to pull off the hood and toss the eagle into the air. Curly was standing with the stuntman, petting the eagle and talking to him.

I felt something was missing and asked Curly when he was going to attach the wire that would keep the eagle from taking off into the wild blue yonder. He told me we didn't need a wire. He had attached an eight pound bag of buckshot under each wing. The eagle could fly but couldn't carry the weight far and would land down in the canyon. He pointed out his assistant down in the canyon. The assistant would pick the eagle up and bring him back in case we needed another take. It made sense to me.

We rolled the camera. The stuntman attached the message. The other stuntman pulled the hood off the eagle and tossed him into the air. The eagle spread his wings and started to fly down the canyon. The only trouble was, he was gaining altitude, and soon disappeared, heading into the wild blue yonder. Curly was disappearing too. He was heading for the equipment and soon a trail of dust from a car told us he was trying to keep his eagle in sight.

From left: Hirman (Bunny) Brown, Jack English, Louie Germonprez and myself. Look at the big production board. The strips between the black borders are one day's work. Each strip represents a complete sequence.

About two hours later Curly was back, eagle in hand. It seems he just saved the eagle's life. He had landed in a farmer's chicken pen and was having a lunch of one of the chickens when the farmer came out of his house with a shotgun. At the same time Curly's car roared into his yard with Curly yelling, "Don't shoot! Don't shoot!" I told Jack about the routine. His comment was, "Eagle bring message—after lunch!"

We got the budget down as much as we could, but we were still twenty-five thousand dollars over what the studio told us we could spend. The day he went down to try to shake the money out of Al Wilson's production department was Bunny's trial by fire. Jack and I both told him to tell Al that we knew we'd have the best serial that Republic had ever made, and I still feel it was number one.

We cast a new actor, Bob Kellard, in the lead, with a real beauty, Luana Walters, as the leading lady and Bill Royle as Sir Nayland Smith. We didn't forget number one on our panic list. John Merton was Fu Manchu's right-hand Dacoit, with fangs and a bald, scarred head.

We had a pair of shoes made for Fu Manchu that he wore on the interiors. They made him at least five inches higher than his six-two, so he towered over the rest of the cast. The shoes were fine as long as he didn't have to move fast. When he was running or moving fast he wore regular shoes.

The stage door opened one day and about ten young men came through with the publicity man. He came to me and asked if I minded if they watched for a few minutes. They were a Texas basketball team and he was showing them around the studio. Now I took a close look at them. The smallest was six-foot-four, and the tallest was about six-foot-six. I looked at Henry Brandon sitting in his chair, his legs stretched out in front of him. He had on his five-inch shoes. I walked over to him and said, "Henry, pull your feet under you and cover them with your long Chinese robe." It came down to the floor. He had two robes, one to war to cover up the special does, and a shorter one to wear with his regular shoes.

I walked over to the basketball players and the publicity man introduced us. I asked them if they'd like to meet Fu Manchu. Their eyes lit up. I motioned to them to follow me. We surrounded the sitting Fu Manchu. I said, "Dr. Fu Manchu, I'd like you to meet these men. They're basketball players from Texas." Henry looked at me, and with his Chinese accent said, "It's an honor and a pleasure." He slowly stood up. He was a couple of inches taller than their tallest. They all looked up at him. One of them said, "Wow," and another asked, "Did you played basketball in China?" Henry sighed and shook his head, "Ah, me too short."

After we finished the picture, Jack and I went down to Hollywood to have lunch. On the way down Hollywood Boulevard to our usual lunch spot, Musso Franks, we passed a theater that had Fu Manchu on the marquee. We had never seen a serial in front of an audience and decided it was time to see if we were pleasing our kid audiences. We had a hard time finding two seats together. The theater was packed with screaming kids and when the main title came on, Jack turned to me, "I hope the main title with the drums, building to a crescendo, doesn't scare them." No worry. We couldn't hear the drums over the screams.

The end of the episode had the Dacoits taking over a train by knocking out the engineer and fireman. The lead and the girl are on the train with a brief-case that Fu Manchu must have if he is to control the world. The passenger train is coming down a long hill. At the bottom we see a Dacoit throw a switch that puts a freight train coming up the hill on the same track. Now the two trains are on a head-on collision course. The cuts of the freight train coming up the hill and the passenger train coming down get shorter and shorter as the trains get closer together.

The kids are screaming. There is a long shot miniature of the two trains coming toward each other, a cut of the unconscious engineer, then another long shot of the passenger train rounding a curve. A loud train whistle is heard over the long shot that seems to be asking for the right of way. Suddenly a little kid about eight years old, sitting right in front of us stands up and yells, "How can the engineer blow the weezle if he's daid?" The two trains crash head on. Come back next week and see how the boy and girl get out of this one.

Over lunch Jack asked, "Did you hear what I thought I heard?" I nodded. I imitated the little kid yelling, "How can the engineer blow the weezle if he's daid?" Jack thought a moment. "Out of the mouths of babes. How in hell did we miss that when we dubbed that last reel? Do you think we should redub the reel and take it out?" I laughed. "Jack, the kids were screaming so loud the whistle never had a chance!"

Two Duds and a Hot Water Tank

My sister's letters were full of war news from Washington. They were talking in Congress about a plan to draft all men between twenty and thirty-six into the service. She urged me to quit Republic and join the marines. She thought that she could get me an appointment to officers' training school in Quantico. When I showed the letter to Maxine, her comment was, "Why don't that redheaded sister of yours mind her own business?" Maxine had declared her own war against Julie.

The *Red Ryder* comic strip was one of the most artistic portrayals of the early days of the Old West that any of us had ever seen. It was drawn by a man who obviously knew horses and what a western cowboy should look like. Fred Harman must have patterned his hero after himself—he had red hair. The writers had been on the script since before Christmas and had come up with an acceptable story. Our start date was set for the end of March 1940.

Jack, Bunny and I had started to look for actors to fill out the cast. We were looking for a lean, craggy-faced western type about six-foot-six. His sidekick was a small Indian boy about eleven. We all thought that a massive man and a small kid would make a pretty picture when they were working together.

We found the kid to play "Little Beaver." His name was Tommy Cook. He had never been on a horse, so I invited him out to our house and put him on Maxine's calm little black mare. He was a natural little athlete, and after a few lessons he was ready to chase any bandit he could find. Red Ryder was a problem, but we kept looking.

One morning the front office called Bunny and told him that they had solved our problem. They had cast Don Barry in the part and had just signed him to a long-term contract. None of us knew Don, so we checked him out with casting. He had been cast in small roles in a mesquiteer series picture and a couple of Roy Rogers pictures. We wanted to meet him.

After we met Don we all decided that he was too short to play the role and his brain matched his size. The only thing he had that was big was his ego. We tried to talk to Yates, but Al Wilson told us that the president of Republic was in New York and wouldn't be out to California until summer. He also told us that he had a new assistant, Bill Saal. Maybe he could help us. We made an appointment with him and when we walked into his office and met him, well, if you ask me what kind of an assistant he was, I'd say he was a fat one.

Bill had been an early producer of the Bill Boyd westerns and had come up from being a picture booker for some theater chain. He knew the picture business forward and backward, and he would be Yates' assistant until the studio folded. You couldn't help but like him. He listened to our story. When we finished, I took one last parting shot, knowing he was a Texan. "If your fellow Texans ever find out you had anything to do with casting a midget for a six-six Texan, they'll take your fancy western boots and your big belt buckle away from you forever."

Bill laughed and put his feet up on the desk. He had on a pair of regular shoes. He opened his sport coat to expose his belt buckle. His belly was big, but the buckle was small. He grinned as he spoke. "They already have, and I'm sure you are right, except I didn't pick him. He was Yates' choice. He feels he'll be the next Cagney. Would you turn down Cagney for the part? Don is a fine actor and can be as tough on screen as Cagney." We were all doubtful, but we could also see we were beating on a dead horse to oppose Yates' choice.

We conceded defeat. When the picture was over, Jack and I decided maybe we should have hit the dead horse a couple of more times. As far as we were concerned, Don stunk. We also decided Bill was like most Texans: full of it right up to his eyebones. I also noted that the next contract for another Red Ryder film included a clause that said the actor playing the part had to be at least six feet tall.

There was one stunt in the picture that has stuck in my memory. There was a fight between Red Ryder and a heavy on top of a running stagecoach. One man is knocked off the top. We were working at a location called Burro Flats in the north end of the San Fernando Valley. The location later became the testing grounds for the rockets that sent a man to the moon.

Dave Sharpe, who doubled Don Barry throughout the picture, was to do the fall from the top of a stagecoach. Davy and I walked down a dirt road to see if we could find a good spot to do the fall. There was a steeply cut bank on one side and a hill on the other. We came to the cut bank and stopped. No stuntman likes to do a fall on flat ground. If there is a hill to roll down after they hit the ground, they can give you a more spectacular fall. Dave looked at me and nodded, "This will be fine with me if it's okay with you." I was kidding him when I said, "Dave, that big sandy hill looks like a big feather bed. You should be able to do a flip or two in the air before you tumble down the hill." Dave didn't laugh. He studied the hill, took a couple of puffs on his cigar, and said, "Will you settle for one?"

Later that day the stagecoach with six horses pulling it came roaring down the road. Dave and another stuntman were standing on top trading punches. When they came to the proper spot, the stuntman hit Dave. Dave fell off the top of the stage, turned over in the air, hit the ground halfway down the hill and rolled to the bottom where the camera was set up. When I said, "cut," Dave got up, picked his cigar up from the rock he had carefully laid it on a few minutes before, and took a puff. He said, "How was it?"

When the picture was finished we decided not to have our usual party. The picture hadn't been pleasant. Jack and I went across the street to have a drink. At the bar Jack turned to me. "Remember when we were wardrobing the midget and I said everything looks too big for him, and that hat he picked was ridiculous? Well, I was wrong. His head grew into the hat. God help the next poor directors who have to work with him. Amen."

I guess Jack and I weren't living right. We caught another dud on the next serial. This time it was our own damn fault. The serial was *King of the Royal Mounted*, another comic strip that was written by my favorite author, Zane Grey.

For our first story the writers had come up with a plot that tied in with the war that we all were sure was well on its way. Canada had declared war on Germany. The heavies were trying to get some ore out of Canada. They planned to use the ore in their magnetic mines in order to blockade any ships from the United States that were carrying guns and munitions to Germany for the Canadians. The German submarines were the heavies and the Royal Canadian Mounted Police were trying to stop them. It was pure and simple propaganda.

The interview for the leading man went well. He had worked in a picture at RKO and seemed like a nice person. I asked what he did for a living before he tried acting. He said he'd been a used car salesman. His name was Allan Lane. Later Jack and I were mulling over our mistake and Jack said, "When he said 'used car salesman' we should have turned him down." When he turned to leave the office we also noted he had a big fat ass. Later we found the ass part fit the whole man.

It was June 1940 and it had been a very rainy spring. We decided that we would be better off going on location. Besides, we needed the big pine trees.

We checked with Doctor Krich, a scientist at Cal Tech whom all the studios hired to give them the daily and extended weather reports. He had discovered the frontal system of weather forecasting. A few years later he would set the date for the invasion of Europe. He missed, but when you guess weather that far ahead and miss, it's easy to forgive.

Doctor Krich gave us a good report on Big Bear Lake. Big Bear Lake is in the San Bernardino mountains. It is about six thousand, five hundred feet above sea level and at that time there weren't too many cabins surrounding it. Today it's wall-to-wall cabins and traffic. There was a small lake and a log cabin settlement that had been built by Paramount Pictures on one end of the lake for *The Trail of the Lonesome Pine*. The small lake was named Cedar Lake, and was higher than Big Bear and drained into it. The location had a small cement dam that Paramount had covered with wood to make it look like a log dam and a big cabin with a water wheel that worked on one end of the dam. It was a perfect spot for the picture.

We picked a girl who had never been in front of a camera before. She was pretty and had that clean, all–American-girl look. She read well for us. Her name was Lita Conway. We took along our regular crew of stuntmen, with Dave Sharpe to double Allan Lane. The rest of them were to play heavies and jump in to double wherever needed. They included Duke Taylor, Ken Terrell, Ted Mapes, Loren Riebe, Earl Bunn, Bud Geary, and Jimmy Fawcett—the best in the business.

The first night on location, for some reason or other, is "party night." I think the whole cast and crew tried to drink Big Bear dry. We all stayed at a big hotel on top of a hill that overlooked the boat docks. The hotel burned down a few years later.

All the stuntmen were drinking at the bar. Jack, Bunny and I were sitting at a table doing the same thing. There was a loud crash and we all jumped to our feet and turned to the bar. Bud Geary's feet were on the bar and his body had disappeared behind it. There was a lot of broken glass. One of the other stuntmen was helping Bud to his feet. "Davy, what's the beef?" Davy looked at me and shook his head, "There's no beef." I looked at Bud and he agreed, "Davy's right. There's no beef." I said, "That sure as hell was no picture punch." Dave shrugged. "Bud said no one had ever knocked him off his feet. I just wanted him to know I could."

I shook my head and said, "Oh boy, oh boy, oh shit. Will you guys go to bed? You're all loaded." I looked at Bud. "Go on, Bud. We'll see the mess is cleaned up." Bud started across the big dance floor. Duke Taylor followed him through the tables. When they got near the door Duke called Bud. As he turned, Duke hit him and knocked him over the table and said, "I just wanted you to know I can knock you off your feet, too."

The next morning the biggest collection of hangovers ever assembled got off the bus on location. Needless to say, all was quiet. A short time later Allan and Lita got out of a car and walked over to a table that had been set up for the makeup man and hairdresser. I walked over to say good morning. They were both new in the picture business and probably a little nervous about the first day of shooting. After "good morning," I asked Lita how she had slept. Her answer was "not too well." I nodded. "Nerves?" She shook her head. "Noise." She pointed to Dave Sharpe. "That nice Mr. Sharpe had a room next to mine. The walls are very thin and he and some men were all arguing over something. Their language made me hold my ears. Then the manager came in and told them to quiet down or he'd throw them out of the hotel. Then there was a loud crash and the manager's head came right through the wall into my room." I didn't tell her that it took the rest of the night to convince the manager not to throw us all out of the hotel. All I could think to say was, "They don't build these summer hotels very well. The walls are all beaver board."

I have seen a couple of pretty good barroom brawls on location. It wasn't always the stuntmen. The crews we had were all hard working people and after putting in fourteen hours in the hot sun and wind, a drink before dinner just seemed part of their lives.

The one fight that I still vividly remember was in Kernville. The bar was later nicknamed the "Bucket of Blood." That was after the brawl. We were all sitting or standing at the bar after an exceptionally long and hot day. At the end of the bar the local farm hands were gathered. They had been at the bar a couple of hours longer than we had and were half loaded. One of them said in a loud voice, "Are you all them faggots from Hollywood?" One of the grips turned and looked at him, then turned back to us. The local said, "Bet none of you ever been in a fight. Faggots ain't got no guts." He spun the grip around only to meet a right hand that nearly tore his head off.

Like I said, after the fight the bar was known as the Bucket of Blood. If it was a five gallon bucket, to my knowledge the fluid count would be Hollywood one gallon, locals four gallons. I can't ever remember Hollywood not still being on their feet when the sheriff arrived to mop up the mess.

The front office had been negotiating to buy the *Superman* comic strip. We were all looking forward to making it into a serial, and we were sure it would be an all-time winner. We had talked it over with the writers and had decided that no mortal man could stand up to him on even terms, so we decided that the heavy would control an army of mechanical steel men. We had gotten a cost for some animation long shots of a mechanical army advancing to attack the big city that Superman lived in, and found we could work the cost into our budget. We were all looking forward to starting the project. Jack and I were sure that an army of steel robots marching on a city with only Superman to stop them would bring alive the motto that we always kidded about: a pair of wet panties for every little kiddie.

We had started to look for an actor to play Superman and had interviewed every bodybuilder in or near Hollywood who was over six-foot-four. We had already decided that Clark Kent, the lead and Superman, should be two people, one smaller than the other, but who looked alike. But when he came out in the Superman outfit, he would be awe inspiring and have muscles bulging. We would dub in the voice of the person playing Clark Kent. The writers were instructed to hold Superman's dialogue down to a few grunts if possible. Things were looking good, we thought.

It was late in the afternoon about four weeks before we were to start when a call came from Manny Goldstein's secretary that Manny wanted to talk to Bunny, Jack and myself. Manny told us that Superman was out and we had to go with another title. They just couldn't make a deal with the Superman people for what we could afford to spend for a title.

Bunny counted on his fingers the number of weeks before we were to start production and shook his head. We can't get a story together in that length of time. Manny said, "what about using the Superman story without Superman?" Bunny shook his head. "The story just wouldn't make any sense. It's based on an army of robots. Can we delay the start for a few weeks?" Manny looked at a chart under the glass on top of his desk and shook his head. "We have a release date to meet. We'll skip the Superman title and," he ran his finger down the chart, "take the next one. It's called *Mysterious Doctor Satan*."

Bunny called all the writers together and told them the bad news. For the first time that I could remember they were all silent. Usually you couldn't shut them up. Jack, Bunny and I decided we should walk across the street to the bar and have a knock so the day wouldn't be a total failure.

Ron Davidson had beat us to the bar. Ron was the lead writer. Nothing ever bothered him. He had one of the most even dispositions I'd ever seen. But that day Ron was talking to his martini. "Instead of seeing an army of robots, we'll talk about building an army of them after the heavy perfects his first one, you know, like building a test model," he said. "Instead of changing into Superman, we'll give the lead a mask. That way we can salvage most of the story we've got just by changing names."

Jack and I groaned. Bunny and Ron looked at us. "What are you groaning about? That way we can get into production on time." Jack took a big long drink. "It's that friggin' robot. You know, the one that looks like a man in a hot

Bob Wilcox fights the hot water heater as Billy Newell watches.

water heater." Bunny nodded. "Let's get with the Lydeckers in the morning and see if we can do something to fix that.

The next morning I was what Bunny always called "wound up," walking up and down the room talking fast, arms waving. "We'll get a midget, have him standing in a big steel tube set on a small platform that is propelled by tracks like a tank. His arms, instead of using the flexible heater ducts, will be hinged with great claws for hands." Babe Lydecker said, "And how do we power these tank tracks?" I was ready for him. "We pull it with wires." Lydecker wanted to know what would keep it from falling over. I suggested that we make the platform wide and long. And how would we get it through the door? I said we could let it knock the door and part of the set down on its entrances and exits. Lydecker said, "I like it." He turned to Bunny with, "I'll need about twenty-five grand and six months to build it.

Needless to say, we got the man in the hot water heater, and the writers went to work changing the script to Ron's idea about talking of the army of robots but never seeing them.

A couple of weeks before we were to start, I came into Bunny's office one morning. He was sitting behind his desk. Jack sat with his back to me, looking at an eight by ten photograph. Neither one answered my good morning. When

I asked if they were sick, they both answered yes. When I asked what was wrong with them, Jack handed me the picture he'd been looking at. It was a girl with long blonde hair and a face that—I was going to say it would stop a clock, but out of deference to her, let's say she was not a beauty.

I made a face and said "uggg" and tossed it on Bunny's desk. It slid across the surface and fell into the wastebasket. Jack said, "Good shot!" Bunny said, "That's no way to treat your leading lady." My reaction was, "Who says?" Bunny smiled. "Yates."

It seems like the circus was in town and Yates had taken it in. This girl, her name was Dorothy Herbert, had a sensational act, and Yates thought she would make a big impression on a serial audience. Jack and his wife, Bunny and his wife, and Maxine and I headed for the circus that night to catch the act. When the announcer introduced the act as death-defying, one of a kind, never before tried, et cetera, et cetera, the lights dimmed and a spot picked up a girl in a silver dress riding bareback on a big black horse with her long blonde hair streaming behind her. She made one turn around the big outside track at a full run. It was a beautiful sight. As she passed by a big five-foot spread jump, it burst into flames. Then she laid back on the horse and it made another turn around the track, headed for the flaming jump, and sailed over the top of it, with the blonde still lying down on the horse's back. It was one hell of an act. Maxine turned to me. "The next time we go to a horse show, why don't you try that? It ought to bring home the money."

Again we were in Bill Saal's office. Yates had gone back to New York. We had pleaded with Bill to hold her for a western. The serial we were working on didn't have any horses in it. Bill said, "I agree with you, but she'll only be in town for a short time and Yates said to use her in the next serial." Bill knew about having to change from the original Superman to another title.

I asked him if he'd met her. He said he was with Yates when he caught the act. My argument was that she wasn't pretty enough or had enough experience to carry a leading part. He thought about it a long moment. "Yates didn't say she had to be a leading lady—just use her in the serial." Bunny and Jack and I all stood up, said thanks and headed for the door with a sigh of relief.

So we left it to the writers to work her in the script. Good old Ron said, "The inventor is wealthy. He has a stable on his estate and the girl runs the stable. We'll find a couple of stunts for her to do on a horse's back. That should keep the front office happy." We still hadn't met her.

A few days later Ron came into the office. "We've worked her into jumping a horse out of a window and they chase her with a car and she does a cossack drag shooting a rifle at the car chasing her." I ask a simple question: "Where does she get the rifle, Ron?" But Bunny said, "Who cares? Write it."

When Ron left, Bunny turned to me. "What the hell is a cossack drag?" I explained that it's a maneuver where a rider swings off one side of the horse, turns backward, locks a knee under the saddle fender, which leaves him hanging onto the side of the horse facing the horse's rear end. Both hands are free. Bunny thought about it a moment. "Oh. I'll call and tell her. She'll probably know what a cossack drag is—I hope."

One afternoon about a week later, the phone rang in Bunny's office. It was the Burbank Police Department. They wanted to know if a Dorothy Herbert worked for him. It seems they had picked her up on the bridle trail in Griffith Park for practicing what she called a cossack drag, riding backwards on the side of the horse, firing a rifle at a full run.

Bunny told the police that it was a stunt she was practicing to do in a picture. Yes, she worked for him and what was wrong with practicing on a public park bridle trail? The policeman asked, "With live ammunition?"

We cast Robert Wilcox in the leading man's role. He had starred in many pictures and we knew he was a good actor. The heavy we picked was Henry Brandon who had done such a terrific job for us as Fu Manchu. The title of the new serial was *Mysterious Doctor Satan*. We had planned some strange makeup for him with a couple of bumps on his head that looked like horns and we were going to give him a Fu Manchu type of accent.

At the last minute he had a chance to play a big part in a major picture. He told us that if we could match the salary of the major picture, he'd rather go with us. We couldn't find the money, so we hired Eduardo Ciannelli, who turned out to be one of the finest actors I ever had the pleasure to work with. I'll always remember him in *Winterset*. He was the gangster they thought they had killed and threw him in the river. But he came back in the end, all muddy and bloody.

We got the script finished in bits and pieces, an episode at a time. It was a stinker. There had been so many changes that Jack and I weren't sure just which pages belonged in the script and which we should throw away. We decided the whole project should go in the trash can.

A few days before we were to start, the headline in the morning paper read, "President signs national draft order—All men must register."

That morning Jack and I walked into Bunny's office with big smiles on our faces. Bunny looked up from some script pages when we stood in front of him and didn't sit down as we usually did. "What do you two find so amusing? Why the big smiling faces?" I asked him if he hadn't read the newspaper that morning. Bunny nodded. "About the draft. Yes, I read it, but I don't see anything funny about going in the army." Jack, still smiling, said, "We've been drafted. Just think: we don't have to shoot this stinking script by orders of the President of the U.S.A." A big smile crossed Bunny's face. "Wait a minute. I'll get my hat and go with you.

We started the picture on schedule. Dorothy worked the first day. She was a very nice person and turned out to be an adequate actress. When I introduced her to Billy Nobles, our cameraman, he looked at her, then at me, and went over to the camera box. He opened a door and pulled out a big round glass filter. I'd never seen him use it before, and asked what it was. He called it a "B disk," and explained that it threw parts of the face just a little out of focus. It took the wrinkles out of the face in the older, once-beautiful, now-wrinkled, actresses. He put it into the matte box on the front of the camera, looked through the lens at Dorothy, turned it this way and that, pulled his head away from the camera, and pulled out the "B disk." He took off the straw hat he always wore, hung it over the lens and said, "Ready."

As soon as production started, Jack and I fell into our usual pattern of working every other day. When we finished the day's work, we knew the other one would be waiting at the bar across the street to talk things over. We both made a lot of changes that we thought might help the tangled script and we kept each other advised so the story continuity would flow along the same lines.

When we finished the serial I registered for the draft, hoping that before I had to put up with the stupid robot again, or to put it in plainer language, "the man in the hot water tank," I'd be drafted.

Captain Marvel

*A*fter all the hassle with Superman being canceled, I couldn't believe the front office buying one that I thought was an infringement on the Superman title. It was called *Captain Marvel*. I thanked the good Lord for putting the man in the hot water heater in back of us. At least the writers would have to come up with something different, and I hoped that the Superman people would hold off a lawsuit long enough for us to make the serial and not have to cancel out at the last minute. A lawsuit did come along. They tried to stop Republic from releasing the *Adventures of Captain Marvel* serial.

I remember a deposition they took from me. My theory was that both Superman and Captain Marvel infringed on the creator of *Popeye the Sailor Man*. Clark Kent went in a phone booth, changed his clothes and became Superman. Billy Batson said "Shazam" and became Captain Marvel. Popeye came years before them to set the precedent. He ate a can of spinach and his muscles bulged and he became Superman and Captain Marvel rolled into one. I don't know if my theory helped, but Republic came out on top of the lawsuits. They released the serial.

We had interviewed an actor named Tom Tyler for the Superman part and liked him. Tom was clean cut, six-foot-four, and had a beautiful muscular body. He'd had his own series and had been in probably fifty or so pictures. You'll probably remember him best as one of the heavies that John Wayne had a shoot out against in John Ford's *Stagecoach*. We picked ex–child star Frankie Coghlan, Jr., to play Billy Batson, who says the magic word "Shazam" to become Captain Marvel. Billy Benedict was his running mate, and a pretty newcomer, Louise Currie, was the leading lady.

The writers had come up with a pretty good story. The first episode explained how Billy Batson is given the power to become Captain Marvel. He can fly like Superman. Bullets bounce off his chest, and he stands for everything that is good.

Frank Coghlan, Jr., had been an actor since he was a baby. He was great as the kid who says "Shazam" and in a puff of smoke becomes Captain Marvel. He is an excellent actor and a gentleman. He has written a book about his early childhood that reads like a history of the silent pictures. The title is *They Still Call Me Junior*.

We had a meeting with the Lydecker brothers. Larry Wickland had started them in the miniature business the same time I was running errands for Mascot. We talked about Clyde Beatty and the *Darkest Africa* serial made five years before and the flying batmen that Larry had designed and flew down from the rocks on wires. The Lydeckers agreed that it was the way to go. They would make several dummies in a flying position, each with an arched back and legs straight out with arms extended in front, using the lightest material they could find.

We decided to make the dummies about a foot larger than the leading man. Either Jack or I would shoot the scenes with the dummies beforehand. They would also make a cradle for the lead to lay in, suspended in front of the process screen. We would shoot the background plates of moving clouds.

We next talked to Dave Sharpe about the best way to get Captain Marvel into the air. Dave had the same perfectly proportioned body as Tom. Dave was about five-foot-ten inches. Tom was six-foot-four. My theory was that as long as Dave was moving, no one could pick up the size. The only time it would be noticeable was if he was standing, not moving. Both Jack and I knew we'd have

This is Dave Sharpe as Captain Marvel taking off.

to be careful about how we handled it. We settled on Captain Marvel running, hitting a hidden beatboard (springboard) and diving over the camera into a net. As he sailed over the camera, the next cut was of either the dummy sliding down a wire, or we would run the film through the camera backward to make him go up to wherever we wanted him to go. We had to be sure the short cape he wore was tied down.

I will not forget one of the funniest things I ever saw—a horse doing a double-take. We were working at Iverson's Ranch. The scene was a horseman riding hard looking back and the dummy sliding down a wire chasing him. The next cut would be Davy diving off a platform onto a horseman and taking him to the ground. When the dummy slid down the wire, it made a high-pitched singing sound. The wire was stretched so tight it acted like a guitar string being rubbed. There were several horses grazing under the wire. A wrangler was leaning up against a rock, keeping an eye on them. They were saddled and bridled, dragging the loose reins as they grazed. When the dummy slid over their heads with its high-pitched sound, they all raised their heads and watched it slide down the wire until it disappeared behind a big rock like an audience watching a tennis match. Then, like a bunch of well-trained chorus girls in unison, they resumed their grazing. Give a count of three, and then one of them reared up, whinnied, and took off for the hills.

Davy's dives into the net were always a thrill. He used a regulation fire net held upright, not in the usual fireman's parallel position. After he hit the beatboard and passed over the camera in the Captain Marvel flying position parallel to the ground, he'd tuck and turn in the air and hit the net flat on his back. The people holding the net, usually the prop men and grips, would lower the net to a parallel position to help break his fall.

We were on top of a cliff at Iverson's Ranch. Davy was to run to the edge of the cliff, hit the beatboard and soar over the camera, located lower down the hill in a bunch of rocks. Dave spotted the net, dug the beatboard into the dirt to hide it and said, "Let's go."

Holding the net were about eight grips and prop men. One of them was Nels Mathias, whom we called the "little giant," a wonderful guy who always had a smile on his face and was always singing. He was one of our top grips. He was holding the net closest to the cliff. We rolled the camera. Davy came on a dead run, hit the beatboard, but somehow didn't get the lift he thought he would. My heart stopped as he sailed out over our heads. I could see he wasn't going to make the net, but that he was going to fall into the rocks. Nels saw it too. He let go of the net, backed over into the rocks in a bent-over position. Davy hit him in the back with his hands and propelled himself into the net. Davy rolled out of the net, came over to Nels and gave him a big hug and my heart started to beat again.

Frank Coghlan and Billy Benedict were fun to work with. Both of them were old pros in the picture business, having started at a very young age. The three of us are still friends today, after over fifty years. Tom Tyler fit the part to a "T." If I had to cast the part again, I'd look for his clone. When the picture was finished, Jack, Bunny and I all decided it more than made up for all the problems we had with the last turkey.

During production on *Adventures of Captain Marvel* we all had a farewell drink with Pete Adreon. He had stayed in the reserves and the marines called him back into active duty. We later had a letter from him. He was in Iceland commanding an artillery company. We all missed him. We called him "Okey Dokey." If you went to him with a script problem, he'd say, "I'll fix it and everything will be okey dokey." I didn't know it then, but I'd be seeing him in the near future.

A loud, pleasant feminine voice yelled, "Bunneee," and a moment later, from out of the jungle an elephant's loud trumpet answered the call. The voice belonged to a beautiful, perfectly formed, long-legged girl named Frances Gifford. The elephant named Bunny was her friend. Republic had bought the title *Jungle Girl* from Edgar Rice Burroughs.

For the first time since sound had come into the picture business, we had a serial built around a girl. In the silent days there were Pearl White and Ruth Roland serials. Now we were hoping this one would have the success that they had. We thought the story could have been better, but we had to admit that the episode endings were different and wild.

When we heard the front office had borrowed a girl under contract to Paramount, we all groaned, but for once we had to admit that after all the mistakes they had made, the law of averages finally prevailed. They had hit the jackpot. She was a beauty. We had fussed over her costume for weeks and finally came up with one that would satisfy the decency code. It was practical for running and doing everything Tarzan could do and still looked like "all girl," which she certainly was.

Instead of being raised by an ape, she was the daughter of a missionary doctor, so that she could have the breeding and social qualities of an educated woman who loved animals. We again used Tommy Cook from the *Adventures of Red Ryder* serial as the native boy. We liked to have a child in the picture because we thought it would give our audience, which was supposed to be all kids, someone to identify with.

We interviewed, liked and hired an actor who had been under contract to MGM. His name was Tom Neal. I'd describe him as a small replica of Clark Gable. Gerald Mohr, a fine actor, was also hired. Having worked with him before, we knew that he would be no trouble. He was to be the heavy.

Lake Sherwood is in the Conejo Valley, a small lake with a dam on one end. It is about a forty minute drive from Republic Studios going west on Ventura Boulevard. We had used it before to jump horses off of cliffs into the water,

Frances Gifford and Bunny, two beautiful ladies.

and we had made the swings of Crash Corrigan and his ape suit in its forest of big sprawling oak trees. Alexander Korda would use it later to make *Jungle Book*. Today it's wall to wall million-dollar homes and a billion dollar golf course.

A few weeks before we were to start, our friend and adviser, old steady himself, cameraman Billy Nobles called us and said he'd like to have lunch with Jack, Bunny and me. It was unusual because between pictures he liked to spend time on his big chicken ranch. He very seldom worked other pictures, just the serials. He told us he was going to retire. Jack looked at me, I looked at Jack. We both turned our shocked faces to another shocked face: Bunny's. It was like having someone say, "I just cut off your right arm." Billy had been so patient with all of us. He had already given his advice of thirty years behind the camera to help the younger green picture makers and was happy to see them go from amateur to professional.

He told Jack and me that we'd get along just fine without him, that we had both turned into pretty damn fine directors. Coming from him, that is still one of the best compliments I've ever had. He laughed. "Just think! You won't have to look for me at four o'clock anymore." At four o'clock sharp he'd disappear behind the set with Nels Mathias, his lead grip, and have a couple of short snorts—just two—to keep him going. We were always invited, but Jack and I always declined. We drank after work, but in my fifty years of picture making I've never had a drink before work or during. Drink was the curse of too many good directors. All you had to do was have a stuntman hurt or an accident on the set. Though you had nothing to do with it, and even if you'd only had a sip of beer, the word went out: the director was drinking. We had a drink with Billy and he disappeared out of our lives.

We all talked it over and decided to go with the cameraman who had replaced Billy when he was sick during the filming of *Zorro's Fighting Legion*. Reggie Lanning was all Irish. He had had thirty or so years in the business and was a good film technician. He was a regular at the studio and after we'd worked with him, we had all become friends.

After we had picked the design for Frances' costume, I asked the head of ladies wardrobe to call Davy Sharpe in and make a costume for him that fit exactly like the costume for Frances. She looked at me like I was nuts. "We're making four sets of the costume for her. Can't he wear one of those?" I shook my head. "Davy is taller than she is and has wider shoulders and smaller hips." She frowned and said, "Is he going to double her?" I said no, that we had hired Helen Thurston for most of the stunts, but there were some things that Davy could do better. She thought a moment and grinned. "What are you going to do about Davy's cigar? Teach Frances to smoke?" I grinned back. "No. That's the way we can tell them apart."

I drew the first day of shooting at Sherwood Forest. The day before Davy and I had gone out with the construction crew to rig some swings from tree to tree. I wanted an aerial transfer from vine to vine and one where Davy flew through the air to catch another vine and swing to a tree. This required a net for safety's sake.

We didn't need Frances until after lunch, but we gave her the same early call the crew took so we could all get acquainted. She stepped out of the wardrobe trailer in full makeup and wardrobe. She looked like a dream come true. She did a little pirouette and said, "Okay?" I wanted to say "you bet," but only okay came out. Frances was just coming out of a divorce from Academy Award winner James Dunn. She was very quiet and didn't seem to make friends easily. I later became friends with Jimmy, who was a wonderful guy, and I asked him how he could let a lovely, intelligent person like Frances ever get away from him. His answer: his drinking.

I watched her a moment as she looked around the activity on the set, then asked her to come with me. We went to the men's wardrobe trailer. I climbed inside. The makeup man was just putting finishing touches on Davy's makeup. As soon as he finished, he gave Davy a tissue and said to press it against his lips to take off the excess lipstick. "You don't want it to come off on your cigar," he said. Davy pressed the tissue to his lips, handed it back to the makeup man and propped the cigar in his mouth. He stood up and said he was ready.

I introduced him to Frances. She studied him for a moment. "I'm jealous. If he took the cigar out of his mouth, he'd be prettier than I am." They became instant friends. Davy headed to check on the rope riggings and the net. Frances followed me to where a big elephant was standing with its trainer. I turned to her. She had stopped about ten feet away. "Come on over here, Frances. I want to introduce you to Bunny. You're going to get to ride her." Frances didn't move. "You mean my double gets to ride her." I said, "I'd rather have you up on her. Come on over and I'll introduce you to her." I held out my hand and the trainer put a big bag full of peanuts in it.

I reached up and rubbed Bunny's forehead. I had worked with her before. She was a doll. She belonged to Goebel's Animal Farm in Thousand Oaks, not far from Sherwood Forest. I held up my head and pouted my lips. "Give kisses, Bunny." She raised her trunk and softly brushed my lips with the funny little prehensile hand on the end of her long trunk. I gave her a handful of peanuts and turned to Frances. I thought to myself that if she wouldn't come near the elephant, Jack and I were going to have a hell of a time making the picture.

"Come on, Frances. You should get along with her as one girl to another." I held out my hand with a silent prayer. Frances stood a long moment, then slowly walked over to me. I told her to pout up and get her kiss. There was another long moment, and then the trainer helped me. "She's as gentle as she is big," he told her. Frances looked at Bunny towering over her, then at me. "Okay, Bunny, give kisses." She turned her face up to Bunny, who held up her trunk and softly brushed Frances' lips. I handed her the peanut bag. Bunny held up her trunk and Frances looked at me with a big smile, turned and filled Bunny's trunk with peanuts. I breathed a sigh of relief. Now for the next step.

I took hold of the harness that hung down from Bunny's face and said, "Trunk, Bunny." Bunny put her head down and raised her trunk. I stepped with one leg in the "v" it formed and Bunny gently put me up on her back. I looked down at Frances. She said, "You've done that before." I invited her to join me up top, promising that the trainer would help her. She looked at Bunny. I reached down for her. She still wasn't sure. "She's big enough to hold both of us, that's for sure, and if you're not afraid of her I guess I shouldn't be either," Frances said. The trainer gave her a few instructions and she gave the "Trunk, Bunny" command, and found herself sitting up in front of me. I asked the trainer to take us for a short walk. Frances turned to me with a big grin. "This is fun." It was not only fun for her, but the start of a beautiful friendship between her and Bunny.

It was summer and Lake Sherwood is located in the Conejo Valley. In other words, it was hot. Every morning when Frances got out of the car Bunny knew that she was bringing a bag of goodies, and every morning both Frances and Bunny looked forward to the "Bunneee—trumpet" reunion. Frances would skip lunch, put on a bathing suit, swing up on Bunny, and the two of them would wade into the lake to cool off. Bunny had a natural shower apparatus built into a long trunk.

Davy did some beautiful swings on the vines, letting go and catching another vine. He doubled her so well that when I saw the dailies I couldn't tell the difference. Tom Neal had a lot of running and jumping to do. He was as graceful as Frances. We had a hell of a team.

That evening when I got back to the studio I went to the bar to give Jack a report. As I slid onto a stood next to him he said, "You look pooped." I told him it was hot as hell out there. "Jack, you won't believe what happened to me today." Jack took a sip of his drink. I told him he'd better take a bigger sip than that, and after he did he asked me what had happened during the day. I took a sip of my own. "I saw a serial leading man with a valet." "A what?" he questioned me. "A valet, Jack. You know, a servant that ties your tie and your shoes, helps you on with your coat, gets you a cool drink, raises the toilet seat." Jack looked at me. "Is this your first drink today?" I nodded, "Just think, I'm the first and probably the last director to ever see a serial leading man with a valet."

Tom kept his valet throughout the picture. Ted, the wardrobe man, thought it was great. The valet took care of all of Tom's clothes. Tom still was a nice person to work with, a good actor and ready to mix into any action.

For the ending of the first episode the leads were trapped in a cave and the heavy opens a gate and floods the tunnel. It sweeps them out of a hole in the cliff onto the rocks below. The cave set had been changed to show a hole with a blue backing in the back of the set, and special effects had built a big dump tank just outside. There was a day's work in the cave set and the water dump necessarily was the last shot of the day. It would take the set several days to dry out. The director got one shot at the water dump sweeping the doubles out of the hole in the background. The director was Jack.

I was waiting at our usual meeting place to have our usual drink and get the daily news. Jack came in and took a stool next to me. The bartender slid his usual Canadian Club and soda down the bar to him. After he'd taken a sip I asked him how it had gone during the day and how the big dump tank worked. His answer was upbeat. "It was one hell of a shot. The water swept the doubles out of the hole in the wall. It was really something—until the rocks came up and started to float out with them."

And then there was Jackie. Jackie had just starred in more pictures than Clark Gable, Robert Taylor, and all of the other leading men put together. You've all seen Jackie a thousand times, but just didn't know his name. He started his career in the early silent days on the MGM logo. You could say he started with a snarl and a roar—Jackie the lion.

There was a sequence where the leading lady, armed only with a dagger, had to fight a lion. Jackie was getting old but he still had all his teeth, and age had made him as cranky and undependable as any good grandpa. I had worked with Jackie three or four times before. We always had the camera in a cage with wide prison type bars and a wider opening to shove the camera lens outside. The cage was inside an even larger cage to confine him, or a large set with four sides. This time it was the cave set. Jackie's trainer was going to fight him.

The first time I worked with him, he tried to crawl through the wide opening for the camera lens. The cameraman, a grip and I were in the cage. His head got stuck in the hole and the trainer had to grab his tail and pull him free. Then he tried to jump in over the top of the cage. He got his front legs over the top and hung there, and again the trainer grabbed his tail and pulled him to the ground.

The next time I worked with him I had Nels Mathias, the grip, put a top on the cage. He used the top of one of the parallels that were always on the truck. We had the old cat beaten this time—or so we thought. He came out of his cage, saw us and jumped on top of the parallel. To him it looked like a kitty litter box, so he used it. "It" dropped through the boards on top of the parallels. We had no place to go. It was like being in a warm shower with one of those pulsating heads.

A few days before I'd asked Nels to put some tar paper on top of the camera cage so that if Jackie used it again for a litter box we'd be high and dry. I'd already talked to the trainer, and we were ready to roll. He had gone to let Jackie out of his cage and shoo him onto the set. I remembered the waterproofing. I hadn't checked it. I yelled for Nels to "come here." He opened the door into the set and ran over to our cage. The trainer shooed Jackie onto the set. I opened our cage door and said, "Get in here, Nels!" He looked at Jackie coming toward him, growling, and came through the door and slammed it shut. "What is it you want?" he asked. Jackie jumped on top of the cage. I looked at Nels' face and asked, "Did you?" He shook his head. "I forgot." Jackie did his thing. When the shower came, Nels said, "I'm going outside. I'd rather face that lion than stay in here with you and Reggie." He opened the door at the same time and took off for the door in the set on a dead run. Jackie was still on top, using the litter box. Reggie, standing in the corner with his jacket held over his head, answered, "He's no dummy."

As I sit here at a desk reminiscing, I realize now that the serial was fun to make. We had no real problems. There is a sad ending for our two leading people and Bunny. She was riding in her big enclosed truck. There was straw on the floor to keep it from getting slippery. Somehow it caught fire. The driver didn't realize it was aflame until it was too late to save her. I read it in the newspaper a few years after the serial finished shooting, and I felt like I'd lost a good friend.

Tom Neal was in the newspapers several times in the following years. He was in a fight over Barbara Payton with another star, Franchot Tone. But he had a full career in good pictures as a supporting actor. Then I remember in the middle sixties that Neal's name was again in the papers. He was accused of killing his wife in their Palm Springs home. He served time for manslaughter and passed away shortly after his release from prison in the early seventies.

Frances went on to have a prolific career under contract to MGM, until it was cut short by a terrible automobile accident. Her head injury never fully healed, and a friend told me it changed her whole personality. She passed away in January 1994.

I can close my eyes and still see the beautiful, lively girl getting out of the studio car with a bag full of elephant goodies and yelling, "Bunnneee!"

The war was closing in on all of us. Hitler had started his blitz against the British, using his superior air force. All of the world thought it would bring the British to their knees in surrender. The papers were full of the death and destruction that were caused by the German bombs dropping by the tons on London. President Roosevelt had told Winston Churchill to "hang on, it's just a matter of time until the Yanks will come to help you." All the United States of America had turned to a full war effort of building planes, tanks, and war ships. There was a feeling of doom in America.

Our next serial had a propaganda theme. It was called *King of the Texas*

Sammy Baugh was a real honest to goodness Texan.

Rangers. I spoke earlier about Bill Saal being a professional Texan. He had signed a Texan who was the best quarterback in football, Slingin' Sammy Baugh, to be our leading man. The "Slingin'" was given to him by the sportswriters. He had come out of Texas Christian University and had an all–American record. In those days, before the platoon system that is used today, players played both offense and defense. Sammy also did the punting.

When Jack and I got the news, we again groaned. Jack said, "Here we go again." We decided that we should be getting more money. We not only were directing the serials, we were running a school for actors. We talked about taking Bill Saal's big belt with the little buckle and hanging him with it.

Bill swore to us that no matter what we thought, we were sure to have a winner. Jack said he hoped the picture would be better than the score on the postseason championship game that year. The Washington Redskins, quarterbacked by Sammy, lost 73–0 to the Chicago Bears.

Mascot Pictures had made a serial with Red Grange, who was nicknamed "the galloping ghost" for his ability to run straight through the other team. I had seen parts of it when I was working in the cutting room. He did a pretty good job. They titled the serial *The Galloping Ghost*.

Bunny, Jack and I had a conference. We decided that we'd better surround him with the best acting cast we could assemble. We picked our old friend Duncan Renaldo to be his sidekick. The girl had more to do than usual for a serial leading lady. We picked a girl who had a world of experience in stage and screen, Pauline Moore.

One of the sequences was to be shot in an oil field. Jack and I found one down near the ocean at Long Beach. It was mostly abandoned, but the derricks were wooden and we both thought they made a better picture than the new steel ones. The lead had to slide down a wire, so I thought I'd better climb up the old ladder to the top to see if a guy wire could be rigged. Jack looked up at the tall derrick and said he'd go up with me. I told him I'd go first to make sure the wooden rungs hadn't rotted to a point that they'd be dangerous.

Jack and I both had on light shirts. I looked up at the tall derrick. "Jack, I'll bet you a drink that your shirt is dirty when you get to the top." Jack looked up and agreed to the bet. I don't know how many of you readers have ever climbed up a tall ladder, but as you get higher, you tend to lean in closer to the ladder. I remember climbing up a tall fire ladder and losing the same bet to a fireman.

When we got to the top and stood on the little platform, we were both out of breath. I looked down at my shirt. It was clean. Jack looked down at his. It looked like he had crawled through a tunnel of oil on his belly. He looked down. The rickety old derrick shivered under our weight. "I'll bet you another drink that it might not be only my shirt that's dirty before we get to the bottom."

A couple of days before we started, we met Sammy, all six-foot-two inches, one hundred eighty pounds of him. There wasn't an ounce of fat on his body. Texans are noted for being noisy, like Bill Saal. After we'd talked to him for a few moments I wasn't sure he was really from Texas. He was the tall silent type.

Jack caught the first day of the picture. They were shooting on the studio's big front lawn. It had been lined up with ten yard markers like a football field. They were shooting close shots of Sammy to cut into stock footage of a big championship bowl game he had played in against Marquette. Sammy was in a football uniform with about a dozen extras in uniform to back him up. Reggie Lanning was lighting a stand-in and Sammy was talking to Jack. As I walked across the lawn, Jack ran downfield and held up his hand. Sammy threw the ball effortlessly, really just let it fly. It hit Jack in the chest and knocked him down.

Sammy was easy to work with, and when you gave him directions he looked you straight in the eye. I guess he was used to listening to his coaches. He also had no trouble learning his dialogue. His memory had been trained by learning the plays out of twenty-page playbooks.

He also proved to be as fine a horseman as I'd ever worked with. The first day I worked with him we were at Iverson's Ranch. I explained the scene to him. I told him to come down the road at a full gallop, pull up, dismount and run behind a tree. He came down the road spurring the horse on, pulled the horse up and stepped off like a professional calf roper as the horse was still sliding on its rump, then dodged behind the tree before the horse stopped sliding.

The stuntmen taught him how to throw a punch. They said you could hear it whistle as it went by their heads. Sammy and Duncan Renaldo became great buddies. Duncan gave him little gestures, like push your hat back, or pause and think a second before you read the line. I believe that if he'd stayed in Hollywood, he would have been the biggest western star ever. He looked like a tall Tom Mix.

One day we were talking football. Sammy told me that he handled the ball on almost every play. I asked him how he stood up under the beating. He said you get rid of the ball by passing it downfield or handing it to someone else. These were the old days when the quarterback also played defense. They put him at the safety position so that he was only involved in the play if a runner broke away from the other safeties or on long pass plays, so he wasn't in a position to get hurt. He said that he had nightmares about Bronko Nagurski breaking away and he was the only man between Bronko and the goal line.

I saw him play the next year when I was in the service, stationed near Washington, D.C. He lived up to all the expectations. When he was named to the Football Hall of Fame during its first year of existence, I was proud to have known him.

Before we finished the picture, Bunny told Jack and me that he had accepted a commission in the U.S. Army Signal Corp. He was going to be stationed at Fort Monmoth, New Jersey, making training films. Bill Saal gave him a farewell party that lasted all night and Bunny went out of my life.

It wasn't the wedding bells that were breaking up that old gang of mine.

Bill O'Sullivan

*T*he studio brought in a new man, William J. O'Sullivan. Bill was a professional Irishman, born in Ireland, raised in New York with a New York accent—you know, instead of "oil" it was "earl." He had worked for Yates in the New Jersey Consolidated Film Lab. Knowing how a laboratory works is a hell of a lot different than producing a film. I told Jack, "I don't need another wild Irishman. I'm married to one."

Bill was almost the exact opposite of me. He wore dark blue expensive suits, white shirts with French cuffs, and large cuff links. He had his hair slicked down and had a manicure every week. He was the only person I know who drank scotch, Chivas Regal no less, the most expensive liquor behind the bar.

He was Catholic, which to me was neither here nor there, and he had made a "novena." I asked a friend of mine what a novena consisted of. It seems like if you've ever done anything really bad, you ask forgiveness by going to church every day. I'm not sure that statement is correct, but it is what I was told. The only things bad the other producers had done was to give us a stinking script once in a while. Jack and I decided that the front office had given us a dud, and wondered what he had done to have to make a novena.

The next serial was another Dick Tracy series with our good friend Ralph Byrd. O'Sullivan had been working with the writers for weeks before we met him. Jack and I thought he was just another writer they had brought in. The title was *Dick Tracy vs. Crime, Inc.* I went into shock when I read the estimating script that O'Sullivan had let the writers dream up. It was about a heavy that could make himself invisible. Jack's impression was the same as mine. Now we knew why he was making a novena. He was probably on dope, or stayed drunk all the time, or else he was asking his maker to make him sane again.

The very idea about an invisible man wasn't new. Look at *Harvey*, about the invisible rabbit. If we had a rabbit for a leading man we might be able to afford to make a movie budget, but on a serial budget? Even then we'd have to cut off his long ears to make it fit what we had to spend.

Whenever our gang—Ralph Byrd, Jack English, and our wives—went anyplace, we'd usually all pile into one car. If we passed a bum walking along the road, one of us was sure to say, "Look, an old serial director." If we made another picture that cost as much as *Jungle Girl*, it probably would be us walking along the road, and some other director saying the same thing.

Jack and I challenged the brand new producer. O'Sullivan sat and listened, then told us not to worry, that he had it all figured out. Jack told him that maybe he should direct it. I told him about the chewing out we got for going over the budget on *Jungle Girl*, and then popped the first question. "How do we disappear the guy out of a scene without using a negative to positive traveling matte at probably three hundred dollars a foot?" O'Sullivan smiled. "We just dissolve him out."

A dissolve is usually used to smoothly go from one scene to another scene. It is a process of overlapping two scenes. One is fading out and the new scene is fading in at the same time. Jack just shook his head. "You can't just dissolve him out; the whole scene will go black. You have to have something fading in at the same time." I turned to O'Sullivan. "You might have a good idea. Let's talk about it." We talked for several hours and the tension eased between O'Sullivan and his two directors.

In the script the heavy pressed a button on a small round machine that started a disk whirling with a weird sound. We would hold on it for a few feet while anyone who was in the scene would freeze into position. When the director said cut, the heavy would quickly step out of the scene and we'd roll the camera again. On action, everyone else in the scene would continue whatever they were doing. Now a dissolve would fade the heavy out, but the people who were frozen into place would be dissolved back into the scene in the same position and could go on with the scene.

We had some wire work where a gun travelled across the room and fired, and papers and things moved out doors, and so on. Roy Wade and Fred Brannon, his assistant, could handle that part with a little extra help that we could afford.

At the end of the script, Tracy uses a red infrared x-ray lamp to make the heavy become visible. O'Sullivan had an answer for how to do that one as well. We'd have the lab make a positive lavender print from the negative, then cut that positive print into the negative that the theater composite prints were made from. When the negative prints were thrown up on the screen, everything that was black would be white and everything that was white would be black. Because of this we decided to have the heavy dressed all in black and wear a mask fitted over his entire head and molded to his facial form. Only his eyes showed through the black mask. He was called the Ghost.

O'Sullivan had the writers use a lot of stock footage from the old Tracy films and also from some Republic features. This gave Jack and me a little extra time. We still figured it was going to be a miracle if we could make the serial in the allotted time.

A start date was set for the first part of September. Ralph Byrd called me and asked if there was any chance of setting it back. He had a major part in Korda's *Jungle Book*, and had been working on the picture for a month or more. When he took the part, *Jungle Book* should have been finished a week before we were due to start. Now they were over schedule. The picture wouldn't be over until after our start date. I told him to get his agent on the problem right away because I was sure we couldn't set the date back. We had a release schedule to meet. Some kind of a deal was worked out between the Korda Company and Republic. We rearranged our schedule so Ralph had a few days off throughout the picture.

This created another hardship for Jack and me. To keep on schedule, we cast Ralph Morgan, Frank Morgan's brother, to play the heavy. Ralph was never as famous as his brother, but I always thought he was the better actor. Frank was the comedian of the family. We picked Jan Wiley, a girl with plenty of experience, to play the usual girl part. Michael Owen was Tracy's sidekick.

The basic story was about how Tracy went about stopping an invisible man from murdering six members of a big city council who had sent his racketeering brother to the death chamber. There was one flaw in the story that the writers and O'Sullivan never could whip. It was imperative that at some time Tracy actually see the Ghost, so they had the machine that made the man invisible run out of power or burn out a tube whenever they wanted to have Tracy face him. Boy, wouldn't the people who advertise the little rabbit that just keeps "running and running" have loved to have gotten in on this one?

When any picture is scheduled, the exteriors are always shot at the start of the picture. A cover set is built on a sound stage from day one so that if it rains the crew can run for cover and not have to sit around outside and lose a day's shooting. We had some weather problems at the first part of the picture and ran for cover into the "city council meeting room," a set where all the men that the heavy is going to kill gather.

After O'Sullivan had looked at the dailies the next day, he came on the set and cornered Reggie Lanning, the cameraman. It seems there was no light under the council table. Reggie looked at me. I coughed, turned by head away and waited for the explosion. Reggie sized up the other Irishman. "Bill," he said, "on these schedules you can have light on the actors' faces or under the table. If you want both, add five weeks to the schedules." Bill O'Sullivan had not made another friend.

We were working in San Pedro harbor on an old freighter tied up to a pier. The scene had the invisible man coming down a rope ladder and getting in a small rowboat with an outboard motor, starting the motor and taking off down the channel. Roy Wade and his crew had worked all morning rigging the wires and weights that would make it work in one scene with no cuts. Heavy weights had been wired under water to the freighter's hull. The weights had pelican release hooks so a pulled wire would release the weights. Another wire had been attached to the weight and to one step of the rope ladder. As the weight dropped from the hull, it pulled down one side of the rope ladder like a man was stepping on it. As the next weight was released from the hull, another wire released the first weight and let the ladder rise on that side. In other words, as the invisible man climbed down the rope ladder his weight pulled down each step.

When the invisible man got to the boat a bigger weight attached to the side of the boat was released from the hull of the freighter and the boat momentarily tipped to the side. Then the weight was cut loose to sink. Roy Wade, straddling an outrigger that the grips had built on the bow of the boat like the bowsprit on a sailboat, rocked the boat. The camera was just cutting him out of the picture. Then he pulled a wire on the outboard motor's pull cord. The engine started and Roy steered the boat with two wires on the outboard, rigged like reins on a buggy horse, down the channel. The camera operator kept Roy—sitting facing the stern of the boat—out of the scene as long as he could, then cut the camera. When the shot was over I waved to Roy to come back.

Roy pulled on the wire to turn the boat back, and the wire broke. Roy fell backward from his precarious position, dropped the wire that would have shut the motor off, and clung to the side of the boat. We all knew he couldn't swim. Lee Lukather, the grip who had jumped off the pier with me in Santa Barbara, said, "Here we go again," and both of us stripped off our coats and kicked off our shoes. We ran to the rail and started yelling to him to climb back into the boat. The boat motor was cocked to one side, and the boat started going around in the middle of the channel. Several big boats coming up the channel changed course to miss him, blowing their horns and sirens.

The boat's turns grew tighter and tighter, and Roy was hanging on now under the bowsprit two by four. Lee and I were both standing up on the railing, ready to hit the water when the outboard ran into the wake of one of the ships, and bounced up in the air, flooding out the motor. It seemed like five minutes before Roy could pull himself back into the boat. He was soaking wet. He sat down on one of the seats and hollered to us, "I hope that was a print. I'll guarantee you there won't be a take two!"

When we finished production, we all went across the street for our usual drink to celebrate the finish of the picture. I guess Bill O'Sullivan didn't know about this ritual because he never showed up. Reggie Lanning said, "Well, you can bet I didn't invite him!" Jack said, "That goes for me too. He made the decision for me." Jack had been threatening to break away from the serials for the last six months. He wanted to go into bigger and better pictures. His decision didn't surprise me. "Why don't you hang around a while, Jack? He might turn out to be a human being, given a little time." Jack just shook his head. "If he does, I won't be around to congratulate him."

We also had a new film editor. Bill Thompson had moved on to features and Tony Martinelli had replaced him. The other editor, Eddie Todd, was still with us. Film editors are a director's best friend, and you get very close to them. They can cover your mistakes. They sometimes see things in a scene that have escaped you in the heat of battle. They have a way of building a scene with various cuts or taking a weak scene and, with a snip here and there with a pair of sharp scissors, can speed up a dull scene or make a chase more exciting. Tony turned out to be an excellent editor. He and I would be a team for the next ten years.

I came in the day after we finished to see the dailies. Bill O'Sullivan was waiting for me, and after we ran them, he asked me if I'd come up to his office. He told me that Jack was going to move on to features, and asked me if I was going to stay with him. I leveled with him, and told him that I probably wouldn't be around for long. I was of draft age. We all felt the war was closing in on us every day. I had answered a letter from Pete Adreon who, because of his background in the picture business, was now in Washington. They had made him a major and put him in charge of the marine photographic unit. He had to build it from scratch and needed help. He told me he was positive he could get me a commission. I had also had a letter from Bunny Brown that said the same thing. He could get me an army commission.

I'd made my mind up and the marines won. I didn't want to get stuck in some army post making training films. I knew that as a marine I'd see action somewhere along the line. I hadn't heard back from Pete, so I didn't know how long I'd be around. Bill thought about it a long time. "Okay, I'm glad you're going to stay with me. You can keep your job here, as far as I'm concerned, until you go on active duty. I'm going to have to replace Jack. Tell me whoever you want, and I'll try to get him."

He waited for my answer. "Jack's going to be hard to replace," I told him. "After all these years we have gotten to think alike. Sometimes when we're cutting a picture, we argue over who shot what. Sometimes I have to finish a sequence he started and vice versa. You've seen some of the serials and they all seem to flow like they were made by one director." Bill agreed that that was true. "Are you suggesting you'll direct the whole serial?" I nodded, "I can handle it, but I'm going to need close cooperation from you." Bill stood up and held out his hand. I shook it and he said, "You've got it."

Thirty years later when I turn on the television in the middle of a picture and suddenly it looks familiar, the technique, the cutting away, the way the action is presented, I know. If I didn't make the picture, I'd bet anybody anything that when the titles come on, the director's card reads "John English."

During the production of *Dick Tracy vs. Crime, Inc.*, my sister Julie moved out to Los Angeles from Quantico, Virginia, with her two-year-old son. She was pregnant again. The two squadrons her husband Cle commanded were moved to North Island at San Diego.

Bert called a family meeting and Maxine came face to face with Julie. There was no air conditioning needed to keep the room cool. They were both overly polite, but frigid.

Bert brought up the subject of the war and the whole family decided to rent out Bert's house on Sunset Plaza Drive and rent a bigger house so that everyone could move in together. Mom could help take care of Julie's yet to be born baby and they could have a victory garden to raise their own fresh vegetables. Maxine had been very silent during the discussion. Now she stood up. "To hell with that. If you think I'm going to move in with her," and she pointed a finger at Julie, "you're all crazy. Thanks, but I'll stay put in Tarzana." Bert said that she couldn't live alone out in the country, but Maxine glared at Julie. "I'm not alone. I've got Cappy and Pete." Bert explained to Julie about Cappy and old Pete. I shook my head and shut up. I knew all the talking in the world couldn't change this stubborn Irish lass. That's the way it would remain until the war was over.

I took a couple of weeks off. Maxine and I would pack a lunch, saddle the horses and take off for the hills. It was October and the weather was mild and warm. The war clouds were gathering and we were sure that it could get nasty at any moment. Maxine and I grew a little closer every day. We talked about being separated and we decided that we could take it in stride as long as we had each other to come home to. That was the one thing we never discussed: "Come home."

The date was December 7, 1941. We took a couple of our dogs to a dog show in Palm Springs. The weather was warm. Around 11:00 the loudspeaker crackled and a voice said, "This morning the Japanese Navy bombed Pearl Harbor." I know this sounds like I'm dreaming this up, but I'll swear it's true. The dogs that always bark all day long shut up. The little breeze that blew across the desert stopped. There was a deadly silence which settled over the entire area for probably a minute. Then all hell broke loose.

We decided we might as well stay for the judging. There was nothing we could do for the people in Pearl Harbor. Barry, our Saint, won the obedience tests and Bootsie, our setter, won the sporting dog group. Usually when you win a group, you stay for the party, but not that day. We headed home.

We were stopped by Army roadblocks four times before we got back to Tarzana. They were looking for anyone Japanese. They were afraid of saboteurs.

Even the gateman's good morning was depressed and quieter than usual the next day. There were about six of us, all directors, gathered in one of the offices. We were talking about how it was going to affect each one of us. All eyes turned to me. I was the only one of draft age. Georgie Sherman stopped in the doorway to listen. Georgie didn't have to worry. At attention a rifle would have just reached up to his chin. He listened to the talk for a few moments before observing, "Anyone who quits Republic and joins the army is a coward."

After the war Georgie was directing Audie Murphy in a picture. They got into an argument and Georgie walked off the picture. I read it in the trade papers. The next time I saw him I asked about the incident. "We got into this argument and he pushed me down into one of the chairs on the set. I looked up. He seemed to tower over me. Here was a guy who had killed thirty-nine Germans. Me, all I did was run over a cat once in Pasadena."

Yes, I got to know some saboteurs. They were the heavies in the next serial. Again Republic had bought a comic book character. This time I'd never heard of him. His name was *Spy Smasher* and as I looked through one of the comic books, the costume he wore made me laugh. The artist who draws Snoopy must have been a serial fan as a kid. He copied the costume when Snoopy is the World War I flying ace. The lead wore an old-time aviator's helmet equipped with goggles, a brown shirt with a black diamond on the chest, and World War I officers' pants and English riding boots. Instead of Snoopy's flowing silk scarf, he had a cape!

O'Sullivan didn't seem to think it was out of line. His arguments were, "Look at *Captain Marvel*, *Zorro* and *Jungle Girl*. They were all big successes!" We were in a shooting war and we're going to send a guy dressed like this to save America? In a costume left over from a costume party from World War I? O'Sullivan still argued, "It's in the contract that we have to dress him like the comic book character." My last words were, "Oh, shit!"

When I read the script I found that the writers hadn't left out anything. They even had the kitchen sink and had added the toilet. There was so much flag waving and propaganda that I thought the whole thing stunk. I remembered what the poverty row producer told Jack after looking at a final cut of another serial: "It stinks! Ship it." So with that enthusiastic thought in mind, we started to assemble a cast.

We cast Kane Richmond in the lead and he fit the part perfectly. He had been in serials before and had made a bunch of pictures for other studios. He

A lobby card for *Spy Smasher*.

was trim and active and seemed like a nice person. Marguerite Chapman had played small parts in a few pictures. I picked her because she reminded me of the beautiful Frances Gifford. She turned out to be just as capable.

Tristram Coffin was added to the cast. I believe he was just coming into the business. He later became a regular at the top of my "very good" list. We

Davy Sharpe dives off the pier at Lake Elsinore.

had some German and French parts that were filled by Hans Shumm and Franco Corsaro.

The story was about twin brothers, both played by Kane. We left the audience to guess which one was Spy Smasher. My theory was: "Who cares which is which when they are both played by the same man?"

The end of the episode was just like the flood water chasing the lead down a tunnel scene in *Daredevils of the Red Circle*, only the writers had changed it to flaming gasoline. We shot it the same way. In *Daredevils* he rode a motorcycle. In this one he had to work harder. He was pumping a handcar in a mine.

We started the picture December 22, which was stupid. It meant we had to absorb Christmas and the New Year holidays in our budget. Boy, did I miss Jack. Now the odds had changed. Before there were the two of us to fight the producer and the front office. Now I stood alone. There was nobody to protect my back.

We started the picture at Lake Elsinore where we had made one of the Tracy segments. Davy Sharpe was in the Spy Smasher outfit. I'd put the camera in a motorboat, shooting back toward the shore. He was to dive off the dock as the boat pulled out, and catch a rope that the boat was trailing. Then he'd pull himself up to the boat. I told Davy just to dive off the dock. There was no way he'd ever find the rope moving in the water. I'd make a cut of him catching the rope and pulling himself to the boat.

The boat pulled out and Davy hit the water perfectly. The scene was over, but before I could yell cut, Davy came up with the rope in his hands. I yelled to the boat driver to hit the throttle, and soon Davy was planing over the water. I yelled cut, and as the boat made a circle to pick him up, I realized he was in trouble. When we came along beside him I reached down and grabbed his arm. One of the grips helped me pull him aboard. He was as white as a sheet. I rolled him on his stomach and pounded his back. He spit up about a gallon of Lake Elsinore. I helped him sit up, and he coughed. "You son of a bitch, you tried to drown me!" I swatted him on the back. "Why didn't you let go?" Another cough. "Because I thought I could pull myself up to the boat." Years later we were at a film festival and Davy told the audience, pointing at me, "Did I ever tell you about the time he tried to drown me?"

We worked at an old brick factory that was still operating. The episode ending was the same old thing, a moving belt with the hero lying on it as it moved toward a big buzz saw, only this time it was a rock cutter.

The plant had a big, unused, brick smokestack that was leaning at a precarious angle. I suggested to O'Sullivan that we see if we could blow the base of the smokestack so it would fall on the hero. The plant manager was all for it, but he said we'd have to get an okay from the main plant in Los Angeles. O'Sullivan wouldn't go for it. That was the difference between Bunny and Bill. Bunny would have said, "Let's find out."

There was a lot of miniature work on enemy submarines and work at a big rock crushing plant. Kane Richmond was tough and held up well under one of the roughest schedules I had ever tried to meet. I can't remember the number of days on the shooting schedule, but I imagine it was over five weeks. We worked sixteen-hour days, each day, wrapping around ten o'clock at night.

Maxine came in to the studio on the final day of shooting to have dinner with me. It had been served on one of the empty sound stages. When we finished we all went across the street to the Little Bohemia for our ritual drink, all but O'Sullivan. I guess he had to make his novena.

We were sitting around the big table in the corner with Kane and several actors, Reggie the cameraman, and a couple of grips and electricians. Suddenly Ralph Oberg, the construction boss who drew sets in the dirt with his foot, joined us. I hadn't had anything to do with him since Mack D'Agostino had started working on our shows. I let Mack wrestle it out with him. I didn't like him and he didn't like me, but he and O'Sullivan had struck up a friendship.

Maxine was sitting next to me. She knew I'd had lots of beefs with him and she nudged me and looked at him. "He's loaded," she said. I shrugged and forgot about him and turned to the rest of our group. Someone said, "Isn't the producer invited to these parties?" Reggie said, "He's probably out looking for the light under the conference table." I said, "You know this is the first picture that they should have shelved the picture and released the producer." Everyone laughed. I got up to go to the can. About halfway back someone grabbed my arm from behind and hit me in the face. I fell back against the wall and covered up. The next punch landed on my arms. Oberg's face came into focus. At the same time Kane Richmond hit him on the chin with a punch I can still hear. Oberg staggered back and Maxine came running at him with a big overhand swing and caught him right between the eyes and he went down. A couple of grips dragged him to his feet. Somebody opened the door and they ran Oberg out through it and threw him out on Ventura Boulevard.

Reggie Lanning picked up his hat and started to throw it out after him. Then he stopped, went into the men's room, and came back after a short wait, carefully carrying something in the hat that he didn't want to spill. He threw it out the door after Oberg. By now my nose had stopped bleeding, so we all bellied up to the bar to celebrate our victory.

One of our electricians was Jack Roper. Jack had fought Joe Louis a few years before in the old Angels Baseball Park. Louis knocked him out in the second round and when the announcer asked him about the fight he said, "I zigged when I should've zagged." Maxine asked him why he didn't get into this fight. He turned all of his six-feet-four inches and looked down at her with a shocked face. "And get me dimples punched?" Yes, he had a big dimple on his Irish chin.

Suddenly Maxine held up her arm. "That dirty no good bum! Look. I've lost a charm off my charm bracelet!"

The next morning the phone rang early. It was Al Wilson, the head of the production department. "I hear you had a fist fight last night with Oberg." The early morning call surprised me. "Hell, Al, it wasn't much of a fight. Maxine knocked him on his ass. You know, Al, I think we should book a fight between Maxine and Charlotte." Charlotte was Al's wife. A year before somebody had taken a punch at Al at the Christmas party and Charlotte had decked him with a right. Al said, "Good thought. I'm going to fire Oberg."

I didn't have to think about that one. "The hell you are. You can't replace him. He knows every board on the back lot. Look Al, this is a personal matter. I'll square it off with the Sunday punching son of a bitch. I've got a black eye to even up with him." Al laughed, "You've got a black eye. You should see him. Both of his eyes are almost closed. He looks like a truck ran over him. I'll bet you that right now every man that works for him on the back lot would vote for you to be the next president."

Al changed the subject. "Mandy Schaefer just called me from the High

Sierra location." Mandy was producing a picture with my beautiful friend Jean Parker, and another friend, Nick Grindle, was directing. It was called *The Girl from Alaska*. The crew had been snowed in for four days and hadn't turned the camera. Mandy wanted to leave half the crew there. An extra cameraman had been sent up a couple of days earlier and he needed another director to shoot the action sequences in the snow. He'd bring the rest of the crew home and start shooting the interiors. I told Al I was awfully tired after shooting *Spy Smasher*. He said, "Mandy asked for you." I hated to turn him down. He had helped me in my early days with Republic and had been a personal friend of mine since I was fifteen. "Okay, Al, send a car for me about 10:30."

Maxine had come into the room and wanted to know what that was all about. I grinned at her. "They're sending a car for me. Al wants to get Oberg and me together to finish the fight." She grinned back. "I'll get my hat and go with you."

The Dog Teams

17

*T*he driver picked me up and handed me a script to read. We got into Bishop, which was at the bottom of the hill, about four o'clock. They had sent another car with chains down from the location to pick me up. Bill Newman and Bud Thackery, the cameraman, were in the car. Two old friends, they appraised my big shiner. Bill had called into the studio earlier. They both said, "Wish we were there." It seems they both would have been happy to take a punch at Oberg.

Buddy said he and Bill had an old friend they'd like to say hello to. He asked if I minded waiting in the car, which I didn't. I could use the time to go over the script again. It had started to snow when they came out of the green house next to the fire station. I knew they'd had a couple of drinks, but that's what old friends are for. It was nearly a week before I found out the green house next to the fire station was the local house of ill repute. I asked them both about why I wasn't invited to go with them. Their answer was that they didn't want to contribute to the delinquency of a minor.

It snowed all the way up the hill. The crew was being housed in a big tavern about a mile on up the hill from the main highway, and the snow was piled up about eight feet deep on either side of the road.

The story had dog sled teams as a background and almost all the work I was to do was with them. There was a dog in the story and I was happy to see the trainer was another old friend, Earl Johnson, with his great dog Ace.

We had a mishap on the first day. Nellie Walker, who was doubling Jean Parker, was walking in front of the lead team. She stepped in a deep snowdrift and fell down. The entire team attacked her. She was wearing a big fur parka that covered her head, and I guess the dogs thought she was a bear. It took a couple of minutes to beat and pull them off. Only a few teeth actually got through the heavy fur. We sent her down the hill to Bishop to a doctor. The next day, though, she was back and ready to get back to work. We all loved Nellie. She had been standing in and doubling all the western gals who didn't ride since the Mascot days. Her fall in front of the dogs earned her a new nickname: Balto (a canned dog food).

When we were filming the altitude was about the eight thousand, five hundred feet, and it was cold. Bud Thackery, the cameraman, took every bit of oil out of the cameras and they were never brought inside because he was afraid of condensation inside the lenses. The dogs were kept in a big garage and one night something happened to the heaters and three of them froze to death.

Earl kept Ace in his room with him. Ace was so well trained that Earl could stand in back of the camera and hold up two fingers, drop a left one and Ace would lay his left ear back. Earl would hold up both fingers again and Ace's ears went back up. He would make a gesture with his hand and Ace would snarl. All these were silent commands.

I had known Earl for several years. He and his wife were always invited to our gang's parties. Both of them were very nice people. Earl was a pretty heavy drinker, but I don't think I'd ever seen him really drunk.

It was two o'clock in the morning and there was a knock on my door. I asked who it was and a voice through the door identified Earl. I got up and put on a robe. It was cold as the devil. When I opened the door Earl came into the room and I asked him what was wrong. He was loaded. He wanted to know if he could sleep on the couch in my room. I suggested he might be more comfortable in his own bed, and he agreed, except that there was one problem. "You know how Ace hates me when I'm drinking. He won't let me come in the room." He spent the night on my couch and in the morning he and Ace came into the dining room for breakfast together. I patted Ace and asked Earl who was training who. He answered, "It's a Mexican standoff this morning."

There were three full teams of eight dogs, plus the leaders. Two of the teams were local. The man who owned and trained them used them to haul supplies back into the mines in winter. The miners in the high back country depended on him for their very existence in the deep snow. These were real working dogs that would chew on your legs if you got too close. The third team belonged to Mister Comport, who supplied any domestic animal that the studio needed. Actors and crew could safely work around them.

Mister Comport also had a lot of oddball animals, like the swaybacked horse that Smiley Burnett rode in the Autry westerns. Comport's sled dogs could also be used as wolves. You dirtied them up with mud and tied their tails between their legs, and lo and behold you had a pack of snarling, dangerous, pettable wolves. He had one old-timer that I'm sure you saw many times. She was blind. You could sit her on a rock or mountain top and she'd have to stay there because she couldn't see. Then everyone would stand still and be quiet. She thought she'd been deserted in the deadly calm. She'd throw her head back and howl. She made many an audience shiver.

Of the two working teams, only one dog was a pet. He was a tough old scarred up fellow that was a leader. His name was Como. Every morning I'd save a bite of breakfast wrapped up in a napkin and would walk up to him, harnessed at the head of his team. He'd see me coming and sit up on his haunches like a trained poodle and beg for his morning snack.

We had a process plate to make shooting forward down the line of dogs following the other team. Buddy mounted the camera on the sled and tied it off. We were going down a hill so the dogs would be running. He was to ride one runner. I was on the other. The dog trainer was on the team ahead of us.

He yelled mush and his team started to run. Then he yelled, "Come on, Como," and our team started with a tremendous lunge as the dogs hit the harness in back of Como, following the other team. Bud and I were really enjoying our crazy careening ride down the hill until...

First let me tell you what they feed these working dogs: frozen fish. It thaws out slowly in their stomachs, giving them enough energy to go all day. It also gives them diarrhea. Halfway down the hill one of the dogs had to go. As he squatted to do his thing the other dogs lifted him off the ground by keeping the traces taut that held him in line. His feet weren't touching the ground. He was suspended in midair. Bud and I were fascinated. Bud said, "Well, I'll be damned." Then, here it came. The slight wind in our face didn't help. Bud and I were more than "damned." We couldn't bail off for fear of the sled turning over and wrecking the camera. When we got down to the bottom the camera, Bud and I were in dire need of a hot shower. I looked at Bud. "You should see yourself," I said. Bud grinned. "You got that wrong. You should smell yourself."

Mandy Schaefer, Buddy and I came out of the projection room. We were all laughing. Mandy said, "That was the crappiest scene that's ever been shot." We had just looked at the process plate featuring the rear end of the dog team. We'd printed it to show the front office what we'd go through to make a picture. Mandy continued, "Too bad we can't use it. It would be like one of those three-D things they shoot to make an audience duck.

Mandy said he'd cleared me with Al Wilson to shoot a couple of more days to try to get him back on schedule. It was up to me, so I worked two more days on the picture, shooting a couple of bear cubs tearing up the inside of a cabin.

When I got home, Cappy gave me a big slurp as I leaned down to pet him. The next kiss was from Maxine, standing in the doorway. I'd been gone about a week. She turned and pointed to a letter propped up against the lamp on an end table. It was from the U. S. Marine Corps Headquarters, Washington, D.C. Inside there were forms to be filled out and a request for three character references.

The first letter was sent out to General William Wallace, U.S.M.C., whom I'd known since I was in grammar school. He was a close friend of the family and was in command of the marine base at North Island, California. The second one went out to Colonel Marion L. Dawson who was in command of the paratroop training command at Great Lakes Training Station. He was also a long-time friend of the family. The third letter went to my old football coach at Coronado High. Then there was the matter of a physical. I knew I was going to have to bluff my way through it if I wanted to pass.

The doctor studied the form I had to fill out, then looked at my left leg. "How long has it been since it was broken?" I counted on my fingers and told him it had been about ten years. He examined my upper leg. It was a little bit smaller than my right one. "How did you break it? Femurs don't break too easily." I told him a horse fell through a jump and turned over on top of me. I couldn't get away from him. He felt my knee. I volunteered some more information. "The deformed kneecap came with the devise that is attached to the styman pin they put through the bone to pull the bone so it won't shorten as it heals. It rested all night on my kneecap because the new rope they used to hold the weights stretched and let the weights rest on the floor." He looked at the kneecap. "That must have been very painful. Why didn't you call the nurse?" I shrugged, "Doc, if you have a broken leg, you figure it's supposed to hurt." He moved to his desk. "Do you want to pass this physical?" I nodded. He started to write, then said, "You know the marines are a rough outfit." I nodded again, and thinking out loud I told him it couldn't be more dangerous than being a serial director. I had tried several times to get an insurance policy and had been turned down because of my occupation. He signed the papers and handed them to me. He held out his hand and as I took it he said, "Good luck."

I hadn't seen Bill O'Sullivan for almost three weeks. When I walked into his office he looked up from his desk. "How was the snow?" I sat down opposite him and told him it was cold. He pushed a script across to me. It was the estimating script of the next serial. He said nothing about the fracas I had been in with Oberg. "We've got the first episode of *Spy Smasher* in pretty good shape. Can you look at it this afternoon with me to see if you want to make any changes?" I nodded.

As I turned the first few pages of the new script, I saw that its title was *Perils of Nyoka*. Of course I knew all about it and also its past history. "What about being sued by Edgar Rice Burroughs over the Nyoka name?" Nyoka was the girl's name in *Jungle Girl*. It seems the Nyoka name was never used by Burroughs in the original book and our writers had dreamed it up so the attorneys were willing to gamble. They apparently told the studio not to use Frances Gifford in the lead. That could possibly bring us into court. I asked Bill if he had started to look for a leading girl. It was going to be practically impossible to fill Frances Gifford's shoes, costume and acting ability. He'd talked to casting about a girl lead, but we couldn't afford the actresses who could fill her shoes. Then he said, "We need two girls." It seems like the lead heavy was also a girl. I hadn't read the script but it sounded like a good idea.

We decided to wait a couple of weeks to do the screen tests to give casting a chance to put the word out to the agents. We also decided to test a bunch of newcomers. They were to wear shirts and shorts with flat heeled shoes. We would put the makeup and hairdress on them and shoot them on the back lot with reflectors, not lights. This would tell us if their eyes could take reflected light without squinting. We were giving ourselves a chance to see the girls under actual shooting conditions. Out of the probably fifty girls we interviewed, we picked about ten to test. We gave them all the same lines to read and at the end of the test I had them run as fast as they could. A girl can look graceful on the tennis court, on the dance floor or in the water, but on a full run it's often a different story. The two girls that we needed for this serial had to run, jump, roll on the ground, and fight. In the script there were several sequences where the lead girl and the heavy girl slugged it out. We tested some beautiful girls, and several of them later became big stars.

We held all the girls in makeup and the assistant would walk the girl who had finished the test back to makeup and walk the new girl down to the set. I watched him disappear around the sound stage with one of the girls who had just finished and sat down to see who was next. I can't remember every name, but it seems to me it was Louise. I remember her interview. She was a beauty. When I looked up, a big limousine pulled up to the set. The assistant got out and held the door open. He looked at me with a smug grin and helped Louise out of the big black sedan with a half bow. I took a good look at her as he led her over to me. She was graceful and had a beautiful figure. When we finished the test she thanked me and got back into the limousine. The assistant got in after her and before he shut the door again gave me a shrug and a grin. The cameraman said, "When I'm reincarnated, I want to be an assistant director." I thought, "Me, too."

We ran the tests the next day. It came down to three girls that we all liked: Louise, a girl who later became a star at Universal, and Kay Aldridge. Someone said Louise was married to a big nightclub entertainer. That and the limo turned me off. The other girl was about five-feet-two. We all thought with what she had to do in the serial her size would hurt her believability, so Kay got the

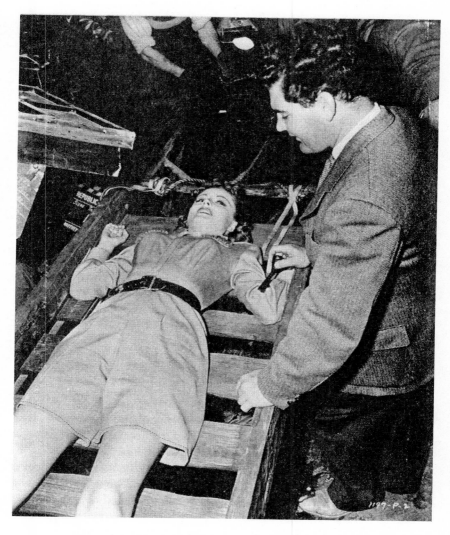

Kay Aldridge and the author on the set. She was quite a gal.

job. She had been a top Powers model and had some acting experience when she was under contract to Warner Bros.

When it came time to wardrobe her, I remembered the problems we had with the censor and the "legion of decency." On *Jungle Girl* Jack and I had spent half our time telling Frances to pull her short skirt down. This time I insisted on a split skirt.

The girl heavy's name in the picture was Vultura. When Lorna Gray walked into the office—even before she said hello—she had the job. She was the exact opposite of Kay. She had dark hair and dark eyes, as well as a figure I'd describe as having a little too much of everything. She was also about the same height as Kay. When we wardrobed her, the decision was made: no split skirt for her. Well, maybe it was a split skirt, long, silk and split clear up to the waist. I figured the little kids wouldn't notice, and the big kids would go home and throw rocks at their sisters. She was just plain sexy.

I found out later that she was also one hell of a good actress. She had been under contract to Columbia and had been in a lot of westerns and a serial. If she could hold up under a Columbia shooting schedule, she would be able to breeze through ours.

We also hired Earl Johnson and his dog Ace. I asked Earl if they had made up after the snow picture. Earl pointed a finger at him and he barked and nodded. We also had an ape in the picture. He was Vultura's bodyguard. I shuddered when I thought of Corrigan and his ape suit that I'd worked with eight years before. I prayed that the moths had eaten it up or Corrigan had put on so much weight that he couldn't get into the suit. Probably both were true. My prayers were answered. We interviewed Emil Van Horn in the ape suit. Emil was a real athlete. He'd been a tumbler in a circus and he was small. The ape suit wasn't as good as Corrigan's, but Emil made up for it. He could bounce three feet off the floor on all fours and strike out at the same time, and he could tumble in the suit, with some good growl sound effects dubbed in. I was sure the kids would love him.

There was also a small monkey. Georgie had been on a long string, tipping his hat and collecting the pennies while his master and trainer, Tony ground the organ before they came into the picture business. As with Earl and Ace, I never did know which was the smarter in that duo.

When Georgie was working, Tony would be behind the camera going through all the motions he wanted Georgie to do. He would jump up and down, wave his arms, make faces. The cameraman had told him many times not to get in front of the lights and cast moving shadows on the set where the camera would pick it up. He'd stop every now and then and turn to the cameraman and nod and say, "Watcha da shad, watcha da shad." I always felt that I should turn the camera around and shoot Tony's antics. They were funnier than Georgie's. In later years I would work many more times with these two delightful characters and whenever I read "a small monkey" in a script, I'd think of "Watcha da shad."

We talked about all of the leading men who were available. At the first meeting of a prospective leading man, I found myself comparing him in size, build and facial looks to Davy Sharpe. The more he matched Davy, the easier my job became. During our casting for this serial, a new prospect with not much experience walked in, but the way he walked, and with his build and good looks, he could have been Davy's clone. His name was Clayton Moore. He didn't know it, but he had the job when he walked through the door.

Clayton turned out to be about the best leading action man any director could ask for. He had been part of a trapeze act when he was younger. He moved well and had guts. The stuntmen, like Davy and Tommy Steele, took him under their wing and about the second day of shooting he was as good at fighting and jumping and falling as they were. When you find an actor who looks you right in the eye and isn't afraid to ask questions, you know you've got your schedule made every day and you're going to have a decent picture. Clayton would work for me twice more before the war closed in on me.

We also picked Tris Coffin from *Spy Smasher*. Tris had ability written all over him. George J. Lewis came in for an interview. George had started in the business during the silent era. He was in a series of college pictures or shorts. I can't remember, but I believe it was called *The Collegians*. I can remember seeing them as a kid. He had also had lead parts in Broadway plays. George came from an old aristocratic California family, of Spanish origin, and he was raised in Coronado, California.

When George came through the door, I stood and shook hands and pointed to a chair. The casting director and O'Sullivan were with me. We sat opposite each other. He was waiting for me to speak. "George, you don't remember me, do you?" I asked. He shook his head. "I know you by name," he replied. I nodded. "You were raised in Coronado, right?" He scowled. "That's right, but I don't remember ever mentioning it in any of my film biographies." The casting director and O'Sullivan became more interested. "Do you remember a couple of pretty girls, one redhead and one blonde you used to take to the big ballroom in Tent City?" I asked. Tent City was on the strand and was next to the Hotel Del Coronado. It was a world famous summer resort. During the war it was torn down and made into the navy amphibious training command. Today only the old boat house stands out in the water near the yacht basin.

George scowled as he tried to remember. "What were their names?" I told him they were Julie and Picky Witney. "Well, I'll be damned. I went to school with them." Now he really looked at me. I laughed. "I'm the little shit that you had to take along to the dance as a chaperone. I can remember you carrying me home half asleep." He remembered and asked, "And what happened to Julie, Pickie and your beautiful mother?" George and I would work together many more times over the next twenty years.

We picked Billy Benedict from *Captain Marvel* to play one of the good guys with Kay and Clayton. My old friend Charley Middleton, with the mean face and wonderful disposition, was selected to play the bad guy. I had surrounded myself with friends, except for the two girls and the leading man. After the first day they all joined in the group of friends.

A week or so into the serial I got an early morning call from the assistant director. We had been shooting the exteriors at Iverson Ranch and I usually drove from home to Iverson's. It was only a fifteen-minute drive from Tarzana. It seemed silly to drive to the studio, get out of my car and into a studio car to go back in the same direction I'd just come. It seems Kay was sick. We would have to take a cover set. Yes, he'd sent the studio doctor to the motel she was living in next to the studio. Yes, he'd stopped the trucks heading to the location at the gate.

I got dressed and was there in half an hour. I can't recall the set we were to use as cover, but it had to be one that Kay didn't work in. It worried me because if she was sick for long we'd run out of cover. She had the lead in the serial. The story was about her. There were few sets that didn't involve her.

About nine o'clock that morning the doctor came on the set. I walked over to him. "Doc, how sick is our girl?" He grinned. "Oh, she's sick, all right." He looked around and said, "I want to talk to her welfare worker." I thought I'd heard him wrong. "Welfare worker!" "For God's sake, Doc, she's over eighteen. Why would she need a welfare worker?" If anyone under eighteen works on the set, a welfare worker must be present at all times. That was the law. The doctor was still grinning. "Are you sure she wasn't telling you a fib about her age? Because she's got a kid's disease called the measles."

Our "kid" was back to work in a couple of days. For a kid, she took the ribbing she got from everybody pretty well.

Ralph Oberg had stayed away from me. If he had a question to ask me, he did it through Mack D'Agostino. On the first day we shot inside I told Mack to have Oberg come on the set and wait for me to finish the day's work. I wanted to talk to him. Mack was a good friend. He looked at me a long time. "You mean 'we' want to talk to him?" I shook my head. "No, Mack, 'I' want to talk to him alone." Now he shook his head. "I won't let you." I cut him off, "Look, Mack, this is between Oberg and myself. I'm going to have to work with him, and I've got to get this settled one way or the other. Now go on and tell him." He stood and looked at me, then shook his head and started for the door. He stopped just before he opened it, and looked back at me. I said, "Go on, Mack. And Mack, don't tell anyone about this, and no peeking around corners with a baseball bat in your hand." He laughed and said okay.

I had just said "wrap it up" when Oberg came through the door. I sat down in my chair and started to make some notes on the next day's shooting. The crew and electricians put their tools away and one by one left the stage.

It seemed like a half hour, but in reality it was probably no more than ten minutes. Oberg stood by the door. The watchman who always came in as soon as the set was empty said hello to me, looked around the empty set to see if everyone had put out their cigarettes, punched his clock and walked out the door Oberg was still standing by, saying hello to him as he passed. Now the set was empty, with only one big light high in the ceiling to put a dull glow on everything that was lit up like a Christmas tree a few minutes earlier. It was like everything that was alive and well just a moment before had died.

I sat in my chair with the script open waiting for Ralph to make the first move. I sat him out. He got tired of waiting for me to open the conversation and moved over a few feet from me. "Wha'd'ya want?" he asked. Now I stood up, closed my cover over the heavy telephone book sized script, and picked it up with one hand, letting it hang by my side. The script cover was as hard as a rock. It had been re-covered several times and I was superstitious about it. It was my good luck charm that I'd bought on my first directing job and I still have it today. I've never made a picture that it didn't hold the pages together. "I want you to take the first swing at me, Ralph, while I'm facing you this time." He stood looking at me. He was thinking about it. He was bigger than I was but fat.

I don't know how long we both stood there facing each other. Finally I said, "Okay, Ralph, if that's the way you want it," and walked past him to the door without looking back. I knew he wasn't following me because I could have seen his shadow move.

Mack D'Agostino was waiting outside the stage. "Mack, I thought I asked you to go home." He smiled. "Just waiting to make sure you could walk out." I gestured with my head at the door. "He backed down." I held up the heavy script. "I think his balls told him not to take the first punch. They could feel this," I shook the script, "aimed right at them."

Over the dinner table the weekend before we were to finish the serial, Maxine said, "You seem to be enjoying this picture more than any you've ever made. You don't seem to be as tired, and you haven't been as grouchy as you usually get the last week of shooting." I thought about the remark before I answered. "I think that instead of having to look at a bunch of dirty old cowboys all day and working with two damn pretty girls instead makes all the difference." Her "oooh" brought me back to reality. I knew immediately I had the wrong answer to her question. "Come on, honey, you know neither one of these girls means anything to me. Is this jealousy rearing its ugly head in our house?" She shook her head. "Which one is it, Lorna? She's the sexy one." I leaned back and laughed. "Lorna's been running around with Duke Taylor since they first met." That ended the conversation and the jealousy bit.

Let's fast forward about a year. I'm in the South Pacific. I haven't seen Maxine for at least six months. She's been doing a bit part in a picture with Lorna. The letter I got from her read:

"I'm sharing a dressing room with your good friend Lorna, Goon. Let me tell you about her. She comes into the dressing room in the morning, puts a partial plate in her mouth to cover a slight gap between her front teeth. The hairdresser puts on some fake hair. The makeup man puts on her false eyelashes. She puts on her brassiere with falsies, wiggles her fat ass into a girdle, finishes dressing, and, by God, she looks pretty damn good!"

The weekend after we'd finished the picture I double-checked all the papers that the marine corps had asked me to fill out. I carefully put them in a big envelope with the letters of recommendation that had come back a few days before, pondered for a moment over the doctor's report on my physical, sealed the letter and started for the door. Maxine's voice came from the kitchen. "Wait a minute. I'll go with you." I watched as the postmaster stamped the package and dropped it in a big basket. As I turned away from the window I looked at Maxine standing in back of me. I think there were tears in her eyes, but I couldn't be sure. I was looking at her through the mist in my own.

Davy Sharpe and his wife Jean dropped by the house to say good-bye. Both Maxine and I would miss them. He had been a good friend. He was going back to Texas to become an army pilot. We sat at the bar and talked about the good times we'd had in the past. We remembered the time we'd all gone to spend a weekend in San Francisco. We were going to the Mark Hopkins Hotel to dance. We were all gussied up in our best suits and the girls in their long dresses. We took a cab from the hotel where we were staying.

On the way over Bud Wolfe said, "Remember the stodgy old doorman that opened the cab door for us the last time we were here?" We all remembered the sour face he'd given us at the small tip he received. Bud and Davy were sitting on the jump seats. Let's both do a fall out as he opens the door. He'll think it was his fault." All the girls protested to no avail. Davy leaned on Bud and Bud leaned on the door. The cab pulled up to the curb. Well, almost to the curb. The stodgy old man in his gold braided coat leaned over and opened the cab door. Davy and Bud went tumbling out in what I'd call at least a fifty dollar fall at his feet. The old man stepped back horrified. Now the girls looked horrified. Now Bud and Davy looked horrified. They'd both landed in a puddle of muddy water.

We remembered another trip we took to the old Grant Hotel in San Diego. It was built in the 1880s and was as elegant as any hotel in America. We all met at the elevator to go to breakfast. The elevator stopped at our floor and the elevator man said good morning as we stepped inside. There were only six of us and the elevator was empty. Davy picked up a paper from a stack sitting on his stool, paid him and said, "Keep the change." The elevator descended to the main lobby. When it stopped and the door opened, we all filed out except Davy.

The elevator man knew he had six people to get in. He waited a moment, then said in a loud voice, "Main lobby." The five of us stopped and turned to watch. The elevator man turned to see why his other passenger hadn't come out. Davy was standing on his head in a corner reading the paper with both hands holding it. The man looked at us. We never cracked a smile. He turned back to Davy. "Sir, first floor!" Davy did a neat little flip to his feet, carefully folded the paper, tucked it under his arm and with a "thank you, my good man," walked out to join us.

Davy and Jean stayed late that night. It seemed we all had a lot to talk about. He left with a handshake from me and a big kiss from Maxine.

Davy became a fighter pilot and flew cover for the bombings of the Trieste oil fields. He told me later that he only got into trouble once, when he was arrested for standing on his hands on the top railing of the Leaning Tower of Pisa.

The war was a frightening time for all Americans. The Japanese had taken the Philippines and Bataan had fallen. When our fleet had engaged the Japanese fleet, we had lost cruisers and carriers. Japan had overrun parts of China and Burma. In the European theater, Poland had fallen and the English were under heavy air attack. France had capitulated and the Germans and the axis powers were in full command of practically all of Europe. Our troops and tanks had gone down in defeat in their first engagements with the Germans in Africa.

I hated to walk back to an empty barn, but there was no way we could keep the horses. Feed was getting more expensive and even with old Pete to take care of them, it would be too much for Maxine to handle. I figured the war would last at least four years. My salary as a second lieutenant would be two hundred twenty-five dollars a month. At that time I was making more than that a week.

I put down my good jumping horse. He was getting a little long in the tooth and I couldn't stand the thought of him being abused. The other horses we gave away to people we knew would take care of them. We gave Trudy, the female Saint Bernard who had won all the obedience tests, to an Army unit heading to Alaska. She had been with them for a month and already she was spoiled rotten. The last we saw of her, she was sitting on the front seat of a big truck leading about ten other trucks as they stopped in front of our house to let us say good-bye to her.

We gave Barry, Cappy's son, to Earl Johnson, the dog trainer, to be used in pictures. We kept Cappy and the champion English setter, Bootsie.

Now everything was taken care of. We put everything we owned in Maxine's name and all we had to do was wait for my orders to report to the marines.

The next serial was another Royal Canadian Mounted Police story with Zane Grey's name on it. The story was all war propaganda about the Axis countries sabotaging bridges and railroads, while Sergeant King tried to stop them. We dragged the airplane "that could float like a balloon" out from the attic storage of the special effects department, put a new tail on it and a couple of wooden guns sticking out of the wings, and to me it still looked like the one we'd used in *Spy Smasher*.

Bill O'Sullivan handed me the script. The title was *King of the Mounties*. It had the same story as the first Mountie serial and used a lot of stock material from it and from some of the other serials. I asked Bill why he developed a story like this. He had a simple answer: money. The studio had cut back on the budget that they handed him to make the picture. I asked him where we could match into stock shots at Big Bear Lake, with all of its pine trees and water, locally. It was obviously a big problem.

O'Sullivan had been given a new assistant. His name was Mike Frankovich. He had been an All-American football player at the University of California a few years earlier. Like O'Sullivan he wore expensive clothes and smoked expensive cigars. I liked him.

We decided to go up to Big Bear Lake and see if all the sets that were used in the stock footage were still standing and get an approximate cost to go there and shoot the exteriors. The next day we took off for Big Bear in one of the studio's limousines. It had been a drought year in California and the lake was lower and the ground was dried out. The fire hazard was high and there were no smoking signs all along the road.

We pulled off the main road onto a dirt side road to check one of the locations that I remembered. Mike lit up a cigar. I told him if they caught him he'd probably go to jail. He said he's be really careful and keep the ashes inside the car. The dirt road left a cloud of dust in back of us and our rear vision was blocked out. Suddenly out of the dust a siren sounded and our driver pulled over to let the siren pass. A Forest Service pickup pulled alongside and stopped. We all looked at Mike. He took the cigar out of his mouth and put it in his jacket pocket.

A forest ranger got out of the pickup and came to the driver's side. The windows were all closed to keep the dust out and the driver rolled the window down. The ranger looked into the car and asked if anyone was smoking. We all held up our hands. I was sure he could smell cigar smoke. He reached in and felt the ash trays to see if they were hot. I looked down at Mike's pocket. The ranger said he was sure that he saw someone smoking. He had been sitting at the crossroads when we turned off.

I was sitting next to Mike. He was in the middle and Mack D'Agostino was sitting next to the window on the other side. I could smell cloth burning. I rolled down the window on my side and coughed several times with the cough pointing out the window, hoping to keep the smell away from the driver's side. The forest ranger asked what we were doing on the road. He accepted O'Sullivan's explanation that we were looking for locations. Mike began to squirm in his seat. I could feel the heat from the burning cloth next to my leg. The ranger wasn't in any hurry.

I sneaked another peak down at Mike's pocket. Now the smoke was starting to drift up. In desperation I said, "That guy we're going to meet to see if we can use the location probably won't wait for us." The ranger wanted to help. He asked what his name was. I picked a name, the only one I could think of was Bill Jones, our head wrangler. The ranger said he didn't know him. We were all squirming now. The ranger said to go ahead. As he stepped away from the car, the driver took off in a cloud of dust. On the first turn he slid to a stop. Three guys bailed out of the back seat, beating at Mike's coat pocket. He jerked off the jacket and when the smoke was out, looked at the hole in a beautiful cashmere jacket. He observed that a new jacket didn't cost as much as the fine he would have had to pay. We all felt we'd won that one.

We got the first budget estimates. It was way over what the studio wanted to spend. O'Sullivan had cut everything he could. We had start and release dates, but we were in big trouble. We had been taking five or six weeks to shoot the serials, depending on whether they were twelve or fifteen episodes. I studied the big production board with the assistant director and cut the shooting days down to twenty-two. Then I asked him if that would cut the budget down enough to meet the studio budget. He said he thought it would, but that we were just kidding ourselves. "You'll never be able to make the loaded schedule without cutting a lot out of the script, and when you do you won't have enough film to meet the number of minutes you need to release the picture."

I pointed a finger at him. "Want to bet? I've got a crazy idea." He threw his hands up in the air. "Here we go again!"

I told O'Sullivan about cutting down the days. He agreed with the assistant. "I've already loaded your schedule and cut the days down to a minimum." I told him what I had in mind. It was daring, but I was sure it would work. We would go on location with just the leading man, take a few doubles who would be able to change clothes and double all the other actors. I'd run the doubles together on location and then shoot a process plate at the exact location and do the dialogue with the real actors on the process stage. We could shoot fights and close shots the same way. We would go with a silent unit, leaving the sound crew home, and use a wild camera, eliminating a couple of assistant cameramen.

O'Sullivan thought about it. "The cost of shooting all those process plates, and the lab work on the film and prints, would eat up what we save." I shook my head. "Who said anything about thirty-five millimeter process plates? We'd use a four-by-five still picture projected on the process screen. We'd need to take along a still photographer." O'Sullivan again was thinking. "The background would be dead." I stood up and pointed out the window to the sound stage across the studio street. "The stage is dead. No movement. The only things that are moving are the bushes and trees in between the stage and the window we're looking through. We put a tree, a branch with leaves between the screen and the people we're photographing. Use the wind machine to blow some action on the leaves, and no one but you and I will know the difference."

Bill got up and looked out the window. "Where did you get this idea?" I could answer that. "From my Mascot picture days. Bud Thackery built the machine that runs water over the still picture to keep it cool so the projection arc doesn't burn it up." Bill walked to the door. "Come on, let's go talk to Buddy."

"Yes, I've still got the machine," Buddy told us, "but it'll need dusting off. And yes, I'm sure it can be done." Buddy continued, "I'd like to be there when the still man shoots the stereo plates." O'Sullivan's eyes were starting to light up.

I had known and liked Buddy since the Mascot days. He had photographed all the process plates and there had been thousands of feet of it used. Since Republic had become a studio, he'd shot second units and miniatures. He was as good a cameraman as anyone in the entire picture business. I was sure he'd like to move ahead to being a first cameraman on feature productions. I turned to O'Sullivan. "Bill, let's see if we can get him to photograph the entire serial. He'll be there when I pick the set up that we have to match into, and he can keep me out of trouble." So another damn good first cameraman was born.

We went to Big Bear with a skeleton crew, and then came home and matched into it on the process stage using the stereo plates. Near the end of the picture, tragedy struck. It hit the stuntmen and myself hard. Gasoline was about to be rationed and a lot of us had bought motorcycles to use to go back and forth to work. Maxine had tried to talk me out of it. She had been in an accident at Warner Bros. It was the tag of the picture. She was on a motorcycle in back of a real policeman as she came by the camera. She was to turn and wave back at the camera. They had built a bump in the road that the motorcycle would hit after her wave and she was supposed to throw her arms around the policeman as they happily rode off into the distance. They hit the bump and the bike went out of control. Maxine had sustained pavement burns on her left leg that left scars she carried throughout the rest of her life.

I bought the bike, and she said, "If it's good enough for you, it's good enough for me." She would climb on the back and we both enjoyed the fresh breezes blowing in our faces.

After shooting fairly late, we all decided that we'd go across the street to our watering joint and have a drink before we headed for home. I think there were six of us, all stuntmen. As we left the studio together after one drink, a stuntman who lived near me and I turned left. Jimmy Fawcett and the other three turned right to head into town. About a half mile from the bar, an automobile suddenly shot out of a motel directly in their path. Three of them laid their bikes over and went behind the car. Jimmy, for some reason, tried to clear it in front. He hit the car head on and died in the accident.

The other stunt people took it philosophically. They had faced death many times in their work. It hit me hard. He had left his wife, Helen Thurston, and a young son. Helen never gave up stunt work. She was still at it thirty years later.

By the way, we picked the same man to play the lead who had been in the other serial, *King of the Royal Mounted.* Allan Lane was better in this one, but he still rode a horse like the saddle was on backwards and he was sitting on the horn. Besides, with all the stock we used from the other serial, we could even use his close shots. His expressions were all the same whether he was doing comedy or tragedy.

Eddy White

*W*hen shooting on *King of the Mounties* finished, I took a week off. We had picked up six separate pieces of property for a cheap price. The man from whom we bought our house was a real estate agent and we had become good friends. Every time a really good buy came on the market, he'd call us and we'd pick it up. None of the empty lots were paid for, so we had to put them back on the market. We also had an extra station wagon to sell.

All of the things that I'd worked for were disappearing from my life. Maxine was holding up better than I was. It seemed that the old nightmare I'd had off and on for years now appeared more frequently: a loose wagon rolling down a hill toward a camera. I'm standing in back of the operator cameraman with my hand through his belt to drag him away from the camera if the wagon got too close.

I had actually done this many times, even though the special effects department had engineered a steering wheel inside the wagon and a stuntman, covered with a black cloth to hide him, steered it. We all knew that if it hit a rock or a little gully it could turn in any direction. He couldn't hold the wagon on a straight course. When I first started to direct, I decided that I'd never ask anyone to do something that I wouldn't do myself, so if the cameraman was to stand in back of the camera, I always stood in back of him with my hand through his belt.

When the cameraman was looking through the camera's viewfinder, his actual perspective of how close the wagon was to him was thrown off by the optical system in the viewfinder. Twice I had waited until the last minute and guessed right which way the wagon was bouncing. Twice the wagon had run over the camera. Cameras can be fixed. Cameramen can't. Once in a while I still have that same nightmare.

I was waiting for the postman every day and still had no news from the marine corps. I guess I was getting on Maxine's nerves. She suggested I go back to the studio and start work on the next serial. It would at least take my mind off my troubles and the war.

I went into the studio the next morning and stopped at the commissary for a cup of coffee. Eddy White, who was new at the studio, came in and looked around, then came over and sat on the stool next to me. I had met him before but didn't know him very well. It seems he was about to produce his first picture and wanted me to direct. He had cleared me with the front office, and they told him it was up to me. The name of the picture was *Outlaws of Pine Ridge*. I told him I wanted to read the script before I could give him an answer.

I read the script. It was written by my old buddy, Norman S. Hall. I knew he'd been hitting the bottle pretty heavy, so I knew before I read it that it would be a good one. I wasn't disappointed. It was excellent. When I went back to see Eddy, Normy was in his office, and before I could tell them my decision, Normy suggested we all go across the street to have a knock or two.

When we sat down at the bar, Eddy excused himself to go to the men's room. Normy turned to me. "Look, Billy, you don't know Eddy, but believe me, he's worth keeping. He's smart, has a good story mind, and when you get to know him, you're gonna like him." Eddy came back and joined us. The bar was deserted. The bartender put his drink in front of him and he took a big swallow, then turned to me, "Well, what did you decide?"

I looked at Normy. I decided that they were setting me up. It was no co-incidence that Eddy went to the can. "Normy, it's a good script—better than your average. Who's going to play the lead?" Now there was a long pause. I waited and took a big swallow. Eddy said, "Don Barry." I coughed and spit the drink all over the bar. Normy swung his stool to face me. "You and I both know Barry is a director's nightmare: he won't say this, wants to change the script, wants to be a director." I knew that Georgie Sherman had made a bunch of pictures with him and suddenly said, "That's it! I've had it!" Jack English made one with him and he told me he'd pulled him up in front of Yates. Yates, after listening to Jack's story told Barry, "I picked you up when you were driving a truck, and I can put you back driving a truck."

Eddy looked at Normy then said, "I asked Normy who he thought would be a good director for the picture. I'm new on the lot. I know the other directors, but Norman knows all of you much better than I do. He told me that you were rough enough to keep Barry in line and not let him change the script."

I liked Eddy's approach, no pleading, just how he felt. I didn't know it then, but later my decision to make the picture would have a tremendous effect on my career, some four years later. "Okay, Eddy, I'll make the picture if you can get George Blair to assist me." George disliked Barry as much as I did and we decided that we'd give the midget something to remember and maybe make it easier on the directors that would have to work with him in the future.

We cast the picture with the best actors we could find. This would make Barry get down and really go to work so they wouldn't make him look bad. We used Clayton Moore and George Lewis. Noah Beery, Sr., played a sympathetic role instead of the usual heavy. Emmett Lynn was cast as an old desert rat who was Don Barry's sidekick.

I had surrounded myself with friends and we were ready and waiting for Don the first day he came on the set. Every time he'd walk up to a horse to mount, one of us would kick an apple box toward him to use if he had trouble mounting. I had a little black book I'd jot things down in, like a report card. If he was one minute late, out came the little black book. If he blew a line, I'd ask the cameraman how many feet were wasted. I'd take time to jot it down. Barry was burning, but he knew we were just waiting for him to blow. He didn't have anyone to cry to because the whole studio felt the same way we did. George and I were having a ball.

Emmett had epileptic seizures once in a while. I had worked with him many times and usually he'd go off by himself if he felt one coming on, and he'd be gone for a few minutes. I would close down the set and wait for him to come back. Nothing was ever said about it. He was worth waiting for.

It was lunchtime. We were working on the western street and I came back from lunch early. Emmett was sitting on the boardwalk talking to the wranglers when he suddenly keeled over and started to choke. I ran over to him, realized what was happening and reached into his mouth to get his false teeth out and to be sure he hadn't swallowed his tongue. Someone called first aid, and in a couple of minutes a car and the studio first aid man were there. We got him into the car and I started to get in with him. The doctor said, "You don't have to come along. He'll be all right in a few minutes." I held up my hand. "But I won't." Emmett had just about bitten my finger off.

When we finished the picture Eddy gave the crew a hell of a party. Eddy turned out to be a great talent. He was an artist by trade, and had drawn the sports cartoons for one of the big New York papers. He had studied art at one of the prestigious New York art schools. But he had one odd little habit. When I doodle on a piece of paper, I draw crosses and lines or circles. When Eddy doodled, he drew girls' breasts. They looked like martini glasses or Easter bonnets or had pretty happy faces. I would come to work in the morning and all I had to do was to look over his shoulder to see what kind of a mood he was in. If it was a bad one, and he was doodling his usual art works, his doodles would be the reverse of those just described.

While I had been making the quickie seven-day picture with Don Barry, O'Sullivan had been finishing the script on the next serial and casting it. The title was *G Men vs. the Black Dragon*. There were no repeat episodes and very little stock footage. It was another propaganda picture, but this time the leading man wasn't dressed like a World War I aviator. No mask, no cape. O'Sullivan had done a good job on the script, and it had some different episode endings. He had already cast it.

Most of the people were new to me. Rod Cameron fit perfectly, all six-foot-six of him. He told me that he was Canadian. Constance Worth was a blonde beauty, not too old and not too young. She was known as the Mary Pickford of Australia. There were several other actors whom I'd never worked with before, and my old friend George Lewis was also part of the cast.

There was a small part for a girl and I asked O'Sullivan if it would be okay to use Maxine. I told him I should be leaving for the marines any time, and I thought it would be good for her to keep busy while I was gone. He agreed. I told the casting office to call her in on an interview, but not to tell her who it was for or what it was about. When I got home she met me at the door. "Guess what? I'm going on an interview." I frowned. "You remember before we were married that we decided that two married people working in the picture business were like ships passing in the night?" She made a gesture with her hands. "Look, this is different. You're going away. There won't be two people working, only me." I nodded. "What studio called you?" She pointed a finger at me. "Republic." I shook my head. "It could be for Jack English, Georgie Sherman, or Joe Kane. They're all friends ready to help." She sat down and started to plan. "I've got to get my hair fixed, and maybe buy a new dress." I sat next to her. "Why don't you call wardrobe and see if you can borrow the dress you danced in, the one I thought you were going to fall out of? That should get you some attention." She laughed. "I would, but I don't think I could get into it after four years." I put my arm around her. It was nice to see her happy again, even for a moment. She'd had my going away on her mind for the last two months. I knew she was worried whether or not I'd ever come home.

"I tell you what. I'll bet you a drink that you get the job." After a big hug she said, "You're on. I sure hope so." The next day the casting director stuck his head in the door and said, "Maxine's here." He opened the door and she came in, stopped, looked at Bill, and then at me. She laughed and said, "You made a bum bet. You owe me a drink." We all wound up at the bar across the street.

We stood looking at the production board. This entire serial was going to cost a lot of money. I asked O'Sullivan how come the studio was so cheap on the Mounties serial and were willing to shoot the works on this one. It seems that the first Mountie serial hadn't done too well, but *Spy Smasher* had hit the jackpot. They thought this one had a chance of doing even better. The front office never told the directors how their pictures had done money-wise. I guess they thought if you made money for them you'd ask for a raise. We all knew that the serials were the backbone of the studio because the money they spent on the features was far less than they spent on the serials.

We decided to go on location. We needed water. The end of the serial was a speedboat chase and it had a submarine sequence or two. The submarines were necessarily miniatures.

Santa Barbara was only about three hours from the studio. We wouldn't lose a day traveling. It had a couple of piers and a harbor to work out of. I'd worked there on *SOS Coast Guard* and felt it would be perfect. There was only one motel that could house the crew, and it wasn't a typical resort hotel. As a matter of fact, it was crummy.

The Warner Bros. special effects department had taken it over a month before to shoot the miniatures on *Action in the North Atlantic*, and they had at least sixty special effects men working. They had large cutouts or silhouettes of a convoy floating out in the bay and destroyers about twenty feet long that the special effects men could sit in and drive through the cutouts. It was the most elaborate setup I'd ever seen. When we checked the location they were moving out, leaving only a skeleton crew to shoot miniature torpedoes going through the water. They looked so damn real. It fascinated me. I knew I'd be aboard ship in the marines. And the ones I'd see would look just like the miniatures, except they would have a thousand pound warhead on their nose.

We couldn't find any motorboats, so we decided to rent them from the Stillwells at Big Bear Lake. We had used them many times before, and they always delivered.

My commission and orders came through several weeks before we were to start production. I was to report to U. S. Marine Corps School in Quantico, Virginia, eight days before the end of production on the serial. I asked O'Sullivan if he wanted me to bow out of directing so he could get another director. He didn't even think about it. "Hell, no. You know the script. We're ready to roll, and besides, you're not going to be easy to replace. I'll finish the last week myself." I grinned at him. "Bill, it's a lot different being out in front instead of sitting back second guessing the director, having a hundred people saying 'where do I stand' or 'I want to change a line.' And the front office sending you nasty notes about shooting too much film and not enough scenes to make your schedule." I paused for a moment. "On second thought, I think it's a hell of a good idea. It'll make you an easier producer to work for. Let's go rearrange the schedule and move what I consider the least complicated sequences to the last week."

We started the picture with the action sequences involving the big speed boats. I designed the chase around the pilings that held the pier up. The first day we wrecked one of the boats. The pilings had just enough room to get through them. The first boat went through at full speed. The second boat almost made it, but the wake of the first boat caught it and slammed it up against a piling. Scratch one boat. Fortunately, we had brought three boats because another boat hit a piling on the second day. We moved to other action sequences while we fixed them.

Rod Cameron's name went to the top of my "great" list. He was a good actor, easy to work with, and threw a hell of a good punch. I would work with him many more times in my life. In my opinion he had one distinction no other actor enjoyed. He was married to a tall, slender, big brown-eyed beauty. He divorced her and married her mother.

Connie Worth turned out to be one of the best actresses that I'd ever worked with. She handled her body well, was a good study, and was as pretty as any blonde in pictures. Unfortunately, she drank.

We were working at a lumber yard. It was a Sunday morning, and a crowd of locals had gathered to watch. We were shooting a fight sequence and Connie had a day off. I felt the crew turn and look at something in back of me and I turned to see Connie coming through the crowd. She had her finger in the neck of a whiskey bottle and was swinging it back and forth like a bell. All eyes were on her. She came over and sat down in my chair and yelled, "Come on, let's all have a party!"

In those bygone days on location we always worked on Sundays. The actors and crew got an extra day's pay, but not on overtime unless they worked over ten hours. It was rough on directors.

Maxine drove up one Saturday afternoon to spend Saturday night with me. The El Patio was a fancy dinner house and nightclub, and I'd made reservations for an early dinner. After a few dances I suggested we go back to the hotel. I was tired and had a 7:00 call on Sunday morning. We hit the sack about 11:00. We were both sound asleep and there was a knock on the door. I got up, slipped on a robe and headed to the door. I opened it a crack and looked out to see who it was. Connie was standing there in a sheer nightgown with a drink in her hand. She said, "I'm lonesome," and started to come into the room. I pushed her back into the hall and closed the door behind me. She said, "Didn't you hear me? I'm lonesome." I stood there in a cold sweat. This didn't look good at all. She said, "Here, have part of my drink." I heard someone coming up the stairs. It was Buddy, our cameraman. He stopped at the top of the stairs and looked at us, then said, "Well, I'll be damned." I pointed to the door of our room. "Buddy, Maxine came up to have dinner with me." Buddy looked at Connie, then at the door. He picked her up in his arms and carried her down the hall. Connie never spilled a drop of her drink. I stood there in shock for a moment, and then went back into my room and crawled back into bed. My heart was going thump, thump. Maxine asked, "Who was it?" through my thump thumps. "Just somebody wanting to know what time the call was in the morning." My heart quit thumping for a moment, and I thought to myself, "Come on, heart, give me at least one more thump."

Maxine Witney, Rod Cameron and Roland Got.

The next morning I thanked Buddy. "It was a real serial ending. The hero was about to die, and along comes his sidekick to bail him out. By the way, I noticed that the sidekick carried the heavy into his own room." Buddy didn't answer the question. "The combat you're going to see in the marines would look like kid stuff compared to the explosion that would have happened if you tried to explain that one to Maxine."

We came back to the studio to finish the interiors. I tried to keep all of the episode endings as exciting as that Saturday night in Santa Barbara.

I was sitting with Rod, talking about the next scene. He said, "Where has everybody gone?" I looked at the set. It was empty. We both turned to the door. The entire crew had gathered around someone who had just come through the door. Rod was puzzled. "Who's the gal?" When I saw through the crowd, Maxine was standing in the middle of the crew. They all seemed to be talking at once. "Rod, the crew considers her their daughter. They feel they've raised two babies into adulthood. I'm the other baby. She's my wife and is going to do a bit with you this afternoon." Rod stood up. "She's pretty as a picture. I want to meet her."

Bill and Maxine Witney.

Maxine finished her part like an old pro and took off long before I was through. When I got home she had a drink waiting for me. She asked, "How did I do today?" I put my arms around her. "You did great." After all, you know the old Hollywood saying: the best way for an actress to get ahead in Hollywood is to work under a great director.

There was a week's shooting left and the crew stayed and had a last drink with me on my final day of shooting. O'Sullivan would take over as director in the morning. I wished him good luck. We shook hands and as I drove out of the gate, Georgie the gate man yelled, "Good luck."

O'Sullivan finished the serial, but not without an incident. On one of his shooting days he had an explosion on the set that buckled the sound stage. No one was hurt, but the stage was a mess. It was a fire sequence in a warehouse and no one checked the empty fifty gallon drums that were being used as props to make sure the plugs were out of the empty drums. One of them got hot and exploded. To my knowledge that was the last time Bill ever directed anything. I worked with him again a few years later and the experience definitely made him a better producer.

There was no going away party, just a few handshakes and hugs. Cle and his squadron were already into combat. Julie was being a true marine wife, worried, but no griping. She was about to have her second child. Bert was looking after all the women—all but Maxine. She had made up her mind to live alone with Cappy and Bootsie. Saying good-bye to my mother was the hardest moment I've ever had. There were no tears. A hug that lasted for five minutes was followed by her soft voice saying, "We'll have a party for you when you come home."

I decided it would be easier to catch the train at the Glendale station. At the big downtown station, Maxine and I would be standing around waiting for the train to leave. It was tough enough just to drive to the Glendale station. The train pulled in, and stayed until everyone was on board, then pulled out. We got there just in time. The train was pulling in. I threw my suitcase up to the porter, turned, and gave Maxine a quick kiss and climbed aboard. The conductor yelled "board!" and waved his arms and the train started to move. And just like the old cliché in the movies, the leading lady was walking, then trotting alongside the moving train as it picked up speed. The hero was leaning out of the vestibule, waving until she grew smaller and smaller, finally disappearing in the far distance.

I found my seat and looked around. The train was loaded with uniforms of all kinds, and on top of the uniforms the faces all looked alike: sad, quiet, thoughtful, frightened. My face blended in with theirs. I thought about Georgie Sherman's remark the day the Japanese bombed Pearl Harbor. "Anybody who quits Republic and joins the Army's a coward."

As we fade out a voice says, "O.S., continued next week."

A Filmography

Serials Directed by William Witney

1937

THE PAINTED STALLION (Republic). *Directors:* William Witney, Alan James, Ray Taylor. *Cast:* Ray Corrigan, Hoot Gibson, Sammy McKim, LeRoy Mason, Hal Taliaferro, Duncan Renaldo. *Stunts:* Babe DeFreest, Duke Taylor, Yakima Canutt.

SOS COAST GUARD (Republic). *Directors:* William Witney, Alan James. *Cast:* Ralph Byrd, Bela Lugosi, Maxine Doyle, Richard Alexander, Lee Ford, Carleton Young, Roy Barcroft. *Stunts:* Yakima Canutt, Loren Riebe, Duke Taylor, Earl Bunn.

ZORRO RIDES AGAIN (Republic). *Directors:* William Witney, John English. *Cast:* John Carroll, Helen Christian, Reed Howes, Duncan Renaldo, Noah Beery, Sr., Dick Alexander. *Stunts:* Yakima Canutt, Loren Riebe, Duke Taylor.

1938

THE LONE RANGER (Republic). *Directors:* William Witney, John English. *Cast:* Lee Powell, Chief Thundercloud, Herman Brix, Chandler George Letz, Sammy McKim, Hal Taliaferro, Stanley Andrews. *Stunts:* Yakima Canutt, Duke Green, Ken Cooper.

FIGHTING DEVIL DOGS (Republic). *Directors:* William Witney, John English. *Cast:* Lee Powell, Herman Brox, Eleanor Stewart, Montague Love, Stanley Price, Hugh Sothern.

DICK TRACY RETURNS (Republic). *Directors:* William Witney, John English. *Cast:* Ralph Byrd, Kynn Roberts, Charles Middleton, Jerry Tucker, Lee Ford, John Merton, Virginia Carroll. *Stunts:* Yakima Canutt, Duke Green, Earl Bunn, Loren Riebe.

HAWK OF THE WILDERNESS (Republic). *Directors:* William Witney, John English. *Cast:* Herman Brix, Mala, Monte Blue, Jill Martin, Noble Johnson, William Royle, Tom Chatterton, Tiffie (Dog). *Stunts:* Ted Mapes, Henry Wills, Loren Riebe.

1939

THE LONE RANGER RIDES AGAIN (Republic). *Directors:* William Witney, John English. *Cast:* Robert Livingston, Chief Thundercloud, Duncan Renaldo, Jinks Falken, Ralph Dunn. *Stunts:* David Sharpe, George DeNorman, Bud Wolfe.

DAREDEVILS OF THE RED CIRCLE (Republic). *Directors:* William Witney, John English. *Cast:* Charles Quigley, Herman Brix, David Sharpe, Carole Landis, Miles Manner, Charles Middleton, Tuffie (Dog). *Stunts:* Loren Riebe, Earl Bunn, Duke Taylor, Ken Terrell, Jimmy Fawcett.

DICK TRACY'S G-MEN (Republic). *Directors:* William Witney, John English. *Cast:* Ralph Byrd, Irving Pichel, Phylis Isley, Walter Miller. *Stunts:* Bud Geary, Tom Steel, Bud Wolfe, Ken Terrell.

ZORRO'S FIGHTING MEN (Republic). *Directors:* William Witney, John English. *Cast:* Reed Hadley, Sheila Darcy, William Corson, Leander DeCordova, John Mertin, C. Montague Shaw. *Stunts:* Ted Mapes, Jimmy Fawcett, Ken Terrell, Yakima Canutt.

1940

DRUMS OF FU MANCHU (Republic). *Directors:* William Witney, John English. *Cast:* Henry Brandon, William Royle, Robert Kellard, Gloria Franklin, Tom Chatterton, Luana Walters. *Stunts:* David Sharpe, Duke Green, Jimmy Fawcett.

ADVENTURES OF RED RYDER (Republic). *Directors:* William Witney,

John English. *Cast:* Don Barry, Noah Beery, Sr., Tommy Cook, Vivian Coe, William Farnum. *Stunts:* David Sharpe, Post Parks, Joe Yrigoyen.

KING OF THE ROYAL MOUNTED (Republic). *Directors:* William Witney, John English. *Cast:* Allan Lane, Robert Strange, Robert Kellard, Lita Conway, Herbert Rawlinson, Harry Cording, Stanley Andrews. *Stunts:* Ken Terrell, Duke Green, David Sharpe, Duke Taylor.

MYSTERIOUS DOCTOR SATAN (Republic). *Directors:* William Witney, John English. *Cast:* Eduardo Ciannelli, Robert Wilcox, William Newell, Ella Neal, Dorothy Herbert, C. Montegue Shaw. *Stunts:* David Sharpe, Helen Thurston, Duke Taylor, Bud Wolfe.

1941

ADVENTURES OF CAPTAIN MARVEL (Republic). *Directors:* William Witney, John English. *Cast:* Tom Tyler, Frank Coghlan, Jr., William Benedict, Louise Curry, Reed Hadley, Gerald Mohr. *Stunts:* David Sharpe, Dick Crockett, Loren Riebe, Ken Terrell.

JUNGLE GIRL (Republic). *Directors:* William Witney, John English. *Cast:* Frances Gifford, Tom Neal, Trevor Bardette, Gerald Mohr, Frank Lackteen, Tommy Cook. *Stunts:* David Sharpe, Ken Terrell, Helen Thurston, Duke Taylor.

KING OF THE TEXAS RANGERS (Republic). *Directors:* William Witney, John English. *Cast:* Sammy Baugh, Neil Hamilton, Pauline Moore, Duncan Renaldo, Monte Blue, Roy Barcroft. *Stunts:* Duke Green, Loren Riebe, David Sharpe, Ken Terrell.

DICK TRACY VS CRIME, INC. (Republic). *Directors:* William Witney, John English. *Cast:* Ralph Byrd, Michael Owen, Jan Wiley, Ralph Morgan, Kenneth Harland, Jack Mulhall. *Stunts:* Duke Taylor, Bud Wolfe, David Sharpe, Ken Terrell.

1942

SPY SMASHER (Republic). *Director:* William Witney. *Cast:* Kane Richmond, Marguerite Chapman, Sam Flint, Hans Shumm, Tris Coffin, Franco Corsaro. *Stunts:* Yakima Canutt, Duke Taylor, Ken Terrell, Jimmy Fawcett, Loren Riebe, Cary Lofton.

PERILS OF NYOKA (Republic). *Director:* William Witney. *Cast:* Kay

Aldridge, Clayton Moore, William Benedict, Tris Coffin, George Lewis.

KING OF THE MOUNTIES (Republic). *Director:* William Witney. *Cast:* Allan Lane, Gilbert Emery, Russell Hicks, Peggy Drake, Abner Biberman. *Stunts:* Jimmy Fawcett, David Sharpe, Ken Terrell.

1943

G-MEN VS THE BLACK DRAGON (Republic). *Director:* William Witney. *Cast:* Rod Cameron, Roland Got, Constance Worth, Nino Pipitone, George Lewis, Maxine Doyle. *Stunts:* John Dahiem, Ken Terrell, Tom Steel, Duke Taylor.

THE CRIMSON GHOST (Republic). *Directors:* William Witney, Fred Brannon. *Cast:* Charles Quigley, Linda Stirling, Clayton Moore.

Feature Pictures Directed by William Witney

1937

THE TRIGGER TRIO (Republic). *Director:* William Witney. *Cast:* Ray Corrigan, Max Terhune, Ralph Byrd, Buck (Dog).

1940

HEROES OF THE SADDLE (Republic). *Director:* William Witney. *Cast:* Robert Livingston, Raymond Hatton, Duncan Renaldo.

1943

OUTLAWS OF PINE RIDGE (Republic). *Director:* William Witney. *Cast:* Don Barry, Lynn Merrick, Donald Kirke, Noah Beery, Sr., Francis

Ford, Emmit Lynn, Clayton Moore, George Lewis.

1946

ROLL ON TEXAS MOON (Republic). *Cast:* Roy Rogers, George Hayes, Dale Evans.

HOME IN OKLAHOMA (Republic). *Cast:* Roy Rogers, George Hayes, Dale Evans.

HELDORADO (Republic). *Cast:* Roy Rogers, George Hayes, Dale Evans.

1947

APACHE ROSE (Republic). *Cast:* Roy Rogers, Dale Evans, Andy Devine. Trucolor.

BELLS OF SAN ANGELO (Republic). *Cast:* Roy Rogers, Dale Evans, Andy Devine. Color.

SPRINGTIME IN THE SIERRAS (Republic). *Cast:* Roy Rogers, Jane Frazee, Andy Devine. Color.

ON THE OLD SPANISH TRAIL (Republic). *Cast:* Roy Rogers, Jane Frazee, Andy Devine. Color.

1948

THE GAY RANCHERO (Republic). *Cast:* Roy Rogers, Jane Frazee, Andy Devine. Color.

UNDER CALIFORNIA STARS (Republic). *Cast:* Roy Rogers, Jane Frazee, Andy Devine. Color.

EYES OF TEXAS (Republic). *Cast:* Roy Rogers, Lynn Roberts, Andy Devine. Color.

NIGHT TIME IN NEVADA (Republic). *Cast:* Roy Rogers, Andy Devine, Adele Mara. Color.

GRAND CANYON TRAIL (Republic). *Cast:* Roy Rogers, Jane Frazee, Andy Devine. Color.

THE FAR FRONTIER (Republic). *Cast:* Roy Rogers, Andy Devine, Clayton Moore. Color.

1949

SUSANNA PASS (Republic). *Cast:* Roy Rogers, Dale Evans, Estelita Rodriguez. Color.

DOWN DAKOTA WAY (Republic). *Cast:* Roy Rogers, Dale Evans, Pat Brady. Color.

THE GOLDEN STALLION (Republic). *Cast:* Roy Rogers, Dale Evans, Pat Brady. Color.

1950

BELLS OF CORONADO (Republic). *Cast:* Roy Rogers, Dale Evans, Pat Brady. Color.

TWILIGHT IN THE SIERRAS (Republic). *Cast:* Roy Rogers, Dale Evans, Estelita Rodriguez. Color.

TRIGGER, JR. (Republic). *Cast:* Roy Rogers, Dale Evans, Grant Withers. Color.

SUNSET IN THE WEST (Republic). *Cast:* Roy Rogers, Estelita Rodriguez, Penny Edwards. Color.

TRAIL OF ROBIN HOOD (Republic). *Cast:* Roy Rogers, Penny Edwards, Jack Holt. Trucolor.

1951

SPOILERS OF THE PLAINS (Republic). *Cast:* Roy Rogers, Penny Edwards, Gordon Jones.

HEART OF THE ROCKIES (Republic). *Cast:* Roy Rogers, Penny Edwards, Ralph Morgan.

IN OLD AMARILLO (Republic). *Cast:* Roy Rogers, Estelita Rodriguez, Penny Edwards.

SOUTH OF CALIENTE (Republic). *Cast:* Roy Rogers, Dale Evans, Douglas Fowley.

PALS OF THE GOLDEN WEST (Republic). *Cast:* Roy Rogers, Dale Evans, Estelita Rodriguez.

1952

COLORADO SUNDOWN (Republic). *Cast:* Rex Allen, Mary Ellen Kay, Slim Pickens.

THE LAST MUSKETEER (Republic). *Cast:* Rex Allen, Mary Ellen Kay, Slim Pickens.

BORDER SADDLEMATES (Republic). *Cast:* Rex Allen, Mary Ellen Kay, Slim Pickens.

IRON MOUNTAIN TRAIL (Republic). *Cast:* Rex Allen, Nan Leslie, Slim Pickens.

OLD OKLAHOMA PASS (Republic). *Cast:* Rex Allen, Slim Pickens, Elaine Edwards.

THE WAC FROM WALLA WALLA (Republic). *Cast:* Judy Canova, Stephen Dunne, June Vincent.

SOUTH PACIFIC TRAIL (Republic). *Cast:* Rex Allen, Estelita Rodriguez, Slim Pickens.

1953

OLD OVERLAND TRAIL (Republic). *Cast:* Rex Allen, Slim Pickens, Roy Barcroft.

DOWN LAREDO WAY (Republic). *Cast:* Rex Allen, Dona Drake, Slim Pickens.

SHADOWS OF TOMBSTONE (Republic). *Cast:* Rex Allen, Slim Pickens, Jeanne Cooper.

1954

THE OUTCAST (Republic). *Cast:* John Derek, Joan Evans, Jim Davis. Color.

1955

SANTA FE PASSAGE (Republic). *Cast:* John Payne, Faith Domergue, Rod Cameron. Color.

CITY OF SHADOWS (Republic). *Cast:* Victor McLaglen, John Baer, Kathleen Crowley.

HEADLINE HUNTERS (Republic). *Cast:* Rod Cameron, Julie Bishop, Ben Cooper.

THE FIGHTING CHANCE (Republic). *Cast:* Rod Cameron, Julie London, Ben Cooper.

1956

STRANGER AT MY DOOR (Republic). *Cast:* Macdonald Carey, Patricia Medina, Skip Homeier.

A STRANGE ADVENTURE (Republic). *Cast:* Joan Evans, Ben Cooper, Maria English.

1957

PANAMA SAL (Republic). *Cast:* Elena Verdugo, Edward Kemmer, Carlos Rivas.

1958

THE COOL AND THE CRAZY (American-International). *Cast:* Scott Marlowe, Gigi Perreau, Richard Bakalyan.

JUVENILE JUNGLE (Republic). *Cast:* Corey Allen, Rebecca Welles, Richard Bakalyan.

YOUNG AND WILD (Republic). *Cast:* Gene Evans, Scott Marlowe, Carolyn Kearney.

THE BONNIE PARKER STORY (American-International). *Cast:* Dorothy Provine, Jack Hogan, Richard Bakalyan.

PARATROOP COMMAND (American-International). *Cast:* Richard Bakalyan, Jack Hogan, Jimmy Murphy.

1960

VALLEY OF THE REDWOODS (20th Century–Fox). *Cast:* John Hudson, Lynn Bermay, Ed Nelson.

THE SECRET OF THE PURPLE REEF (20th Century–Fox). *Cast:* Jeff Richards, Margia Dean, Peter Falk.

1961

THE LONG ROPE (20th Century–Fox). *Cast:* Hugh Marlowe, Alan Hale, Jr., Robert Wilkie. Color.

MASTER OF THE WORLD (American-International). *Cast:* Vincent Price, Charles Bronson, Henry Hull. Color.

THE CAT BURGLAR (United Artists). *Cast:* Jack Hogan, June Kennedy, John Baer.

1964

APACHE RIFLES (20th Century–Fox). *Cast:* Audie Murphy, Linda Lawson, Michael Dante. Color.

1965

THE GIRLS ON THE BEACH (Paramount). *Cast:* Martin West, Noreen Corcoran, The Beach Boys. Technicolor.

ARIZONA RAIDERS (Columbia). *Cast:* Audie Murphy, Buster Crabbe, Michael Dante. Technicolor.

1967

40 GUNS TO APACHE PASS (Columbia). *Cast:* Audie Murphy, Michael Burns, Laraine Stephens. Color.

1970

TARZAN'S JUNGLE REBELLION (National General). *Cast:* Ron Ely, Manuel Padilla, Jr., Sam Jaffe. Feature version of a two-part TV episode, THE BLUE STONE OF HEAVEN. Color.

1973

I ESCAPED FROM DEVIL'S ISLAND (United Artists). *Cast:* Jim Brown, Christopher George, Paul Richards. Color.

1975

DARKTOWN STRUTTERS (New World Pictures). *Cast:* Trina Parks, Edna Richardson, Bettye Sweet. Color.

Television Episodes Directed by William Witney

STORIES OF THE CENTURY (1954-55). Belle Starr, Billy the Kid, Frank and Jesse James, Geronimo, Quatrill and His Raiders, Cattle Kate, Sam Bass, Johnny Ringo, The Dalton Gang, Doc Holliday, The Younger

Brothers, John Wesley Hardin, Joaquin Murietta, Tiburcio Vasquez, Chief Crazy Horse, Black Bart, Henry Plummer, Bill Longley, Harry Tracy, The Wild Bunch of Wyoming, The Doolin Gang, Little Britches, Black Jack Ketchum, Tom Horn, Ben Thompson, Clay Allison, Burt Alvord, The Apache Kid, Tom Bell, Kate Bender.

ADVENTURES OF DR. FU MANCHU (1955). Dr. Fu Manchu's Raid, The Death Ships of Dr. Fu Manchu, The Counterfeiters of Dr. Fu Manchu, The Master Plan of Dr. Fu Manchu, The Satellites of Dr. Fu Manchu, The Assassins of Dr. Fu Manchu.

FRONTIER DOCTOR (1956-57). The Homesteaders, Three Wanted Men, The Crooked Circle, The Apache Uprising, Danger Valley, Double Boomerang, Mystery of the Black Stallion, South of the Rio Grande, The Twisted Road, Fury of the Big Top, Outlaw Legion, A Desperate Game, The Great Stagecoach Robbery, Iron Trail Ambush, Shotgun Hattie, Trouble in Paradise Valley, Shadows of Belle Starr, Illegal Entry, Sabotage, Belle of Tennessee, Bitter Creek Gang, Broken Barriers, The Woman Who Dared, Storm Over King City, Law of the Badlands, Uncharted Trails, The Big Gamblers, Strangers in Town, The Big Frame Up, Strange Cargo, Man to Man, The Confidence Gang, The Counterfeiters, Gringo Pete, Superstition Mountain, The Elkton Lake Feud, Drifting Sands.

LASSIE (1958-59 season). Tartan Queen.

RESCUE 8 (1958-59 season). Flash Flood, Initiation to Danger, International Incident, Nine Minutes to Live.

SKY KING (1958-59 season). Frog Man, Runaway Truck, Dead Giveaway.

ZORRO (1958-59 season). Welcome to Monterey; Zorro Rides Alone, Horse of Another Color, The Senorita Makes a Choice, Rendezvous at Sundown, The Runaways, The Iron Box, Spark of Revenge.

MIKE HAMMER (1959). Another Man's Poison, Evidence on the Record, Curtains for an Angel, Dixie Is Dead, M Is for Mother, Doll Trouble, I Remember Sally, Now Die in It, Merchant of Menace, A Mugging Evening, Siamese Twinge, Wedding Mourning, Bride and Doom.

S.A. 7 (1959). Jason and the Double Fleece, Material Witness, Male Order.

STATE TROOPER (1959). The Judas Tree, Let 'Em Eat Smoke, The Patient Skeleton, Pistols for Two, While Jerome Burned, So Early in the Morning, Love on the Rocks.

M SQUAD (1959-60 season). The Velvet Stake-Out.

RIVERBOAT (1959-60 season). Face of Courage, Landlubbers, The Treasure of Hawk Hill, Three Graves, The Night of the Faceless Men.

WAGON TRAIN (1959-60 season). The Stagecoach Story.

CORONADO 9 (1960). The Groom Came D.O.A., Three's a Shroud, The Day Chivalry Died, Loser's Circle,

Obituary of a Small Ape, Alibi Bye, Run, Shep, Run, Wrong Odds, Hunt Breakfast, Doomtown, The Spinster of Nob Hill, The Day Ramon Fell, But the Patient Died, Gone Goose, Run Scared, Careless Joe.

OVERLAND TRAIL (1960 season). Sour Annie, The Reckoning, The Most Dangerous Gentleman.

BONANZA (1960-61 season). The Tax Collector, The Gift, The Infernal Machine.

TALES OF WELLS FARGO (1960-61 season). The Hand That Shook the Hand, That Washburn Girl, The Remittance Man, The Jealous Man, The Lobo, Rifles for Red Hand.

THE TALL MAN (1960-61 season). Dark Moment, Rovin' Gambler, Hard Justice, The Story of Millionaire McBean.

WALT DISNEY PRESENTS: ZORRO (1960-61 season). El Bandido, Adios El Cuchillo.

BONANZA (1961-62 season). The Lonely House, The Burma Rarity, The Auld Sod, The Jackknife, The Gamble, The Long Night.

FRONTIER CIRCUS (1961-62 season). The Deaths of Fear, Lipizzan, Patriarch of Purgatory, Coals of Fire.

TALES OF WELLS FARGO (1961-62 season). Winter Storm.

BONANZA (1962-63 season). The Deserter, The Deadly Ones.

LARAMIE (1962-63 season). Broken Honor, The Marshals.

THE VIRGINIAN (1962-63 season). The Devil's Children, Say Goodbye to All That.

WIDE COUNTRY (1962-63 season). Step Over the Sky.

THE ALFRED HITCHCOCK HOUR (1963-64 season). Final Escape.

THE VIRGINIAN (1963-64 season). A Time Remembered, Man of Violence, A Man Called Kane.

WAGON TRAIN (1963-64 season). The Fort Pierce Story, The Robert Harrison Clarke Story, The Bleecker Story.

BONANZA (1964-65 season). The Wild One, Between Heaven and Earth, The Saga of Squaw Charlie, The Trap, Lothario Larkin.

THE VIRGINIAN (1964-65 season). Big Image, Little Man, Man of the People, The Old Cowboy.

WAGON TRAIN (1964-65 season). The Jarbo Pierce Story.

BONANZA (1965-66 season). The Lonely Runner, Ride the Wind (2 pt.), Peace Officer.

BRANDED (1965-66 season). McCord's Way, The Ghost of Murietta, The Assassins (2 pt.).

LAREDO (1965-66 season). Limit of the Law Larkin, The Treasure of San Diablo, Sound of Terror, A Taste of Money.

THE WILD WILD WEST (1965-66 season). The Night of the Deadly Bed, The Nighit of Sudden Death.

BONANZA (1966-67 season). Horse of a Different Hue, The Pursued (2 pt), Tommy.

DANIEL BOONE (1966-67 season). River Passage, The Williamsburg Cannon (2 pt.), The Fallow Land.

LAREDO (1966-67 season). One Two Many Voices, Hey Diddle Diddle, Walk Softly.

TARZAN (1966-67 season). To Steal the Rising Sun.

THE VIRGINIAN (1966-67 season). Beloved Outlaw.

BONANZA (1967-68 season). Sense of Duty, The Sure Thing.

THE HIGH CHAPARRAL (1967-68 season). The Firing Wall, Survival.

HONDO (1967 season). Hondo and the Singing Sire, Hondo and the Apache Kid, Hondo and the Death Drive.

TARZAN (1967-68 season). Blue Stone of Heaven (2 pt.), The Fanatics, The King of the Dwsari, Rendezvous for Revenge.

THE HIGH CHAPARRAL (1968-69 season). The Stallion, The Deceivers.

THE VIRGINIAN (1968-69 season). Incident at Diablo Crossing.

THE COWBOYS (1974 season). Death on a Fast Horse, The Accused, The Indian Givers, Requiem for a Lost Son.

Index